Psychology of
Financial Planning

Psychology of Financial Planning

The Practitioner's Guide to Money and Behavior

Dr. Brad Klontz, CFP®
Dr. Charles Chaffin
Dr. Ted Klontz

WILEY

Published by John Wiley & Sons, Inc., Hoboken, New Jersey.
Published simultaneously in Canada.

For general information on our other products and services or for technical support, please contact our Customer Care Department within the United States at (800) 762-2974, outside the United States at (317) 572-3993 or fax (317) 572-4002.

Wiley also publishes its books in a variety of electronic formats. Some content that appears in print may not be available in electronic formats. For more information about Wiley products, visit our web site at www.wiley.com.

Library of Congress Cataloging-in-Publication Data is Available:

ISBN 9781119983729 (Hardback)
ISBN 9781119983743 (ePDF)
ISBN 9781119983736 (ePub)

Cover Design: Wiley
Cover Image: © VectorMine/Shutterstock (modified by Wiley)

SKY10035917_091222

To past, present, and future financial planners. You are helping heal the world of one of the biggest sources of stress, conflict, and well-being—money.

Contents

About the Authors

Bradley T. Klontz, PsyD, CFP®

Dr. Brad Klontz is an expert in financial psychology, financial planning, and applied behavioral finance. He is a clinical psychologist and a Certified Financial Planner® practitioner. He is an award-winning academic and practicing financial planner and owner of a Registered Investment Advisor (RIA) firm, where he works directly with clients in a financial planning capacity. His unique background and perspective have helped make him a leading expert in financial psychology, creating educational content that goes beyond just theory and can be directly applied into a real-world financial planning context.

Dr. Brad Klontz is an associate professor of practice at Creighton University Heider College of Business, co-founder of the Financial Psychology Institute, and managing principal of Your Mental Wealth Advisors. He is co-author/co-editor of eight books on financial psychology, including *Money Mammoth: Unlocking the Secrets of Financial Psychology to Break from the Herd and Avoid Extinction* (Wiley, 2020), *Facilitating Financial Health: Tools for Financial Planners, Coaches, and Therapists* (NUCO, 2008; 2016), and *Mind over Money: Overcoming the Money Disorders That Threaten Our Financial Health* (Broadway Business, 2009).

Dr. Brad Klontz is a Fellow of the American Psychological Association (APA) and a former president of the Hawaii Psychological Association. He was awarded the Innovative Practice Presidential Citation from the APA for his application of psychological interventions to help people with money and wealth issues and his innovative practice in financial psychology for practitioners across the country.

Dr. Brad Klontz has been a columnist for the *Journal of Financial Planning*, On Wall Street, and PsychologyToday.com. His work has been featured on ABC News' *20/20* and *Good Morning America*, and in *USA Today*, *The Wall Street Journal*, the *New York Times*, the *Washington Post*, the *Los Angeles Times*, *Time*, *Kiplinger's*, *Money* magazine, NPR, and many other media outlets. He has an avid social media presence of over 1,000,000 followers across platforms including LinkedIn, Twitter, Facebook, Instagram, YouTube, and TikTok.

In 2019 he was appointed to the CNBC Financial Wellness Council and received the 2018 and 2021 Montgomery-Warschauer Award from the *Journal of Financial Planning*, honoring the most outstanding contribution to the betterment of the financial planning profession. He has partnered with organizations including Capital One, JPMorgan Chase, Mutual of Omaha, and H&R Block in efforts to help raise public awareness around issues related to financial health and financial psychology.

Dr. Charles Chaffin

Dr. Charles Chaffin's work encompasses a broad range of fields, from educational and cognitive psychology to financial planning. He has served as the author or lead editor of six different books within financial planning and cognitive psychology, helping practitioners become more client-centered and helping individuals and companies address the pushes and pulls on attention in the workplace. He has taught at the undergraduate and graduate levels, as well as in a variety of executive education programs.

Prior to *The Psychology of Financial Planning: The Practitioner's Guide to Money and Behavior*, Dr. Chaffin wrote *Numb*, which focuses on life in the Information Age, ranging from confirmation bias and tribalism to choice overload and compassion fatigue. *Numb* is designed to help readers use information, and the technology that goes along with it, as a tool for better productivity, deeper relationships, and authentic experiences . . . as opposed to a destination.

For over a decade, Dr. Chaffin worked as director of academic initiatives at CFP Board, developing instructional programs, books, and research initiatives that directly or indirectly related to financial planning practice. He served as co-academic director of the client psychology program at Wharton Executive Education as well as program lead for the financial planning teaching seminar at Columbia University. He consults with financial service firms and is a regular keynote speaker at a variety of conferences.

Ted Klontz, PhD

Paul T. (Ted) Klontz, PhD, associate professor of practice of financial psychology and behavioral finance at Creighton University's Heider College of Business, founder and CEO of Klontz Consulting Group and co-founder and director of the Financial Psychology Institute®, is based in Nashville, Tennessee. He has a 40+-year career in counseling, consulting, and advising that has included authoring, co-authoring, and contributing to six financial psychology–related books: *Money Mammoth: Unlocking the Secrets of Financial Psychology to Break from the Herd and Avoid Extinction*; *Mind over*

Money: Overcoming the Money Disorders That Threaten Our Financial Health; *Wired for Wealth*; *The Financial Wisdom of Ebenezer Scrooge*; *Facilitating Financial Health: Tools for Financial Planners, Coaches, and Therapists*; and *Financial Therapy: Theory, Research and Practice*.

Dr. Ted Klontz is a published researcher, professional speaker, and trainer with corporate groups focusing on communication skill development and anxiety management. He is a designer and facilitator of workshops (including "Exquisite Listening®," "Ultimate Listening," "Touching Mortality," and "Experiential Tools for Change"); consultant to major entertainment management groups; consultant to the United States Defense Department; and has a private practice focused on working with professional athletes, entertainers, and financial professionals.

Dr. Ted Klontz has served in expert roles as an advisor to Congressional committees and is regularly quoted in national and international media including *The Today Show*, CNN, *Good Morning America*, *Larry King Live*, *The Oprah Winfrey Show*, NPR, *The Wall Street Journal*, *Money* magazine, and the *New York Times*. Ted's Healing Money Issues Workshop was featured on ABC News' 20/20 and *Good Morning America*. He was also featured on the Oprah Winfrey Network. He has served as one of the founding executive officers of the National Financial Therapy Association, and is co-founder of Your Mental Wealth®, a direct-to-consumer personal finance brand.

Introduction

Successful financial planners understand one crucial thing about their clients: Personal finance and psychology are inextricably linked. If someone is not good with people, they're not going to be a good financial planner. Because when a planner gives their client advice, they are facing off against hundreds of thousands of years of human psychological conditioning, as well as their client's unique beliefs, behaviors, habits, and background. Knowledge of clients' financial psychology has never been more essential to the practice of financial planning. As technology continues to advance, making information more and more accessible to clients, there is a greater need for each financial planner to maximize their relevance through a keen ability to understand, respond, and in some cases predict, their client's behavior relative to a variety of circumstances and life events. The financial planner is no longer the gatekeeper to client data, and clients are not interested in receiving cookie-cutter advice. The value and future of this great profession is on the human side, being able to understand each client's circumstance – financial and otherwise – so that they are adequately heard and served in their own unique way by a trusted advisor.

Getting to know your client sounds like a simple proposition: Schedule a time to meet, ask about their goals, and just listen. But, as accomplished planners will tell you, it is so much more than that. Today's financial planning is about more than just portfolios and products. The field has evolved to take into consideration all of the areas in a client's life that are impacted by money: their pursuit of meaning; financial goals that are in line with their values; and concerns about the impact of money on those who matter most to them. At the same time, a less-evolved financial planner will say to us, "I have been doing this for 10 years now and I know my clients." That may be true. They may serve their clients well, build relationships with them and their families, and help them meet their financial goals. But what about the client who did not return after the discovery meeting? How about the client who didn't follow through on every aspect of their financial plan? More importantly, what about the clients the planner hopes to add to their practice who may bring different life experiences and perceptions than their own or the colleagues at their firm?

THE IMPERFECT HUMAN

The truth is, our primal brains are not wired to make smart money decisions. They are wired to survive in the moment, grab instant gratification, save nothing, and share everything. Our smartphones, tablets, apps, and computers all get regular software updates, but our brains have essentially been the same for tens of thousands of years. We are still wired like our tribal ancestors, designed to exist in the harsh wilderness. In prehistoric times, there was no way to save the meat of a woolly mammoth for later. The tribe needed to consume it quickly before it spoiled. If a member of the tribe refused to share the meat with others, they would be banished and ultimately die. That hunter-gatherer, tribal mentality is still alive inside our modern-day minds. Centuries of these experiences created the social creatures who, in many cases, struggle to think of the long term because of short-term emotions such as fear, FOMO, and the countless biases that impact our decisions and, ultimately, our financial and overall well-being. Stacked on top of this are our backgrounds, beliefs, and experiences around money – all of which shape our unique financial psychology.

There is an old adage in education, "telling isn't teaching." This means that true learning comes from experience and engagement with content, not from someone reciting facts for the purpose of passing an exam. A similar philosophy holds true with financial planning: Merely telling clients the right thing to do is not enough to bring value in this competitive market. Furthermore, there are countless online sites and media "experts" who tell people to "buy low and sell high," to not drink expensive lattes, or to just save more than they spend. People already know this. They know they should save money, avoid revolving debt, make smart investments, and live within their means. Yet, so many people struggle with these basic concepts because of their financial psychology: They *know* better, but they just can't seem to *do* better.

Consider the following examples:

- Our epidemic of overspending and undersaving
- Buying when the market is high and selling when it is low, doing the exact opposite of what's in their best interest

- Trying to get rich quick
- Having a lack of diversification
- Saying they want one thing but failing to follow through
- Having trust issues around money
- Blowing a bonus, inheritance, lottery win, or even a big sports contract
- Failing to put a will or trust into place
- Getting rid of money out of feelings of guilt
- Providing financial support to adult children when the client can't afford it *and/or* the children misuse the money
- Having trouble saying "no" to requests for money from family and friends, even when the client knows they should
- Chronic money conflicts with spouses, partners, and family members
- Lying about or hiding financial actions from a partner or spouse around money
- Failing to follow through on financial advice, even when they requested it
- Feeling too anxious to spend money even when they can afford to
- Sacrificing health, relationships, and emotional well-being in the pursuit of more, even when by all objective evidence they have enough
- Avoidance around money issues
- A lack of motivation, creativity, and passion in occupational pursuits

OUR VALUE AS FINANCIAL PLANNERS

So, given all our imperfections as they relate to money, financial planners must equip themselves with the knowledge and tools to help clients overcome these mental obstacles. Being knowledgeable is not enough. Financial planners must then use this knowledge to understand their clients' unique personal, family, and cultural backgrounds and how they impact their financial goals. To do this, financial planners must first understand their own psychology of money, including the worldview and biases they bring to the client relationship. This will enable them to be sensitive to each client's unique worldview and biases. Finally, the practitioner's knowledge, as well as their understanding of their client, must be enacted with a variety of tools and techniques that help the planner lead the client toward their goals.

We considered all of the above as we were writing *this* book. Our goal was to bring relevant research from various disciplines, understanding, and compassion to financial planning. We provide a broad overview of everything that makes the financial planning client "tick," what motivates them, hinders them, and affects their biases, beliefs, and behaviors. Next, we wanted to help you as a financial planner better understand your own worldview and biases, enabling you to better engage and retain clients, most notably ones who differ from you. Finally, we wanted to be specific in providing tools and techniques that you can use in your practice to better serve each and every client with whom you work. *The Psychology of Financial Planning* combines the science of the mind with the science of money, demonstrating proven techniques to help clients feel, think, and behave in a financially healthy and responsible way. Just as importantly, it is designed to help you help your clients based not on your worldview and experiences, but theirs. If we are going to be client-centered, it needs to be about the client! We believe this book can help you do that and ensure that both you and your clients are successful.

HOW TO USE THIS BOOK

The inclusion of the psychology of financial planning in the requirements for current and prospective CFP® professionals is another step forward for the profession in becoming more client centered. We've organized this book into five sections, focusing on key elements that impact a client's financial psychology, incorporating all of the learning objectives and, more importantly, bringing contexts, tools, and solutions to addressing each of them. We do not just "cover" them. We dive deep into what they mean, why they are important, and, most importantly, what to do when addressing these objectives in real-time. Our goal is not only to explain financial psychology and how it contributes to problem financial behaviors, triggers, flashpoints, beliefs, and cognitive biases, but to provide exercises and tools designed to help facilitate behavioral change in a compassionate and effective way. Planners can fall into the trap of asking the wrong questions, therefore impeding or even halting a clients' progress. *The Psychology of Financial Planning*, along with the accompanying toolkit, helps financial planners, investment advisors, financial counselors, money managers, coaches, financial therapists, clergy, and psychotherapists—including psychologists, psychiatrists, social workers, counselors, and marriage and family therapists—avoid common pitfalls and get to the root of financial difficulties with their clients. When a planner gets inside the client's mind, they'll get a glimpse of the best ways to help them break free from problem financial behaviors so they can enjoy financial freedom.

We envisioned this book with the practitioner, and future practitioner, in mind, with the intention that it will be referenced throughout the career of the financial planner, specifically when you have a difficult issue with a client or are feeling as if your firm is not being as responsive or client-centered enough in some way. It is designed to make practitioners know, and ultimately serve, their clients better. This book is a bit of a paradox of sorts. It is all about your success as an advisor because the book is all about your clients and your relationship with them. We hope this book contributes to the further success of you, your client, and your firm.

Now, let us begin the journey.

PART I

THE PSYCHOLOGY OF MONEY

Evolutionary psychology and research in behavioral finance have shown us that we are naturally bad with money. The instincts that helped us survive and thrive in prehistoric hunter-gatherer tribes often hurt us in our modern financial lives. Delaying gratification, saving for the future, acquiring resources without sharing with our friends and family members, and suppressing our instinct to flee with the herd in the midst of a stock market correction all challenge our natural hardwiring. Our brain has not received any software update in thousands of years. Our Stone-Age brains are designed for hunters and gatherers, not accountants, plumbers, lawyers, and all of our other occupations. This certainly holds true with managing our finances as well.

We developed the *Klontz-Chaffin Model of Financial Psychology* to illustrate the factors that impact money and behavior (Figure I.1). This model is a comprehensive overview of all that influences, motivates, and impacts our financial behaviors as well as what may hinder our ability to meet our financial goals. This model is a representation of the content of this book and accompanying advisor toolkit.

In Part I we answer the fundamental question: "Why are human beings so bad with money?" We explore our prehistoric development and its impact on our cognition, with a focus on why what helped us back then hurts us now in our relationship with money. We also explore the impact of our environment on our cognitive biases. We encourage you to read the entire part (Chapters 1–3) as one module.

1

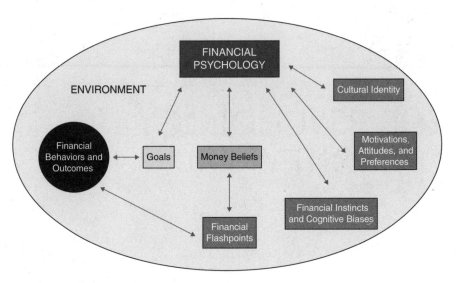

FIGURE I.1   Klontz-Chaffin Model of Financial Psychology

CHAPTER 1

Financial Instincts: Why We Are Bad With Money

In the late twentieth century, economists began to come to terms with what psychologists had known for hundreds of years: Human beings do not always act rationally and in their own best interests. In 2000, then-future Nobel laureate Richard Thaler predicted that the field of economics would evolve to incorporate this basic acceptance of human psychology. Rather than assuming that human beings are rational financial actors, he believed that economics would shift to developing more realistic assumptions about actual financial behaviors. Specifically, he anticipated that economics would focus more on the exploration of human cognition and emotion and how they impact financial decision-making [1]. If we want to understand, predict, and help shape financial behaviors, we need to understand how humans think and feel, and the impact of cognition and emotion on financial behaviors. In this chapter we focus on the impact of financial instincts on our financial psychology, as illustrated in Figure 1.1.

THE SURVIVAL INSTINCTS OF OUR ANCESTORS

When it comes to money, food, exercise, or anything that takes us outside our comfort zones, our brains are wired to do it all wrong. As we said, they are in desperate need of a software update, because we are designed for

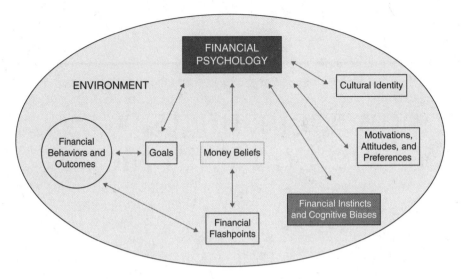

FIGURE 1.1   Klontz-Chaffin Model of Financial Psychology

hunting and gathering and not the complexities of modern life. When the power of our primal instincts are considered, it's a miracle any client follows the advice of a financial planner. Overspending and undersaving are not the result of some tragic character flaw. Financial mismanagement occurs because of hundreds of thousands of years of neural programming in the human brain. When a client stays on the right financial track, they are doing so because they have been able to override their natural, instinctive impulses. These impulses have a powerful hold on human behavior. Our prehistoric ancestors lived in small groups of closely related nomads facing harsh conditions of scarcity and danger. If they were to survive, they had to work together with the rest of the tribe. If one member went against the group, they faced banishment, which equaled death in such a dangerous environment.

Human beings are optimized to survive in small, 100- to 150-person groups. Our brains helped our ancestors survive by keeping the tribe closely related and dependent on each other, which made sense back when we were early humans on the plain, but now explains our penchant for self-destructive financial behaviors. Once a financial planner understands this important factor, they can help clients work around their survival instincts so they can make better financial decisions. It can be helpful to normalize the instinctual destructive financial thoughts and behaviors clients have, because all human beings are vulnerable to them.

SHARING IS CARING . . . AND SURVIVING?

The indigenous people of the Northwest had a culture and economy that were based on the principle of sharing. The members of the tribe who gave away the most were often regarded as having the highest status in the tribe. In some native cultures, if a member of the group stole something, they were punished, but the person they robbed was also punished for failing to see that a member of the tribe needed or wanted something they possessed. Many indigenous people continue to rely on a culture of sharing within their communities and families rather than saving for themselves. The pressure to share is alive in today's communities and cultures, especially in places where financial disadvantages and a lack of resources are prevalent. In some cultures and communities, people will look down on members of their families if they don't share what they have with other members if the group is in need.

There are many examples of professional athletes who come from humble beginnings who lose millions in earnings because they gave their money away. They sometimes have difficulty saying "no" when family members ask them to carry the financial burden for the entire family. Sharing is how less affluent communities survive, whether it is food, labor, medical expenses, childcare, transportation, or money. In today's world, it is unlikely that a person will face certain death if they are banished from the tribe. However, the brain instinctually thinks we will die if we don't stay closely intertwined with our people. This makes it difficult to change course from deeply ingrained cultural norms. Even if the tribe may be moving against our own best interests, our instincts tell us to stay with our group.

In addition to contending with a long history of expected sharing, the human brain releases feel-good chemicals whenever we do give to others. Some may find it more convenient to overlook those who are struggling and need help, rationalizing that it's okay to feel comfortable while others are doing without because they "work hard and deserve" what they have. But most people enjoy giving back to their communities, whether that's through donating to charities, volunteering, or just helping the person in front of them. Compassionate contribution is in our DNA. We are hardwired to give to others. In one study, researchers found that the mesolimbic reward system, which includes the parts of the brain that are activated by stimuli such as food, sex, drugs, and receiving money, also becomes activated when giving to others [2]. In other words, charitable giving gets people high. For those who struggle with giving too much to family and friends, a reasonable charitable donation could help these clients curb that urge and still activate the feel-good chemicals in their brains without depleting their savings in an endless cycle of sharing.

THE ANTI-SAVING INSTINCT

Compounding the sharing instinct's potential impact on wealth accumulation is the anti-saving instinct. The concept of saving is relatively new in human development. Our ancestors, and, in some cases, our current communities and family systems, value sharing over saving. Thousands of years ago, the act of saving for oneself would have been considered antisocial hoarding. Not only were our ancestors discouraged from saving for themselves, they also could be expelled from the tribe or even killed for being selfish. Hoarding would have threatened the survival of the whole group, so it was often forbidden. In addition, one of the most important resources for our ancestors was food. Without modern appliances, saving food today for safe consumption later was difficult. Therefore, for thousands of years, we consumed and shared without even thinking about saving. If saving was the result of a genetic trait, then according to Darwin's theory of evolution by natural selection, those traits would have died off with the killed or exiled hoarder. Therefore, the saving gene would not have been passed down in great abundance to future generations. The idea of saving was punished out of our primal relatives. Now, hundreds of thousands of years later, it is no wonder most of society struggles to save money. The true psychological wonder is that anyone saves at all. That's why it is crucial for financial planners to help clients override this deeply ingrained biological programming.

To this day, anti-saver bias still has a powerful hold on our society. It is evident in the anti-rich sentiment in the United States. People envy the rich and famous, but they also love watching them fall from their thrones. Ironically, there is a strong link (a correlation coefficient of 0.45) between beliefs that rich people are greedy and money corrupts and simultaneously wanting more money and believing that money will solve all of one's problems [3]. Researchers have described this simultaneous loving and hating money as "money ambivalence" [4]. They hypothesize that the psychological discomfort of money ambivalence can trigger cognitive dissonance, where in order to decrease their psychological discomfort, people create a narrative in which having money makes someone bad so they can feel better about not having as much.

Similarly, when someone comes from humble beginnings and achieves wealth, they may feel a sense of guilt as they have become what their family and friends have labeled as bad or corrupt, leading to all kinds of poor decisions and behaviors. In other words, when someone has something we want but don't have, we are likely to experience feelings of envy. To cope with those uncomfortable feelings, we disparage them. As such, those who advance above the middle class are often looked at as greedy, selfish, corrupt, or evil. People soothe those feelings of envy or jealousy with a balm of moral superiority. Society still shames and shuns people who hoard wealth rather than sharing it for the greater good. However, those who are shunned and shamed are no longer plucked from the gene pool. They can now pass those saving traits on to the next generation. As humans moved into the agricultural age, saving became crucial and thus more acceptable. A *future orientation* – the extent to which one plans ahead and thinks about the future consequences before taking action – becomes critical to survival. Farmers who saved a portion of their crops could invest in the following year's planting, contributing to the survival of the community. Still, from an evolutionary standpoint, the human being-as-saver concept is still in its infancy.

I WANT IT NOW!

We live in a world in which instant gratification has become the norm. We can get almost anything we want instantaneously, be it food, blue jeans, or lumber, all delivered to our front door within moments. We even have apps that can order up a potential mate who will show up at our house, one whose appearance and occupation we already know. Businesses of all kinds have worked to make our lives as frictionless as possible. The easier it is to buy something, the more we buy it. Forget worrying about cash, we do not even need to take our credit card out of our wallet to pay. With instant gratification comes changes in the neurological pathways in our brains. Once we receive a reward, we want that reward again and our brain will alter its neurological pathways to help us get it again.

In 1972, Walter Mischel and colleagues sought to examine the connection between a child's ability to forgo instant gratification (a marshmallow or pretzel) in favor of a larger reward later (a second marshmallow or pretzel). Children ranging in age from three to five years old were placed in a room with one treat in front of them. The researcher told the children they would receive an additional treat if they waited until the researcher returned.

The researcher then left the room for 15 minutes while the children had the reward sitting in front of them. They found that the children who were able to delay their gratification to achieve the additional reward tended to have a series of better outcomes later in life, including higher educational attainment, SAT scores, physical fitness, and a host of other factors. Certainly saving, investing for retirement, and diet and exercise exemplify the benefit of delaying gratification. Putting away a larger portion of our salary for an emergency fund or forgoing that second helping of mac-and-cheese are ways we can think about the long-term rather than short-term satisfaction. Our distinguished colleague Hal Hershfield at UCLA discusses the power of thinking about your "future self," imagining in very concrete terms what your savings, body mass index (BMI), or relationships can be like in the future if you avoid the pitfalls of instant gratification. As planners, it is up to us to find ways to help our clients think about the long-term goal and, in some cases, be specific about what the future will be like if sacrifices are made in the short term.

In modern society, it's considered smart and savvy to save money. Whether this is a learned behavior, a genetic anomaly, or a combination of both, there are some people who have a knack for saving. In fact, some save too much and become hoarders. Those with a hoarding disorder place saving above everything and everyone else, often sacrificing relationships, physical and mental health, and emotional well-being. In that instance, it is important for the financial planner to recognize this as something that needs attention from a qualified mental health professional. But in general, saving has proven to be beneficial for the individual and, therefore, their families. Families who master the ability to save over time pass down this mindset to their children, creating multigenerational wealth. However, savers seem to be few and far between, especially in the United States. Financial planners who can help clients overcome their primal programming and help them learn to save and grow wealth are contributing to a financially literate and prosperous society.

HERD INSTINCT

At the Black Hills Wild Horse Refuge outside Hot Springs, South Dakota, the thundering hooves of wild horses shake the ground. The horses at the head of the herd lead the charge. If the leaders gallop in any direction, the entire herd follows. The herd doesn't know what is driving the run – if the leaders are galloping because they sense a mountain lion, or if they just want to let off some steam. Where the leaders go, the herd follows. The herd trusts the leaders blindly. They could be guiding all the horses to safety, or they could be headed for the crumbling edge of a cliff. They won't know for sure until it's too late to change course. What they *do* know is that they don't want to be left behind. The herd is a protective force against predators, but only if they stay together. To stay safe, a horse doesn't have to be the fastest, they just can't be the slowest. Falling behind means death. Predators pick off the most vulnerable members that can't keep up with the rest of the herd, so the risk of plummeting off a cliff is much lower than the risk of being attacked from behind.

Just like those wild horses, we have a herd instinct. It ties into our tribal hardwiring. Humans and horses are biologically programmed to stay together, avoid straying, and follow a leader. This prehistoric instinct is alive and well in us today. Yet, it often operates outside our conscious awareness. When the herd instinct is activated, it hijacks the rational brain, throwing logic and reason aside in the name of primal survival. In modern society, we see examples of herd mentality in riots, gang violence, bullying, and even human stampedes. Think of the long list of soccer and Black Friday shopping disasters over the years. As the old saying goes, "When the whole world is running toward a cliff, he who is running in the opposite direction appears to have lost his mind."

The herd instinct applies to financial behaviors as well. In fact, every stock market crash and bubble can be explained by a herd mentality. Once stock prices rapidly decline, everyone runs to sell, sell, sell. When the housing bubble was at its height, people were buying homes they couldn't afford because the herd was rushing into a home-buying frenzy. Many of these behaviors, which may seem random and irrational, are the result of a predictable social dynamic that is baked into our DNA. It's easy to look at these incidents from afar and think, "I would never behave that way." But anyone who has experienced the frenzy of collective human panic knows just how powerful that instinct is when activated.

WHAT'S YOUR FINANCIAL COMFORT ZONE?

There is intense pressure to stay within the financial circumstances that have been created for us by our families and socioeconomic cultures. The desire to stay with the herd prevents us from breaking free from our financial comfort zones: the socioeconomic herd with which we are most familiar and feel most comfortable. For people to break free, they must go against thousands of years of conditioning and leave the herd, embarking on a journey to new territory. If they are unable to resist the herd, they will often continue to subconsciously self-sabotage and gravitate toward harmful financial behaviors that keep them in a perpetual cycle of drifting back to their socioeconomic herd. This helps explain why so many people blow lottery winnings and other sudden increases in income. Even though many of us would say we would like to have more money, the social and relational pressures that come to bear when we start to rise above the socioeconomic conditions of our family and closest friends can be too much.

The pressure exerted on us from others to stay within our financial comfort zone is often referred to as the crab-barrel effect. Live crabs that have been caught and placed together in a barrel don't need a lid to keep them contained. If any determined crab scrambles to the top to escape, the other crabs will claw and pull it down in their own attempts to reach the top and free themselves. Regardless of the intent, it results in an "if I can't have it, neither can you" scenario. If a crab continues to try to free itself, the other crabs may even attack it, breaking its claws and making it impossible for the crab to escape. Communities in human society do this, too, except they don't use claws. They use sharp tongues, the threat of social isolation, and sometimes violence to keep everyone in check and within the confines of the financial barrel. A person's financial comfort zone is formed by the circumstances, communities, and families in which they are born and raised. Since they grow up in this environment, they consider these circumstances normal and familiar. The financial behaviors, beliefs, and situations of the herd plant themselves in the psyche, becoming second nature. But if the unhelpful financial beliefs and behaviors are never challenged, they become a barrel from which there is no escape.

Jim was able to break free from the financial constraints of his family and community. As one of eight siblings growing up on a farm with parents who barely made enough money to feed the family, Jim found familiarity in scarcity. However, from an early age, Jim decided there was no future for him on the family farm. So he worked after school and on weekends, saving everything he could to go to college and get his business degree. Farm life had taught him how to work hard, so he succeeded in the business world. After years of dedication and hard work, he finally became wealthy. He managed to break free from his financial comfort zone, much to the chagrin of his parents, siblings, aunts, uncles, and cousins. Each summer, Jim would visit his family at the farm. The reaction of his family was that of the crabs in a barrel, trying to pull him back down with verbal attacks and vicious gossip, saying things like,

"He is flying in, probably first class, just to show off how much money he has."

"Guess he's too good to let us pick him up in the farm truck. No, he has to take some fancy car from the airport, wasting money when other people are starving."

"He's probably too high and mighty to stay on the farm. He's probably racking up room service bills at the Four Seasons."

"He's just doing all of this to show off because he thinks he's better than us."

While Jim did what he could to break free from the financial constraints within his family, it came at a price. In exchange for escaping "the barrel," he faced ridicule and ostracization. This social punishment is often strong enough to pull a person back into "the barrel." Those who left their financial comfort zones may subconsciously sabotage themselves. As a result of the pressure from his family, Jim ran the risk of engaging in poor financial decisions and behaviors, such as overspending, giving away his money, or accumulating large amounts of debt. He worked against generations and millennia of ingrained thinking to do otherwise.

Even if a person manages to get out of their financial comfort zone, they may behave as if they are still in the same circumstances. Take, for instance, a previously highly compensated executive who lost their job and is struggling financially, yet continues to live a lavish lifestyle, or a self-made millionaire who rides around in a used pickup truck that constantly breaks down. Both situations are potentially unhealthy and can compromise the person's well-being. Whether a client has moved above or below their financial comfort zone, they may be feeling a great deal of stress from losing their place within the herd. They may be wondering who they are if they no longer belong and may struggle to fit in their new financial environment. It is important for people in this situation to examine some questions:

- How do they identify themselves now that they are outside their original socioeconomic class?
- What will people they know think of them?
- What do they think of themselves?
- What does it mean to become a person who exists outside their financial comfort zone?
- What are the social rules and norms of this new zone?

Getting clarity around their new socioeconomic status and their place within it will help them steer clear of poor financial choices. Herd instincts are powerful, invisible barriers to the financial freedom so many are seeking.

FEAR OF MISSING OUT (FOMO)

FOMO, or fear of missing out, is anxiety caused by not being included in an exciting or interesting event that others are experiencing [5]. FOMO is often aroused by posts seen on social media, but it's actually an ancient survival instinct. When our ancestors brought food to the tribe, everyone benefited from taking notice and joining in on the feast. FOMO can also alter behavior in motivating the individual to act when they might otherwise not do anything. This applies to financial planning as well as parties and social events. Take, for instance, cryptocurrency traders, who tend to score higher on the FOMO scale [5]. Studies have shown that Bitcoin investors tend to be younger than typical investors, sharing a higher risk propensity, and an irrational optimism about getting rich quickly and easily, similar to problematic gamblers. These investors tend to be more sensitive to rewarding experiences, thus aligning with studies that suggest FOMO is a crucial driver in cryptocurrency investment settings [5].

Perhaps the tendencies of risk-taking, irrational optimism, and enthusiasm served ancient tribal hunters. Surely these traits would enable hunters to take big risks in the face of danger. An irrational optimism is necessary to believe they would succeed in killing a huge woolly mammoth with tusks that could impale them at any second. However, if the hunter's behavior was too risky, they would quickly be killed and unable to pass on their swashbuckling genes. Risking all of the tribes' resources for a shot at something bigger could mean death for the members of the tribe. Any entrepreneur can attest that taking risks may be necessary to have a shot at success. Yet, making risky investments without adequate knowledge of the market or accurate assessments of the probability of success can be detrimental. The way we communicate in this information age certainly fuels FOMO in our clients. Perceived victories in the market can be communicated instantaneously through texts, news outlets, and social media. But perhaps more importantly, our innate desire to present ourselves as strong and competent motivates us to share victories far more frequently than we share defeat. If our clients are only hearing about the rewards and not the consequences of risk, then FOMO can become a powerful force in fueling decisions that may not be in their long-term interests. Successful investors and entrepreneurs must strike a delicate balance between risk and reward, which requires open-mindedness and flexibility in thinking.

SOCIAL STATUS AND RELATIVE DEPRIVATION

Do you consider yourself rich? We are wired to be acutely aware of our status within our reference group. In other words, what people think about us matters – a lot. While we like to think that we shouldn't care or that it isn't important what other people think, we just aren't wired that way. Within the tribe, awareness of social status was critical to our ability to survive and thrive. If individuals were perceived as somehow better than others in some way, then it was assumed on some level that they would receive more resources than others. In fact, managing how we are perceived by others takes up a lot of our time and mental resources. Social status can consume our time in doing everything from holding on to our class status to how we present ourselves on social media. Thousands of years ago, our status within the group meant more food; today, it can mean anything from more income and attention to more likes on Instagram.

Although such findings have been disputed by others, and they are in no way conclusive, some studies have suggested that there appears to be a magical cutoff between money and happiness [6]. For example, a 2018 study from Purdue University found that the desired annual income for optimal happiness is $95,000 for life satisfaction and between $60,000 and $75,000 for emotional well-being [7]. Perhaps it is no coincidence that the median annual income in the United States in 2018 was around $64,000 [8]. The concept of relative deprivation may be the reason for this correlation between median income levels and happiness. The theory of relative deprivation posits that our sense of well-being is not based on objective reality, but rather on our perceived status relative to the perceived status of others around us [9]. When we believe we are not enjoying similar benefits as others in our community, we tend to have feelings of anger, resentment, and entitlement. If everyone is making around the same amount of money, they are either relatively well-off or relatively deprived. Older generations attest to this with statements like, "We were all poor, but we didn't know it." They weren't aware of their poverty because everyone around them was also poor. However, in today's world of social media, celebrity magazines, and reality TV shows about wealthy heirs to family fortunes, the relative deprivation effect is not likely to occur unless someone lives in a village untouched by technology and knowledge of the outside world. It illustrates that wealth and happiness are relative, depending on our socioeconomic groups, and that these groups impact our money beliefs, flashpoints, and behaviors.

TWO SYSTEMS

In his book *Thinking, Fast and Slow*, Daniel Kahneman refers to two systems in the mind. The first system "operates automatically and quickly, with little or no effort and no sense of voluntary control" [10]. The second system "allocates attention to the effortful mental activities that demand it, including complex computations. The operations of System 2 are often associated with the subjective experience of agency, choice, and concentration" [10]. According to these descriptions, System 1 is our instinctual part of the brain. It's the part of the brain that senses danger, solves simple math problems, and recognizes familiar phrases and places. It is responsible for spatial awareness and quickly locating the source of a sudden sound. System 2 shares the control over which things the brain gives attention. However, System 2 is responsible for carrying out tasks that don't come naturally. When System 2 is focused on an activity that requires concentration, it can make a person blind to external stimuli that would normally catch the attention of System 1. For instance, if a driver is concentrating on a winding road on the edge of a cliff, the passengers may stop talking for fear of distracting the driver. Chances are, because of System 2, the driver would not hear or process anything the passengers said at that moment anyway.

The concept of the two-system brain, while simplistic enough to make any neuroscientist worth their salt cringe, can be useful in the practice of financial planning. If a client's brain is dominated by System 2, it may miss critical elements of financial planning and be unable to take in new information. If a planner gave their client a complex math problem to solve while trying to discuss investment options, the client would likely not hear what the planner is saying, nor would they be capable of processing that information. System 2 is also responsible for consistently monitoring behavior. It prevents us from blurting out offensive remarks or making mistakes. System 2 is like the parent of the brain. It takes over when things get complicated or difficult, and it usually has the last word [10]. The first system of the brain is efficient and often accurate. However, it has biases, likely tied to primal survival and quick, efficient thinking. System 2 oversees self-control, the part of the brain that financial planners must reach if they want to impact their clients' thinking and behaviors. Understanding the two-system brain can help us learn to recognize situations when mistakes could be made and try to avoid these mistakes when the stakes are high [10].

UNDERSTANDING FINANCIAL INSTINCTS

People may never be free of the ancient instincts tying us to a herd or tribe to survive. It would be impossible to expect a client to rewire their brain to change their financial behaviors. However, understanding a client's financial instincts can help a planner create space between the impulses of the primitive parts of the brain and the actions of the client. This is where simple interventions can help calm down emotional flooding in our System 1 brain to bring our System 2 brain back online, including the following:

- Delay making an important financial decision for at least 24 hours.
- Ask yourself a series of questions before making a purchase, such as: (a) can I afford this?, (b) where will I put it?, (c) how will I feel about this purchase tomorrow?
- Engage in some relaxation exercises such as taking 10 deep breaths, going for a walk, or listening to music.
- Consult with your financial planner before making a big financial decision.

This chapter has established that our brains are wired based on many evolutionary traits that, although they served us well as hunters and gatherers, have created challenges for us in modern life. Highly functional, financially successful people would have been punished in the early tribal days. If a person is successful at saving, keeping their spending in check, making wise investments, and stepping outside of their financial comfort zones, it is because they were able to overcome hundreds of thousands of years' worth of primal instincts and genetics. The financial experiences of our clients, whether growing up in wealth, in poverty, or experiencing financial trauma, will have an impact on their financial beliefs and behaviors for the rest of their lives – and for generations to come. For the financial planner, this creates both a challenge and an opportunity, understanding clients' instincts and most importantly, discovering ways to help the client overcome them to achieve financial success. The rest of Part I will explore many of the hurdles and influences that affect all of our decisions, worldview, and perspectives as they relate to money and overall well-being.

KEY CONCEPTS

- We are not wired to make good decisions with money.
- Our brains were developed to thrive in hunter-gatherer groups, and thus, are not wired for us to save and invest for the future.
- We rate our financial status less on objective numbers and more on how we compare ourselves with others.
- We have a natural tendency to follow the herd, which leads to predictable patterns of investing mistakes.
- FOMO, or fear of missing out, can cause us to act when we otherwise would not, particularly as it relates to social status or investments.

CFP BOARD LEARNING OBJECTIVES COVERED IN THIS CHAPTER

H.66. Behavioral finance

a. Identify how cognitive biases and heuristics can impact financial decision-making.
b. Describe how a client's psychology, such as their financial comfort zone, socialization, money beliefs, and past financial experiences and behaviors impact their objectives, goals, understanding, decision making, and actions.

CHAPTER 2

Behavioral Finance: Understanding Cognitive Biases and Heuristics and What to Do About Them

Financial psychology is the application of many fields of psychology to personal finance. These fields of study include, but are not limited to, behavioral psychology, cognitive psychology, developmental psychology, neuropsychology, personality psychology, social psychology, cognitive psychology, clinical psychology, abnormal psychology, marriage and family psychology, and multicultural psychology. Financial psychology seeks to integrate science, theory, and practice to understand and predict financial behaviors, as well as to promote sound financial decision-making and good financial health.

Behavioral finance seeks to understand people's instincts regarding money and, at the risk of oversimplification, figure out why they tend to make poor financial decisions [11]. Much of the early work integrating psychology and finance grew out of the field of behavioral finance, which applies just one branch of psychology to personal finance – the cognitive. Instead of diving into specific experiences, family patterns, and relationships, and how specific beliefs can impact a person's relationship with money (which we will explore in great detail, along with the planner's role in addressing it, in the

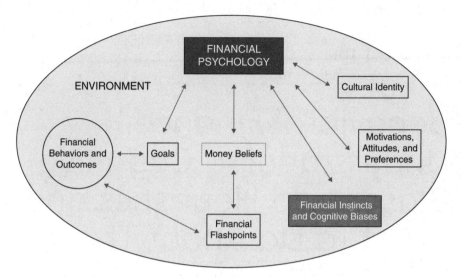

FIGURE 2.1   Klontz-Chaffin Model of Financial Psychology

rest of this book), behavioral finance hones in on common human cognitive and emotional biases and the ways we make sense of the world around us. It examines how *normal* human cognitive processes influence, explain, and predict individual and collective financial behaviors. In this chapter we focus on how cognitive biases impact our financial psychology, as illustrated in Figure 2.1.

WHAT ARE COGNITIVE BIASES AND HEURISTICS?

A cognitive bias is a systematic error in thinking that arises from our attempts to make sense of a complicated world. Many of these ways of thinking helped humans survive and thrive throughout human history. However, in today's complex world, cognitive biases can result in errors in thinking, perception, memory, and attention. In contrast, a heuristic is a process for doing something, which in many cases is defined as a rule of thumb. A heuristic may or may not be ideal but is a readily accessible strategy to solve a problem or analyze a situation often based on previous experiences.

While the thoughts, emotions, and behaviors of clients may vary widely, there are some common cognitive biases and heuristics that inform human behavior when it comes to financial decision-making. These biases are the result of genetic coding passed down from our ancient ancestors, inborn instincts, and how we, as human beings, perceive the world around us. There are several steps a financial planner can take to mitigate these biases and help the client stay focused on their long- and short-term goals. At the same time, it is important for the financial planner to recognize their own potential biases. This section explores cognitive biases seen in financial planning to help make sense of commonly seen self-destructive financial behaviors, based on our shared human history. We hope that you, as a financial planner, will reflect upon each of these biases to better understand yourself in relation to money. This inward-facing process will be most helpful so that you may then better help your clients. Although there is a long list of biases, in this chapter, we cover some of the primary ones that have the most significant impact on financial planning practice.

Anchoring Heuristic

Anchoring is an irrational bias toward an arbitrary figure, such as a purchase or listing price, in impacting one's decision making [11]. Anchoring can cause investors to purchase an undervalued investment or sell an overvalued one. Anchoring can also be caused by historic values of investments, impacting the investor's decision making when it comes to buying and selling.

A common investment mistake is when an investor anchors onto the purchase price of an investment and views it as what the investment is "worth." If the investor wants to sell and then the investment drops in value they may hold on to it longer than they should, waiting for it to go back to where it "should be" (i.e., the purchase price). Another common example is when an investor is onboarded by a financial planner. Even though the client's funds may have been invested in the market for years, the amount transferred on that particular day could be looked at by the client as the anchor point for the portfolio and for the advisor's performance. The problem is that this new anchor point is arbitrary and does not take into account what's been happening in the market before and after the transfer. For example, even though the value of the initial investment may have dropped, the planner could be doing an excellent job of outperforming the market. However, a client's anchoring bias may cloud their recognition of this fact, due to their attachment to the number on the date of the transfer.

Often, anchoring bias is used strategically as a negotiating tactic. This is another reason clients would benefit from having a working understanding of cognitive biases. For example, a salesperson could name an initial price for a good or service and that initial price will impact future negotiations. Let's say Sheila is looking at buying a used car from an individual seller. After significant research on the make and model of the car being sold, she is prepared to buy it for approximately $12,000. When meeting with the seller, he first quotes a sales price of $15,000 in negotiating with Sheila. Hearing that initial quote, Sheila immediately adjusts her budget for buying the car up to $13,500. The seller set an anchor of $15,000 that impacts the rest of the negotiation with Sheila. Anchoring bias can also influence our behaviors at restaurants and stores. For example, we may think that a $50 steak is expensive. However, if we see it on the menu below a $75 steak, the $50 steak can feel like a bargain. Seeing an item in a store marked down from an anchor price of $100 to a sales price of $80 can also make us feel like we are making a good financial decision.

We can avoid anchoring bias by first taking time to evaluate the initial figure that might be contributing to the anchor. In the example of Sheila, it would be best for her to walk away after the seller asked $15,000 so that she can consider carefully how the seller's asking price is far beyond her $13,500 target. We can also avoid anchoring bias by recognizing our own biases and own vulnerabilities. If Sheila knows what anchoring bias is and that she is susceptible to it, she can remind herself to stay firm on her target amount regardless of the owner's initial asking price. Finally, we can avoid anchoring bias by taking the initiative to make the first offer. Perhaps Sheila could have started the conversation by saying, "I will give you $13,500 for the car and not a penny more!"

Affinity Bias

Every time the latest smartphone or tech gadget comes out, people flock to the stores to be the first to buy it. There is obviously no shortage of working smartphones in society, so why the rush to get the newest model? Affinity bias may have something to do with it. People want to be perceived as being on the cutting edge of technology. Having the newest gadgets from popular companies gives off the appearance of success and wealth. There is an affinity toward certain companies that are perceived as the best, most exciting, or leaders in innovation. People also make purchases and investments according to their values. Another example is when hiring a prospective employee, a manager may think an individual who worked at similar companies as them or has the same educational or socioeconomic background is the best person for the position.

Financial planning clients may be vulnerable to making unwise investment decisions such as keeping their portfolio full of domestic holdings, even if a more diversified, global portfolio would offer greater returns. The affinity bias causes people to sacrifice wealth for the "benefit" of patriotism or other values. While it's good to invest in companies that share a client's values, it is beneficial to look at the soundness of the investment and whether it makes objective sense in the client's portfolio. When emotions and biases lead the charge in making financial decisions, the results are often not ideal. As a financial planner, it's important to know when to rely on logic and rational thinking as opposed to emotion, and when to harness those biases and emotions and use them for the benefit of the client.

Availability Bias

Availability bias is a distortion that emanates from the use of information that is most available or vivid in our memory, as opposed to what is more representative. The most common example of availability bias is people's fear of flying due to airplane crashes. Some people see television coverage of airplane disasters, including the vivid images of debris and the mention of fatalities and injuries, and it distorts their view of the safety of flying. Television crews do not go to airports with breaking news regarding the thousands of flights that land safely each and every day, but the attention devoted to the disasters distorts some people's view of flying. As William James wrote in *Principles of Psychology*, "An impression may be so exciting emotionally as to almost leave a scar upon the cerebral tissues; and thus originates a pathological delusion." For example, "A woman attacked by robbers takes all the men whom she sees, even her own son, for brigands bent on killing her" [12].

Bandwagon Effect

In 1848, Dan Rice, a circus clown, invited then-presidential candidate Zachary Taylor to ride in his bandwagon (literally a wagon on which a band or ensemble would perform while moving) during his presidential campaign. As Taylor gained popularity as a candidate, the expression "jump on the bandwagon" was coined to identify individuals who were adding their support for Taylor for president. Given Taylor's success, politicians in later campaigns emulated Taylor's bandwagon in their campaigning and the expression became a household phrase.

The bandwagon effect was first described in economics in the 1950s, describing "the extent to which the demand for a commodity is increased due to the fact that others are also consuming the same commodity" [13, p. 189]. In other words, it represents the desire people have to purchase things that are seen as fashionable, stylish, or simply belonging to a larger group that they view as fashionable or "in the know." The bandwagon effect helps explain the never-ending cycle of market bubbles and crashes. We have a tribal instinct to buy when everyone else is buying and sell when everyone else is selling. At our core we just don't want to be left behind, as our emotional brain experiences it as a threat to our survival. We see this in everything from cryptocurrency to politics to sports fanatics. For example, many individuals tend to buy the latest fashion because it is so popular, regardless of whether they need more clothing.

We can counter the bandwagon effect by thinking objectively about purchases, investments, and even politics. Financial planners can help their clients explore both the positives and negatives of investments and offer reminders that in many cases, the successes of investments like cryptocurrencies are highlighted on social media without the sharing of the losses.

Confirmation Bias

"I know I'm right and I'm ready to prove it!" Often, our beliefs are self-fulfilling prophecies. If we believe that people are inherently selfish or evil, we'll likely struggle to form open and trusting relationships. We may be suspicious of others, questioning their intentions. This suspicion can push people away, confirming the belief that others can't be trusted. If we believe that the world is a dangerous place, we'll notice danger all around us and miss safety cues. We may not be willing to take risks because nothing feels safe.

Confirmation bias is a mindset that can hinder our growth and cause harm to ourselves and others. It sifts experiences through the filter of preexisting beliefs. This bias explains the human tendency to seek out evidence to support our beliefs, while simultaneously ignoring or failing to notice evidence that challenges those beliefs [14]. Confirmation bias occurs in all aspects of our lives. A German study of 75 psychiatrists and 75 medical students found that 13% of the psychiatrists and 25% of the medical students showed confirmation bias in diagnosing a patient's disease. Those who demonstrated confirmation bias developed a theory of the malady in their minds and then searched for new information based on that idea, which in most cases merely reinforced the theory. They were not looking for information to better understand the disease. They were looking for information to reinforce their initial diagnosis. Confirmation bias can also make us surround ourselves with people who think exactly like we think, act like we act, and share the same core beliefs. Social media amplifies this tendency with algorithms that direct us toward the news articles, groups, and political pages to which we seem responsive. This constant reinforcement can make us become far more dogmatic in our beliefs because we are essentially being told every day that our opinions are right and that opposing viewpoints are wrong.

The only way around this bias is to accept – on a mind-bending level – that our beliefs about "reality" are subjective. In other words, our beliefs about people, money, politics, and so on are based on our opinions and feelings, and are not objective, universal truths. Accepting the subjective nature of reality is such a difficult psychological task that it creates significant amounts of anxiety in most people, so much so that many can't even entertain the possibility that their beliefs are not objective. This anxiety can spur them to double down on their beliefs, seeking more people and books and websites to confirm that their opinions are true and correct.

In his book *Sapiens*, historian Yuval Noah Harari credits the human ability to construct and share an intersubjective reality with others with spurring the "cognitive revolution" [15]. Our ability to create and propagate a shared "reality" allowed *Homo sapiens* to cooperate in large numbers around things that exist just within our imagination – including ideas such as human rights, money, and politics. He credits this unique ability as one of the primary factors that led to the flourishing and dominance of *Homo sapiens* over other prehistoric human species, such as the Neanderthals. Beliefs can be hard to change, especially if they have strong emotions attached to them. Confirmation bias makes us closed-minded. The challenge is to invite ourselves and clients to be more open-minded. Certain beliefs may make a client feel safe and offer some self-satisfaction but open-mindedness is associated with higher income, net worth, and overall success in life [16]. As financial planners, it's a good idea to consistently practice open-mindedness so you can help clients do the same.

Cognitive Dissonance

Being faced with conflicting beliefs makes us uncomfortable. For example, studies have shown that people who hold negative beliefs about wealthy people are also more likely to want to be wealthy themselves [16]. We experience cognitive dissonance when we become aware of conflicting beliefs; it causes us psychological discomfort, which we will typically seek to alleviate [17]. As a result we may arrive at a rigid, nonnuanced, or erroneous belief. Studies have found that cognitive dissonance has been associated with investors irrationally holding on to investments they should probably have sold [18]. Optimal financial health requires us to be open-minded and flexible in our thinking to adapt to changing times and circumstances.

Disposition Effect

The disposition effect is a phenomenon in behavioral finance that causes people to sell assets that are gaining value while holding onto assets that are losing value [19]. The disposition effect is tied in with other biases, such as loss aversion, regret avoidance, and mental accounting. A client wanting to cash in on an investment because its value was rising but refusing to part with a stock that was losing money is likely being influenced by the disposition effect. Financial planners know that it's ideal for the client to hold on to medium to high gains until they become long-term capital gains, selling losses as they happen, since an investment's future performance is irrelevant to its purchase price [19].

There are ways to combat the disposition effect to ensure that your client maintains a healthy investment profile. Some proven methods include encouraging clients to avoid making hasty decisions and applying tolerance bands and/ or stop-loss orders [20]. It is also beneficial to normalize and discuss this effect with the client before this situation arises. For instance, a planner might explain how the disposition effect drives our human tendency to want to sell winners and hold on to losers. This conversation will be much more impactful if the planner has it before the client has the chance to latch onto this bias rather than after they have already bought into it and are ready to defend their stance [20].

Endowment Effect

How much is your favorite coffee mug worth? Chances are you're wrong because your estimation is significantly higher than the mug would be worth on the open market. This seems like a minor miscalculation, but the psychology underlying it can wreak havoc on your financial life. The endowment effect is where an individual places a higher value on an object or investment they already own than the value they would place on it if they did not own it. It is often caused by some emotional attachment to an object, or it is symbolic of something that is especially valuable to the owner. In some cases, the endowment effect occurs merely because we have the object in our possession. For example, Rita could purchase a painting for $500 and after owning it for a few years, she refuses an offer to sell the same painting for $1,000. It could be that Rita overvalues the object given the location of the painting in her home or some nostalgia that occurred in relation to the painting. The endowment effect is a product of loss aversion. We value what we have, particularly food, water, and shelter in order to survive. In a famous experiment, researchers handed out mugs to half of the participants free of charge [21]. Researchers then asked the half who received the mugs how much they would sell the mugs for and the other half who did not receive the mugs how much they would pay for the same mugs. The group that received the mugs said they would sell the mugs for somewhere between $5 and $7 and the group that did not receive the mugs said they would buy one for only around $3, indicating that we tend to overvalue what we already have in our possession.

As this study illustrates, the endowment effect can lead to miscalculations of over twice the value of what someone else would pay for something in our possession. In practice, financial planners may see clients hold on to an investment, even though they want to sell it, because they are convinced that the rest of the market is undervaluing it. The endowment effect can also be seen in real estate transactions, where a client who claims they want to sell rigidly adheres to an asking price, even though the market has shown that the property is overpriced by a lack of interest or an offer of a dramatically lower amount. In a downward-moving market where the owner needs to sell, this can have dramatic financial consequences as the seller keeps dropping the price slowly, but not to the level the market has set. In extreme cases a seller can ride the market down 10–20% or more until they finally come to their senses and sell at actual market value.

Financial planners can help clients counter the endowment effect in several ways. First, they can educate their clients about the effect prior to discussing whatever financial decision is at hand. Utilizing stories of past clients (changing names and details to ensure anonymity) or studies such as the one just discussed, can be helpful in this regard. Second, they can ask their clients to imagine life without the possession or investment. Would their lives be seriously harmed by not having the item in their lives? This process can help the client to evaluate the item more objectively. Third, when it comes to investing, the endowment effect tends to be most exaggerated with inexperienced investors. As clients gain experience (and the losses that can come from the endowment effect), they can actively work to avoid overvaluing their investments. Financial planners can continue to remind clients of past experiences that can help them examine their investments more objectively.

Familiarity Bias

We have spent most of human history in hunter-gatherer tribes without the benefit of the scientific method. We had to learn by trial and error, which was often quite dangerous. An unfamiliar plant or mushroom could have led to either a delicious meal or poisoning and death. As a result, it's likely that many of our ancestors who favored the unfamiliar were less likely to pass down their genes. Better to just stick with familiar foods than risk one's life, right? Additionally, being around unfamiliar faces often meant exposure to new diseases and/or violence. As such, it makes perfect sense why we have evolved to favor the familiar and be wary about the unfamiliar.

Familiarity bias can cause us to favor known quantities over what is new, novel, or less well known. When current situations appear similar to previous situations, we tend to regress to whatever state of mind we had previously held. For example, in evaluating numerous applications for an open employment position, a manager might favor applicants who graduated from the same alma mater the manager did. In many cases, familiarity bias occurs when an individual is experiencing a high amount of cognitive load or is stressed. In this case, the manager may be overwhelmed with applicants so this familiarity can help them in sorting through the resumes. In terms of investing, it is not uncommon to see portfolios that are overweighted with stocks from well-known companies, even when lesser-known companies may be better investments at any given time. Residents of countries all over the world have a tendency to hold portfolios that are overweighted with domestic investments, and it's common for employees of publicly held companies to be overconcentrated with their company's stock in their 401(k)s. Investing in something we are familiar with can make us feel more at ease even though it may be placing us at great risk due to a lack of diversification.

Flat Rate Bias

Flat rate bias is a customer preference to pay a flat rate as opposed to a pay-per-use approach, even when the costs are equal to or greater than the actual usage. Companies of all types utilize this approach with customers. Studies have found that even purchasing professionals fall prey to this bias, even when pay-per-use options are cheaper [22].

Gambler's Fallacy

Also called the Monte Carlo fallacy, the gambler's fallacy refers to the erroneous thinking that an event is more or less likely to happen based on previous events. Given its name, this phenomenon is most common in casinos, where individuals will assume that a roll of a dice will go a certain way because it did or did not in previous rolls. The gambler's fallacy has been observed in laboratory settings as well as in real-life gambling scenarios. For example, after gamblers experience a streak of five or more occurrences, they place significantly more bets on that occurrence happening a sixth time versus it not happening [23].

Law of Small Numbers Bias

Tversky and Kahneman are credited with first describing the law of small numbers bias [24], which is when someone makes sweeping generalizations about a group based on the behaviors or other qualities of one or a small handful of people. Sometimes referred to as "painting with a broad brush," this bias tends to manifest itself in groups that have different identities of sorts. For example, people of one race, gender, or ethnic group can be susceptible to the law of small numbers bias if they are exposed to only a small number of individuals who differ from them in some way, shape, or form.

Loss Aversion

"The thrill of victory, the agony of defeat." This unforgettable statement from the opening of the *Wide World of Sports* TV show perfectly sums up *loss aversion* bias. People hate to lose more than they love to win. Our brains are wired to seek pleasure and avoid pain [11]. The psychological pain of losing something is twice as powerful as the joy from winning something of the same value [25]. In finance, when we don't want to admit to taking a loss because it's too painful, we may hold on to an investment longer than we should. Holding on to a losing investment inevitably leads to even more loss and more pain. This is also common in failing business ventures, which we describe soon in greater detail as the *sunk cost fallacy* [26]. It is difficult for people to part with something when they've invested a large amount of time, energy, money, and resources into it.

It is natural to want to avoid loss, shame, guilt, embarrassment, or grief. But in trying to dodge the pain, many entrepreneurs will wind up going down with the ship. They'll sell off assets, withdraw from their retirement plans, and go down a spiral of repeatedly borrowing money to keep a failing enterprise afloat. Studies on the psychology of wealth have shown that ultrawealthy people have less of a tendency toward loss aversion than those in the middle class [4]. The ultrawealthy are more willing to admit when an investment has failed and are more readily able to cut their losses sooner, preventing the losses from continuing to hurt their portfolios so they can recover more quickly. It may help clients to understand the tendencies of the ultrawealthy so they can work to adopt a similar mindset and avoid the pitfalls of loss aversion.

Mental Accounting

Imagine a woman who just won the lottery. She was a frugal saver before the lottery winnings, with an account for her child's college fund, a grocery budget, and a little bit set aside for retirement. Instead of investing or saving her winnings, she goes on a cruise, buys a bunch of expensive clothes, dines at the finest restaurants, and blows all her winnings in a matter of a few years. She squanders her lottery winnings because she put them in a category of "throwaway money." She kept all her hard-earned money, but the lottery jackpot was money she never intended to have and didn't work to earn. Therefore, she placed a different value on those winnings. It was easier for her to part with them. This person isn't necessarily bad with money, she is just up against a common cognitive bias called *mental accounting*. This behavioral economics concept was first introduced by Nobel Prize–winning economist Richard Thaler [27]. It points out that people tend to place different values on money based on biased criteria, often to detrimental effect [28].

Mental accounting also comes into play with credit cards. In 2020, Americans owed $73 billion in credit card debt. It is much easier for a person to throw down a credit card to pay for something than to withdraw from savings or keep track of how much they can spend in a checking account. Funds from a credit card may feel like "free money," because people may not be paying attention to the interest they are paying on their balance. Some find they are paying hundreds of dollars each month in interest fees, money that could go into a savings account and earn interest.

People are prone to categorizing money differently, even though the value of money doesn't change. They put money in mental buckets based on ideas – often irrational. One bucket might be for bills. Another bucket could be a general savings account. A different bucket might be for retirement, but since that seems far away, many people ignore that bucket and leave it empty for much too long. The general savings account bucket is problematic because there is no specific purpose for it. Anytime something comes up, whether it is a car repair, a big birthday celebration, or a vacation, it's all too easy to dip into that general savings fund.

In some circumstances, mental accounting can be harnessed for our financial benefit. For example, if a person were to label a savings account specifically, such as "Jasmine's College Savings Fund," it would be harder to justify pulling from that savings to go on vacation. Similarly, a client may choose to open a separate savings account labeled "Italy 2030" to motivate them to save for a family vacation. The more specific a person gets with labeling their subaccounts, the higher their success will be in achieving their saving goals, and the less likely they will be to withdraw from the accounts for unexpected emergencies or frivolous spending [11]. It's a good idea to encourage clients to imagine themselves succeeding in their goal. If they have a plain "vacation" fund with no real destination in mind, they will be less motivated to save. But if they imagine themselves seaside, eating delicious pasta at a beautiful Italian restaurant, they will save with enthusiasm and stay committed to the goal.

Another way financial planners can use mental accounting for a client's benefit is by presenting the performance of investments in different categories, represented in different graphs. For example, a client's portfolio could be divided into two buckets: 50% in equities and 50% in fixed income. In the event of a market downturn, a client might benefit from seeing these asset classes displayed as two separate bars in a graph. While seeing news of a market drop of 20%, represented by their equity allocation, they may take comfort in seeing the fixed income portion of their investments down by only 2%. The planner might use mental accounting to remind their client that if needed, they could draw from the fixed income portion of the portfolio for years before they would need to tap into the equity portion, giving it time to recover.

Overconfidence

Most people have been guilty of overconfidence at one time or another. It is human nature to overestimate our abilities and our level of control over a given situation. According to a study by AAA, 8 out of 10 male drivers consider their driving abilities to be above average [29]. Statistically speaking, this is quite unlikely. It would suggest that many, many above average drivers are crashing into one another yearly. So why do we tend to overestimate our abilities? One explanation is a cognitive error called the *illusion of control*. This term was originally introduced by Ellen Langer in the *Journal of Personality and Social Psychology* [30]. Langer explained that people have a common instinct to overestimate their role in successful outcomes and to downplay their part in failures. People don't like to believe that chance has anything to do with it because the lack of control makes human beings uncomfortable.

The illusion of control is a factor in financial decision-making as well. One prime example of this phenomena's influence in finance is in cryptocurrency trading. The illusion of control is a dominant feature in those who engage in crypto trading, day trading, and sports betting [31]. For cryptocurrency traders with a propensity toward the illusion of control, favorable market conditions will only reinforce this illusion of control, which may contribute to greater risk taking. As the market drops, due to their tendency to downplay their role in failures while overestimating their role in any success owing to a favorable market, they risk losing their whole investment. The more time and effort people put into picking a stock, the more they believe they have insight for predicting the future of that stock as well as the direction of the entire stock market [11]. The illusion of control leads to overconfidence in investing insight and abilities, which could cause financial ruin. Advisors can help address this overconfidence by discussing the limited control that comes from things like crypto trading and sports betting. Lecturing your client is not advisable but helping them gain a longer-term view can potentially open their eyes to the lack of control they actually have with their money when investing in activities where the outcome has little rhyme or reason.

Persuasion Bias

Persuasion bias describes our susceptibility to making decisions based on social influence and the repetition of information. Specifically, it describes the phenomenon by which we fail to fully account for the impact of information we hear repeatedly on the formation of our beliefs and behaviors [32]. Whether the information is right or wrong, the more we hear it the more likely we are to believe it. This helps explain the powerful impacts of social media, marketing, airtime, and even censorship on the impact of belief formation and behaviors. The impact of persuasion bias is linked to social influence, where the people who have the most airtime and reach in a particular social network are able to exert the most influence.

Recency Effect

The *recency effect* is the tendency to best remember the information that was presented last. The most common example of the recency effect is memorizing a list that was presented verbally. Attorneys focus largely on the recency effect as they plan their closing arguments to a jury. In terms of investing, a recency bias plays out when investors incorporate more recent events into their decision making around investing, even when past events may be more important in understanding the wisdom of the decision [32].

Regret Aversion

The fear of regret can be crippling. Many of our cognitive biases reveal that our brains just don't like to feel the effects of negative outcomes. Regret aversion is another example of the brain trying to protect us from the bad feelings of regret [33]. This bias can prevent a client from making a decision for fear that it will be the wrong one. Regret-averse people also regret taking no action at all. It's a double-edged sword. Loss-aversion bias, which we discussed previously, causes people to focus more on avoiding making bad decisions than on trying to make good decisions. Regret aversion isn't all bad. It helps us make lifestyle changes, for instance, when the doctor recommends cutting down on fatty foods and exercising to bring down cholesterol. It can also be used to motivate clients to save more for their futures so they don't regret retiring without a proper nest egg. But when regret aversion freezes a client from making decisions or taking action, it can be helpful to discuss acceptance with clients. Research shows that people tend to overestimate the weight of future regret [34]. Practicing acceptance of outcomes and understanding the natural human tendency to overestimate regret can help clients get over the hurdle of regret aversion [35]. To a certain degree, regret aversion is healthy and keeps us from making bad decisions. As long as it is properly managed, rather than a hindrance, it can be an asset, in financial planning.

Representativeness Heuristic

A representative heuristic is when we tend to label something because of its connection to a larger group with similar characteristics. For example, investors may conflate a successful company with being a successful investment. As we know, those are two very different categories within a given period of time, but because they are based on the identity of one company, it is common to conflate reputation and investment. Representativeness can impact our investing decisions in other ways, too. For example, researchers at a brokerage firm looking at 40,000 households found that investors preferred stocks that had recently had abnormally large positives, suggesting that they thought these recent returns were representative of future returns [36].

Salience Bias

Psychologists in the 1970s found that one's literal point of view in observing social interactions has an influence on how others are perceived [37]. Specifically, when we are watching two people talk, we ascribe more causality in the interaction to the person whose face we are seeing than to the person for whom we can only see the back of their head. This cognitive bias has since been called *salience bias*.

Salience bias is our tendency to focus on the information that is most vivid and in our face. For example, when consumer sentiment news is reported, it can have a disproportionate impact on more salient, well-known stocks given the attention of news reports and analysts [38]. The problem with salience bias is that even though what is grabbing our attention may be the most poignant, it is often not the most important. This is why financial planners will often encourage clients to not spend excessive time watching the ups and downs of the markets. For example, news that stocks are on a tear may be exciting, but it is often irrelevant to the client's financial plan. Instead, acting on that information could go against their best interests.

Status Quo Bias

We're all lazy. It is okay to admit it. It's in our ancestral programming. When presented with the opportunity, our brains will seek out the path of least resistance every time. Long ago, laziness was a tool of survival. Due to our primitive instinct to conserve energy and avoid exertion, we typically prefer to apply the least amount of physical and mental effort in any task [11]. In cognitive psychology, this tendency is referred to as the *status quo bias*. For example, chances are you've had the same cell service for several years and even though you complain about the occasional dropped calls, high fees, and limited customer service, you stick with the same carrier. You see advertisements for other services that offer financial incentives to change, but it is easier and simpler to just stick with the company you already are using.

The status quo bias served our ancestors well. They struggled to survive in scarcity, not knowing when or where they would get their next meal. By conserving their energy, they could stretch the sustenance from their latest feast as far as possible. However, in modern society, the status quo bias isn't necessary for humans to survive. We live in an age where food comes to our doors at the tap of a button. Instead of hunting for woolly mammoths, many people sit at their desks for most of the day. The status quo bias has become something we must often override to do what is best for us.

Exercising is an example of a way human beings must override this inherent bias to conserve energy. It takes a conscious effort to overcome our laziness and build a healthy habit of physical fitness in our modern world. Ancient humans would probably laugh and sneer at modern-day people, needlessly running in circles, lifting weights, or rowing a boat that goes nowhere. But with the rise of obesity and heart disease, it is necessary to our survival for us to exercise. The tables have turned. Now human beings must fight against the laziness instinct and make it a priority to get to the gym.

Human beings are also genetically programmed to conserve mental energy. We have a list of cognitive shortcuts we use every day to exert the least amount of mental energy as possible. One of these shortcuts is to stick with the status quo, hence the term *status quo bias*. Our natural tendency is to keep things the same. Don't rock the boat. Anyone who has ever tried to break a habit knows the power of this tendency. The human brain prefers to stick with the known rather than the unknown, the familiar over the unfamiliar, with outcomes on which it can rely, whether healthy or not. It's easier to just keep doing things the way we've always done them.

Sunk-Cost Fallacy

Have you ever stayed in a relationship too long? Deep down you knew it wasn't going to work but you kept putting off its end. After all, they knew your friends, they had your favorite hoodie, and your parents even liked them. You knew it was over but who wants to go through the drama? Admitting to yourself, to them, and to the world that it was a bad relationship was hard, and you weren't looking forward to the smug look from your best friend who had been telling you your partner wasn't good for you. Perhaps you even made up some excuses like "I can't end it now, it's their birthday next month" to delay the inevitable.

The *sunk-cost fallacy* is our tendency to follow through on something even though the costs outweigh the benefits [33]. In financial planning, this often manifests as difficulty in letting go of a bad investment or a failed business into which one has put their valuable time, energy, or money, regardless of whether the current costs outweigh the benefits. In many cases, the decision to continue with an experience or investment goes against any evidence that suggests that following through is the best decision. It is irrational to consider irrecoverable costs in making a present decision. For example, Bryant prepaid a dinner for him and his partner for Valentine's Day at a local restaurant. Halfway through the meal, the couple was not having a good time as the restaurant environment was loud and uncomfortable. Instead of leaving, Bryant insisted they stay since he had already paid for the experience. Neither staying nor departing was going to recoup the invested money in the dinner, but the couple was investing more time in an experience that they were not enjoying. Organizations are also susceptible to the sunk-cost fallacy when they invest in projects that go over budget or even lose their desired objectives partway through the project. Due to their already committed resources, they follow through despite the costs or potential impact.

Financial planners can help their clients avoid the sunk-cost fallacy by first keeping track of resources that have been invested and the necessary resources needed to finish whatever investment or experience they are engaged in. Perhaps most importantly, planners can continue to remind their clients of the big picture and how continuing on the same path may impact their short- and long-term goals.

THE ROLE OF THE FINANCIAL PLANNER

Financial planners can help limit the negative impact of cognitive biases. To be most effective, the planner must continue to listen and help the client better identify their biases and, perhaps most importantly, take some of the emotion out of their financial plan. Bringing objectivity to the conversation is critical. The planner can work to develop an environment that not only eliminates friction in helping the client act in their own best interests, but even capitalizes on some of these cognitive biases to be used for the client's benefit, such as the strategic use of mental accounting to ease anxiety in the midst of market turmoil or to increase a client's motivation to save toward a meaningful goal. Financial planners can also create an environment in which there is open dialogue, allowing the planner to identify some of the biases a client may exhibit. With this in mind planners can proactively inoculate clients against many of these biases by open discussion and education around how human beings are wired to do money wrong – especially in times of heightened emotion. Introducing these conversations early in the relationship can facilitate the creation of a shared language and make it easier to refer to them when the biases rear their ugly head.

ELIMINATE THE FRICTION

One way we can counter our laziness, whether at the gym or mentally, is by eliminating the friction that makes it more difficult for us to do the things that are in our best interests. For example, people who go to a gym five times a month have an average commute of 3.7 miles, whereas those who only went to the gym once a week had an average commute of 5.1 miles [39]. There is less friction, in this case a commute, for people to get to the gym to exercise. Many online retailers do an incredible job of making purchasing as easy and frictionless as possible. No reentering credit card numbers or even selecting what to buy! Their system knows what you purchased before and with one or two clicks, the product is back at your door and your money is on its way to the CEO of the retailer! Frictionless. We can alter our environment to eliminate the friction to help us do the things that are going to make us happier and healthier.

Since human beings have an innate desire to keep things the same, how can we increase the possibility for success in helping our clients meet their financial goals? One way to address the status quo bias is to use that instinctual laziness to the benefit of the client by eliminating the friction and making doing the right thing as easy as possible. For instance, let's say that a client wants to invest more into their retirement. By engaging a financial planner, they have taken the first step in overriding their status quo bias and are excited about taking action to achieve their goal. The client has decided how much they want to contribute each month. The worst thing a financial planner can do is to establish a system in which the client must write a check or transfer money into an account every month. This requires too much effort for the ancestral brain. The client will inevitably forget to make the transfer, or when something unexpected comes up that requires extra money (and something always comes up), it will be too easy to stop contributing. A more successful strategy is harnessing the status quo bias and automating the contributions. Whether this is through autotransfers the client sets up ahead of time or salary deferrals that occur without the client thinking about it, this method will short-circuit the cognitive bias to keep everything the same and resist extra effort. When a client automates contributions, they will need to make a conscious effort to sabotage their saving and investing goals. Stopping the contributions will require extra mental energy and complex processes, which we know the brain hates. Automation will help the client harness the power of their mental laziness, therefore serving their financial well-being for the long term [39]. In modern society, we need to outsmart our cognitive biases and get them working in our favor, rather than against us. The status quo bias is just one of many that can hold a financial planning client back.

TECHNIQUES FOR OVERCOMING BIASES

Soll, Milkman, and Payne offer techniques that can help financial planners and clients overcome their cognitive biases in three areas important to decision making: (1) thinking about the future, (2) thinking about objectives, and (3) thinking about options [40].

Thinking About the Future

1. *Make three estimates.* When trying to make predictions about the future, the price of a particular stock, for example, try to come up with three estimates: low, medium, and high. Coming up with three numbers can help you compensate for being overly optimistic or pessimistic. Often the middle number will be the closest to reality.

2. *Think twice.* Another hedge against poor decisions is to make two guesses. Make your first guess, set it aside, and then come back later and make another guess without referring to your first. Then average them out.

3. *Use postmortems.* In a twist on thinking through a failure, Soll et. al (2015) encourage people to imagine a future failure and then deconstruct (ahead of time) what went wrong. This approach can help curb excessive optimism and help you come up with a backup plan.

4. *Take an outside view.* Try to view the situation from an outside perspective, such as if you were going to advise a friend on how to proceed.

Thinking About Objectives

1. *Cycle through your objectives.* Once you have made a list of your goals, spend some time looking at each one of them individually and develop a plan for meeting that goal rather than approaching them all as one.

2. *Seek advice.* This is where financial advisors play such a critical role. Once you have a clear idea of your goals, seek objective advice from others to help expand your point of view.

Thinking About Options

1. *Use joint evaluation.* Rather than evaluating options in isolation, try to look at them together. Often pursuing one option precludes the other. Take some time to consider what you will be missing out on if you choose one option over the other.

2. *Try the "vanishing options" test.* Once we decide on an option we may move forward without fully exploring alternative options. You can avoid this problem by pretending that the option you have chosen no longer exists, asking yourself: "What else could I do?"

Perhaps most importantly, financial planners must become aware of their own biases and their vulnerability to falling prey to them. With knowledge of their own biases, the planner can not only be more vigilant in detecting them with their client, but also share that they themselves may be susceptible to similar biases and behaviors. Illustrating this level of openness and vulnerability can go a long way in establishing a deeper relationship with the client, which can ultimately lead to more impact in helping them meet their financial goals.

KEY POINTS

- A cognitive bias is a systematic error in thinking that arises from our attempts to make sense of a complicated world. A heuristic is a process for doing something that may or may not be ideal.
- The planner must recognize their own biases so they can bring objectivity to their work with clients and their own decision process.
- The planner must work to better identify client biases that will inform many aspects of the client's behaviors as it relates to their financial plan.

CFP BOARD LEARNING OBJECTIVES COVERED IN THIS CHAPTER

H.66. Behavioral finance

a. Identify how cognitive biases and heuristics can impact financial decision-making.

CHAPTER 3

The Environment

Consider two professionals sitting at a conference table. While they are in the same place now, dressed similarly and perhaps even working for the same firm, they come from two very different backgrounds. One grew up wealthier than the other; they are of different races; and one experienced psychological trauma that the other didn't. If you were their financial advisor, would you want to approach your relationship with them in the exact same manner? Without working to better understand their clients' backgrounds, many planners could make a number of erroneous assumptions based on their initial behaviors or appearance in your first meeting. Given their different backgrounds, how might their priorities and worries differ? Could there be potential triggers that might elicit some emotion in one of them but not the other? What assumptions might you make about their worldviews based on their appearance, dress, or demeanor? Between any two clients, we can see these dramatic differences in backgrounds and life experiences manifest throughout the financial planning process. There are a variety of strategies a planner can use to help build a solid, trusting relationship with clients and to help them meet their financial goals. But before we dive into the strategies it's important to understand our clients and how their environment has impacted their financial psychology.

We are immersed in an environment that shapes our thinking and experiences around money. The impact of this environment can be extremely difficult to see from the outside. In some cases, we are like fish swimming in a pond. Until we are exposed to other bodies of water, we think our pond is "just how the world is." Our fundamental subconscious assumptions,

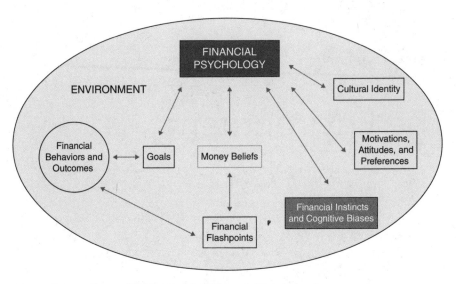

FIGURE 3.1   Klontz-Chaffin Model of Financial Psychology

without disconfirming evidence, will be that other people are having similar thoughts, feelings, and experiences as we are.

Mark Twain touched on this notion when he spoke of the benefits of traveling: "Travel is fatal to prejudice, bigotry, and narrow-mindedness, and many of our people need it sorely on these accounts. Broad, wholesome, charitable views of men and things cannot be acquired by vegetating in one little corner of the earth all one's lifetime" [41]. In this chapter we focus on the impact of our environment shaping our financial psychology, as illustrated in Figure 3.1.

ENVIRONMENT: CULTURE, GENERATION, CLASS, AND COMMUNITY

Our environment has the power to impact everything we say, do, feel, or think, often without our even being consciously aware of it. As the famous psychologist B.F. Skinner once wrote: "I did not direct my life. I didn't design it. I never made decisions. Things always came up and made them for me. That's what life is."

Although many of Skinner's conclusions have been challenged in the decades following his work on operant conditioning, there is a great deal of truth to his assertion that our environments have a powerful impact on shaping all aspects of our lives. Our environment directly influences our beliefs about money. It plays an enormous role in developing our sense of normalcy, influenced by our country, state, city, neighborhood, religion, culture, socioeconomic background, and whether we grew up in a rural or urban environment. These can all be key factors in determining the nature of our relationship with money. While some environments nurture positive money habits and outcomes, others can be destructive. A person's money beliefs and financial behaviors may be based on false narratives and inaccurate information. We need to understand the environment a client experienced as a child if we want to help them overcome any inaccurate or destructive beliefs, habits, or tendencies they may have. Aspects of their environment worthy of consideration include their culture, generation, socioeconomic class, and community.

Culture

The culture in which we are immersed has a tremendous impact on our relationship with money. Being raised in a particular country, being a member of a particular ethnic group, adhering to specific religious beliefs and practices, and being raised according to established gender norms all have a profound impact on our financial experiences and resulting beliefs. Our majority or minority status in any or all of those groups also impacts our experiences. We explore the impact of majority and minority status on financial planning in detail in Chapter 15. Cultural norms and values impact, for example, how much an individual experiences a desire, or external pressure, to share their financial resources with their families and communities. Going against that culture could result in banishment, similar to the times of our hunter-gatherer ancestors. While we would not likely die from being exiled from our families or communities today, our brain still believes that banishment equals death. It can be challenging for a person to go against the culture in which they were raised, and a financial planner must take care in honoring a person's cultural values in the development of a financial plan.

If you're a practicing financial planner, what is the makeup of your current clients when it comes to culture? What backgrounds do your clients emanate? Do you work with clients from different backgrounds? This book dives deeper into ways to engage clients from a broad range of cultural backgrounds. The people with whom we work and spend our free time can help us see the world through a different lens.

Generation

Given that cultures shift over time, the generation in which we are born can also have a profound impact on our experiences. Norms and values shift over time and entire generations experience events that can shape their approach to money. For example, the Great Depression was accompanied for many by scarcity, and a lingering penchant for frugality. The Great Recession resulted in a generation of young people who had less trust in the stable value of real estate and the stock market. While people in a particular culture and generation may experience these differently, the environment in which one is immersed will impact their financial behaviors.

The average age of a financial planner is 55 years old, with approximately one-fifth of the workforce at over 65 [42]. What is the average age of the advisors in your firm? What is the average age of the clients in the firm and are you looking to attract younger clients? Conversely, are you a younger planner (or still in school studying to become one) and looking to discover avenues to connect with older clients? It is important to consider generational influences on a client's values, goals, beliefs, and behaviors.

Socioeconomic Class

A person's socioeconomic status while they were growing up also heavily impacts their views and behaviors around money. For example, climbing the socioeconomic ladder comes with challenges. When one member of the family becomes wealthy or successful, it can make them feel alienated from their family, especially if that family is poor. Instead of offering support and encouragement, the wealthy family member may feel estranged, disparaged, or used because of constant requests for financial support and loans that may never be repaid. Sometimes the wealthy family members will subconsciously sabotage themselves just to feel like they belong within their tribe. Psychologically, there is a strong pull to stay at the same socioeconomic level as the rest of the family. So they may give away their money or lose it all in bad investments, just so they don't have to feel the sting of the family's hostility and estrangement [11].

Social Exchange Theory

A greater understanding of shared tribal bonds can be gathered from the perspective of the *social exchange theory*, which asserts that there is a human tendency to seek a natural balance between give and take [43]. In order for tribal relationships to be worthwhile, each member must feel they are receiving value that is equal to or greater than the amount they sacrifice and/or invest in the tribe. If the balance is off, if resentment and discontent fester, the individual's bond with the tribe can be harmed. For instance, if one member of the tribe contributes significantly less than other members, they risk banishment. On the other hand, if one member is giving significantly more than the rest of the tribe, they may begin to feel bitter, taken advantage of, or held back from their full potential. In the latter instance, the individual may find a new tribe that aligns more closely with their values. As a planner, it is crucial to understand the cultural dynamic at play in a client's life in order to navigate the sometimes-choppy waters of family and community relationships. Chapter 6 covers how to learn about a client's cultural background, discover how much they are influenced by it, and navigate that sometimes tricky territory so they can make the best financial decisions possible.

Community

Being from a small town in a rural area can lead to very different experiences around money than while growing up in a larger town. One could argue that being exposed to a larger worldview could provide a more diverse environment that can influence and shape our belief systems. Regardless of where you live today, the rise of social media has widened our exposure to other ways of being. Instead of growing up in small communities, we are now exposed to lifestyles of people from all different classes, cultures, and levels of wealth. Our modern world went from keeping up with the Joneses to keeping up with the Kardashians. People flaunt their wealth on social media, making a person of average means and a more humble upbringing feel inadequate. Individuals see the curated posts of the people they follow on Instagram or Facebook and feel compelled to achieve the same, not realizing that so many create images of themselves that are only loosely based on the reality of their lives. This creates feelings of FOMO and inadequacy even though people are measuring themselves against something that may not even exist! This inadequacy gives rise to people living beyond their means, hiking up credit card debt to buy the latest fashions and gadgets, and neglecting things like savings and retirement. The environment of social media has had a major impact on society's financial beliefs, values, and behaviors. If a client wants to make sound financial choices, who they follow on social media may be just as important as where they were born and raised. Following people on social media who can empower and motivate you toward your goals can be far more helpful than devoting attention to people who only make us crave more things that we may not even want in the first place!

WHAT'S NEXT

When a financial planner is in a room or in a virtual meeting with a client, they are not just facing the client. They are dealing with generational messages, ancestral programming, cognitive biases, and influences from their culture, gender, the socioeconomic status in which they were raised, their financial flashpoints, money beliefs, and their financial outcomes to date. There is a lot to unpack. But with the proper tools and a knowledge of psychology, a planner can help clients to understand their own biases, tendencies, beliefs, behaviors, and habits. Once the planner and client share an understanding of the intricacies at play in the client's financial life, they'll be able to harness those factors and use them to propel the client toward achieving their financial goals.

KEY CONCEPTS

- Environment has a powerful influence on a client's financial psychology.
- Environment impacts culture, generation, class, and community.
- In order to establish a solid, trusting relationship with a client, the advisor needs to have a keen understanding of the client's background as it relates to past experiences and environment.

CFP BOARD LEARNING OBJECTIVES COVERED IN THIS CHAPTER

H.65. Client and planner attitudes, values, biases

a. Analyze a client's degree of risk tolerance and loss aversion and ensure recommendations are consistent with a client's risk propensity, attitudes, composure (e.g., past behaviors during market corrections), capacity, knowledge, and needs.

b. Explain how a client's psychology, background, preferred learning style and values (socially conscious investor, etc.) impact the financial planning process.

c. Explain how a client's values, including cultural and religious values and attitudes, may impact their goals and the financial planning process.

PART II

UNDERSTANDING A CLIENT'S FINANCIAL PSYCHOLOGY

As we've discussed, when a financial planner is meeting with a client, they are not just facing the client, they are dealing with a host of generational and cultural messages, biases, and influences, the outcomes of which they may or may not be aware. In Part I we explored why human beings are naturally wired to be bad with money and the impact of the broader environment on their financial psychology. But these universal human tendencies are just part of the financial psychology story. Our financial psychology is also influenced by individual factors. Our experiences around money, beliefs about money, and our financial behaviors all help shape our relationship with money. We have unique individual, family, and generational experiences around money, which we refer to as financial flashpoints. To make sense of these experiences, we develop beliefs around money, which we refer to as money scripts®. These beliefs, in turn, influence our financial behaviors and outcomes. Our financial outcomes give us new financial flashpoints, and the cycle continues.

In Part II we explore the intersection of financial flashpoints, money scripts, and financial behaviors in shaping our financial psychology. We dedicate a chapter to each of these topics. Utilizing our model of financial psychology (Figure II.1), our hope is that you are able to better make sense of the individual factors impacting a client's relationship with money.

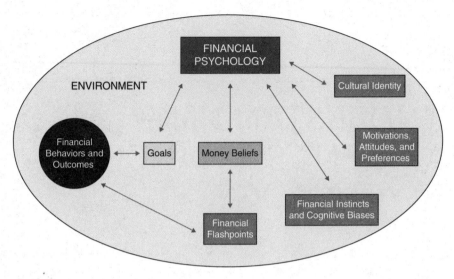

FIGURE II.1   Klontz-Chaffin Model of Financial Psychology

CHAPTER 4

Financial Flashpoints: Exploring a Client's Financial Background

At 11:30 p.m. on a Tuesday night, Ted collapsed into bed and uttered to himself, "At least they can't call me lazy." He was exhausted from a day that had started at 3:30 a.m. tending horses. After that, he was off by 5:00 a.m. to the gym he owned, where he began preparations to open the doors by 6:00. He left the gym by 7:00 to get to his full-time job, teaching high school and coaching basketball and baseball. After a full day of teaching and coaching, he was back to the gym to close up at 10 p.m. and then return to the horses to feed them once again. His average workday spanned nearly 20 hours. At the end of each day, when he finally made it to bed, he would utter the same phrase to himself, "At least they can't call me lazy."

Years later, Ted examined this voice in his head. He learned that this belief had been passed down from his great-grandparents to their children and through the generations to Ted. After doing some digging into his family history, he learned that his paternal grandfather hadn't worked much, possibly due to an injury. Whatever the reason, Ted's grandmother would complain about his grandfather to Ted's father when he was a young boy. She admonished him for how little he worked to support his family. Ted's father internalized this experience and decided to help neighboring farmers when he was six years old, gaining the praise and approval of his mother and everyone in town. Ted remembers his father having several jobs and always working. From this story, Ted absorbed the idea that being called lazy was the worst thing someone could say about a person.

As he got older, Ted also worked harder, always focused on proving that he wasn't lazy rather than being paid appropriately for his labor. He often worked on his maternal grandfather's farm baling hay. One day, at 10 years old, Ted mustered up the courage to ask his grandfather if he would be willing to pay him one dollar per day for his work. He knew that his grandfather paid other neighborhood boys a dollar per hour for doing the same work. He also knew his grandfather would never give him a dollar per hour but thought maybe a dollar a day would be reasonable. His grandfather's words became the guiding principle of his life for the next 30 years. He said, "I will decide whether or not I think you're worth anything, and if I do, I'll pay you. You should feel lucky that you have something to eat, a place to sleep, and clothes to wear." Ted never got a cent from his grandfather. At every job he worked after that, for the next 35 years, Ted let other people decide what he was worth and what he should be paid.

Our financial psychology is forged through our experiences, and the environment, culture, and socioeconomic situation in which we live. Traumatic experiences as they relate to money can also impact our financial psychology. When examining a client's financial behaviors, it can be helpful to first learn about their financial beliefs, digging deeper to find the source of these stories, and deciding together whether these beliefs are serving the client or causing harm to their financial lives. The source of many of our clients' beliefs are their financial flashpoints, which consist of their specific background and experiences around money. Financial flashpoints can be unique events experienced by the individual and/or family – such as a job loss or bankruptcy – or a universal societal event, such as the Great Recession or Great Depression. As illustrated in Figure 4.1, financial flashpoints lead to the development of our money scripts. These events shape our financial psychology and our subsequent financial behaviors and outcomes. Our financial behaviors and outcomes, in turn, give us a new set of financial flashpoint experiences – whether positive or negative – that either reinforce our money scripts or give us opportunities to challenge and change them.

The purpose of this chapter is to build on the factors that influence our perceptions and behaviors and focus on how our unique experiences around money shape our financial beliefs.

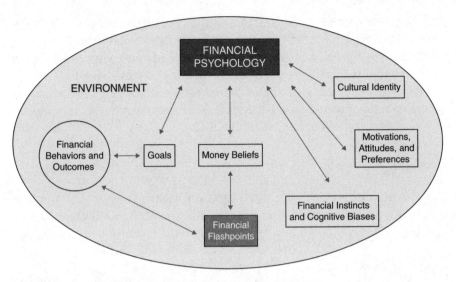

FIGURE 4.1   Klontz-Chaffin Model of Financial Psychology

FINANCIAL FLASHPOINTS

Ted's experiences around money, from watching his father get praised for hard work to his grandfather telling him he wasn't good enough to get paid, represent his financial flashpoints, which shaped his money beliefs and his own work-related behaviors. Financial flashpoints are life events (or a series of events) associated with money that are so emotionally powerful that they leave an imprint that lasts into adulthood [44, p. 8]. This imprint has an impact on our beliefs, attitudes, and relationship with money.

Financial flashpoints could be specific to a person's family situation, culture, or cultural or societal events, such as the Great Depression or the housing market crash. Flashpoints can also occur from the socioeconomic status in which an individual was raised, their religion, their majority or minority status, and even gender. For instance, parents are still bringing their male children into financial conversations and situations – such as requiring them to work outside the home – before their female children. This causes female children to be behind in learning about things like balancing a checkbook, budgeting, and saving. All of these factors lay fertile ground for financial flashpoints early in a person's life. Some financial flashpoints can be traumatic, which, if left unchecked or unchallenged, can cause a client to make poor financial decisions that could harm their financial future. Other flash-points could be a bit more mundane, but still have a powerful impact on a person's life. It is imperative that the financial planner work to develop a deeper relationship with the client to uncover any of these potential barriers and experiences that can dramatically impact a client's view on money. We explore several approaches to eliciting these stories from clients in financial planning later in this chapter.

Growing Up Poor

Growing up poor is often a traumatic experience, one of scarcity and fear that there will never be enough to survive, impacting people's beliefs about money and their financial outcomes. It is a logical conclusion for someone who grew up in poverty and, at their core, assumes that there will not be enough. A scarcity mindset can have a powerful impact on so many aspects of our lives, from our money to relationships to time. Essentially, the experience of scarcity leads to scarcity beliefs, which unfortunately lead to more scarcity. When people grow up believing there is not enough money, they can go in two radically different directions:

1. **A person becomes a saver and a hustler.** This individual works exceptionally hard so they don't fall back into poverty. These types of individuals often accrue significant amounts of money and make up a significant percentage of financial planning clients. Many become avid savers and manage their personal finances well. Ironically, in trying to avoid a life of scarcity, many wind up living a life of subjective scarcity and anxiety around money. Often these clients struggle to retire or begin to take distributions from their accounts.

2. **A person will fall into a pit of learned helplessness.** This is a psychological condition that causes people to think that no matter what they do, it doesn't matter. In a series of experiments using electric shocks on dogs, psychologist Martin Seligman found that when experiencing uncontrollable and inescapable trauma, animals will become passive. However, when the situation changes and escape *is* possible, the previously traumatized animals will still remain passive, refusing any attempts at escape [45]. This type of mindset is also often referred to as an "external locus of control," and studies have shown that such a mindset is associated with worse outcomes in life, including lower net worth and self-destructive financial behaviors [46]. Similar to the

dogs in the Seligman study, a person with this attitude will not be motivated to take action to make life better because they falsely believe it won't matter what they do. A person operating from a place of learned helplessness will accrue high credit card debt, because to them, what's the point of trying to have good credit anyway since they will never have enough? They max out their credit cards the moment they get them, thus causing more debt, which leads to even more scarcity.

Growing Up Rich

Kristen rarely spent time with her parents. Her parents felt more like grandparents, people who would occasionally visit but have little impact on the daily lives of Kristen or her siblings. The children's caretakers were "hired help," including nannies, tutors, chauffeurs, and chefs. The staff often told the children that if they didn't behave, they would lose their jobs and the children would be sent to an orphanage. They would reprimand, "You're so lucky to have money. Stop complaining and look at what you have!" Kristen heard these phrases often as she grew up. She and her siblings were surrounded by eight hired employees in a huge house, yet they experienced an overwhelming sense of loneliness. Kristen felt a huge hole in her life and developed an inability to connect with others. She was embarrassed by her wealth and actually tried to hide the fact that she was dropped off at school by a chauffeur. This ongoing flashpoint taught Kristen to associate money with shame, guilt, disconnection, and alienation from others.

In her adult life, Kristen's beliefs about money caused several negative behaviors. She served on over two dozen nonprofit boards, which required her to travel constantly. Although she overworked herself, there was a nagging feeling that nothing she ever did was of value. She began to drink excessively and eventually, her marriage ended and her children stopped having any contact with her. It was hard for Kristen to trust people because she couldn't tell if they were genuinely interested in being her friend or just liked her for her money. At the same time, she never felt like she belonged anywhere, which perpetuated her feelings of loneliness.

People, whether growing-up rich or poor, tend to get stuck in the socioeconomic class in which they were raised. Growing up either poor or rich can become tied to a person's sense of self-identity, which can cause them to cling to it. Even if circumstances change, people will continue living as if they are still in the old socioeconomic status. It's not uncommon for people who grow up in poverty to manifest a life of scarcity even after they become wealthy. For Kristen, she still tried to live and spend like a rich person as an adult, even after she lost her wealth.

Financial Rescue

One Saturday morning when Molly was 12 years old, she was told to choose six of her favorite toys and pack them in a car because her parents told her they needed to move. They had received news that the sheriff was coming later that morning and they were not going to be able to live in their house any longer. As she was carrying her treasures to the car, she saw her grandparents pull into the driveway. They gave her a hug and asked her to come inside with them. As she neared the house, she saw her mom and dad waiting at the front door. As she recalls it, her grandmother said: "Good news!" and handed her dad an envelope. He opened it, looked up, and began crying. Inside was a check that would cover not only the cost of their missed mortgage payments but the price of the entire house. Her grandparents had secretly sold a piece of property and gifted her mom and dad with the proceeds. Her mom began screaming and jumping up and down with joy.

Molly thought it was a miracle, and her parents supported that idea by saying "God is good" and "God always provides." Fast-forward 50 years and Molly is self-employed. She lives on the verge of defaulting on her house payment, her car payment, and credit card balances. When asked how she plans to tackle these financial problems, she responds: "I'm not worried, because the Universe will provide."

When a person gets into financial trouble, it is helpful to reach out to friends and family for a one-time loan or financial support. However, this behavior can become problematic if the financial trouble keeps repeating and this person becomes dependent on being rescued financially or merely expects things to "work out" on their own without a plan or taking action. Being bailed out frequently can lead to a mindset of apathy. People who repeatedly get bailed out by friends and relatives may start to think they don't need to worry about taking responsibility for their own financial lives because they always get rescued. This belief leads to financial dependence, which is not good for the person on either side of that situation. In Chapter 6 we explore, in depth, the dynamics between the financial enabler and the financial dependent.

Death or Divorce

At 50 years old, Bruce realized he had been sabotaging himself when it came to money but didn't understand the reason behind it. As soon as he would start to become successful in a business venture, he would psychologically crumble and destroy the opportunity. When he was invited to dig deeper into his past, he remembered an experience he had when he was around 11 years old. A sports car drove up and a well-dressed man (the country doctor) got out of the car. The doctor confronted Bruce's dad, asking him to pay his hospital bill. To Bruce's surprise, his dad slammed the doctor against his car and told him if he ever came to ask for money again, he would kill him. After the doctor drove away, Bruce's dad told him that all the doctor cared about was money and not the life he destroyed.

The hospital bill that the doctor was referring to was from when Bruce's mom was rushed to the hospital with complications from pregnancy. She lost the baby, and Bruce's dad blamed the doctor. He believed the baby died because the doctor wasn't there to treat his wife. The doctor was reportedly playing golf at the time of the incident, or so the story went. Clearly, that experience had a huge impact on Bruce. From that moment forward, Bruce had a negative association with money. Subconsciously, he didn't want to make his father violently angry or cause the death of someone else by caring too much about money. This manifested in his life in a self-destructive way, in the form of sabotaging his business ventures.

Otherwise Unremarkable Happenstance

Not all financial flashpoints are the result of trauma. Sometimes we pick up messages from random places in our childhoods, like board games. Can a board game change somebody's life? In this case, it did. A successful entrepreneur shared that his entire family went to university. Everybody except him. When asked why he decided not to go to college, he recalled playing the *Game of Life* as a kid. He learned that he could make money faster by skipping college and going straight into the workforce. This left an imprint on him, and his entire adult life, he subconsciously based his financial future on a board game he played as a child.

Ancestral Flashpoints

A client's relationship with money can be influenced not only by their own life experiences, but also from the experiences of their grandparents, great-grandparents, and beyond. The experiences of our ancestors become genetically encoded in us even if we don't know the full story. For instance, a person seeing a slithering snake will probably jump away from it. They would do this even if they had never been bitten by a snake or warned about them by their parents. At some point in humanity's ancient past, our ancestors learned that avoiding snake bites was beneficial to survival and passed down this instinct to future generations. In modern times, a person doesn't need to know the history of snake bites and how they harmed earlier generations; the brain's fight-or-flight response automatically kicks in, protecting a person from potential snake bites [11]. As we've discussed, our genetic coding that was necessary for survival in previous generations is meant to protect us in the present, which is why our instinctual responses to perceived threats can be passed down through generations without the direct experience of the offspring and grandchildren.

Our experiences in childhood leave us vulnerable to developing beliefs that are not 100% accurate, of which we are often not consciously aware, and that can have a profound influence over our lives. Our childlike brains lack perspective, nuance, and context, and in our attempts to make sense of what's happening, we can easily draw inaccurate conclusions. Since money is a taboo topic, we are rarely provided with the opportunity to discuss and explore these beliefs, and as such, many go unchallenged well into our adulthood, often having a profound impact on our financial behaviors and outcomes.

Financial flashpoints are the underlying cause of many self-destructive money behaviors. Studies show that disordered money behaviors are often a result of a history of trauma, related to money or otherwise. For example, studies have found a link between childhood trauma and gambling disorder [47]. Compulsive hoarding has also been linked to a history of traumatic events experienced in childhood [48]. Trauma has been closely linked to a host of chronic self-defeating, self-destructive behaviors.

Gender

Many women grew up learning that they shouldn't think about, deal with, or even earn too much money. They were taught that men should be the primary breadwinners, and that a woman doesn't "have a head" for math or business. In fact, research has found that the more a wife outearns her husband, the greater the chance of infidelity, marital instability, and lower levels of marital satisfaction [49]. Girls are socialized from a young age to be much more comfortable with the idea of being financially dependent on their partners [50]. This ongoing financial flashpoint leads to money scripts such as, "I need a man to take care of me financially." Women who were raised with this mindset may grow up without even the most basic financial knowledge and skills, such as balancing a budget or reading bank statements.

In addition to the conditioning girls receive from a young age about money, they are also strapped with more responsibilities at home as adults. Women are often pushed to sacrifice their own careers for their families while men enjoy the full potential of their occupations [51]. This comes with dire financial consequences for women, leaving them with as much as $1,055,000 less cumulative wealth in retirement than their male counterparts [52]. The fact that women make less money than men has continued to set women back financially. Considering that women tend to live longer than men, later in life they are more likely to need long-term care and more retirement savings than men. Yet, many women feel uncertain when it comes to investing and are climbing an uphill battle of making less money, unequal family care responsibilities, as well as having to take more time off from work to care for family. This can lead to career disruptions including missed promotions and having to take lower paying jobs which can impact their retirement and social security.

Men are also shouldered with expectations around work and money that can be limiting and even harmful. Many are taught that if their spouse earns more money than they do, they are failures. This belief can lead to discontent and even infidelity. The harmful and constricting belief that a man's only value is what he earns can play out in unhealthy ways in adulthood. In a culture steeped in the worship of wealth and success, men are often under enormous pressure to not only provide for their families, but to shoulder the financial burdens of the whole family. Rigid gender roles around money in our society harms everyone.

The financial flashpoints just discussed lead to money beliefs, or internal scripts that play on repeat in a person's mind due to their adverse, and not so adverse, money experiences early in life. It can help financial planners to understand these money scripts so they can understand how to counter them and lead a client to better decisions about their money.

Stress and Trauma

In their "Stress in America™" survey, the American Psychological Association has consistently found that money ranks as one of the top sources of stress in the lives of Americans. Add into the mix experiences steeped in intense emotion or even trauma, and it can become difficult to help a client overcome limiting or self-destructive money beliefs. It is important to note that during the traumatic event, a certain money belief may have been 100% accurate. But as time goes on and circumstances change, that belief, once adapted by the client to survive, may no longer be true or relevant. Take, for instance, the Great Depression. During that dark time in history, many people lost everything. They trusted banks with their money, and the banks lost their hard-earned life savings. For many people, the belief that arose out of that traumatic event was, "You can't trust banks with your money." In the time of the Great Depression, that was 100% true and accurate. But as time went on, regulations were put in place to prevent such a catastrophic event from happening in the future. This did very little to restore a generation's faith in the banking system, so many people report finding hidden money all over their deceased grandparents' property: coffee cans buried in the yard, rolled-up bills in the freezer, money under the mattress, and so on.

Intense emotion can make money beliefs rigid and difficult to change – a mindset of "I'm never going to let that happen to me again," no matter what. This is why some people who grew up in poverty never feel like they have enough to feel safe and secure. It might be why older generations are less willing to take risks, whereas younger generations, who have not had direct experiences of devastating market corrections or loss, tend to be more willing to take risks. Ideally, a client will be flexible and open to change. But if they are having trouble overcoming these limiting beliefs about money, it might be time for them to consider seeing a psychological professional for help.

Cultural Events

Events that occur on a national or global scale also have an impact on the individual, like that of a tribe. Those who live through economic recessions, depressions, or other types of shared economic hardship are likely to pass along to younger generations fear or anxiety about not having enough money, and the values of saving. The tech bubble is another example of a large-scale phenomenon that has had significant cultural impact. With the emergence of online trading tools available to everyone, many inexperienced investors became "traders," and when the markets tanked, many sustained significant losses. More than one such investor swore off investing as being too risky and proceeded to miss out on the biggest bull market in history.

Financial trauma can occur when global events impact an individual economically over an extended period. The psychological effects of the Great Depression or hardships related to the Great Recession do not just disappear when the period of hardship subsides. Such events can create behaviors and habits that can live with the individual, or in some cases a generation, for the rest of their lives. As we have described, many of our clients' grandparents were known to save or even hoard due to the Great Depression. Those who lost money during the dot-com bubble may have developed a fear of the markets or an aversion to investing. Generation X and Y can be perceived as far more pragmatic when it comes to saving, spending, and even how they earn their living due to their experiences related to the Great Recession of 2008–2011.

Research has shown how such worldwide economic events have impacted individuals and the collective psychology and financial behaviors. The effects of financial crises are often first experienced through threats to emotional well-being. For example, foreclosures during the Great Recession in 2007 were found to be associated with increased rates of depression not just in the individuals who were losing their homes but in the community overall, including higher rates of community depression and hospital visits [53]. The psychological impact of the Great Recession was even worse for those who were more vulnerable prior to the crisis, including people who were older and/or poorer precrisis [54].

The effects of cultural financial events can also lead to mass traumatization. For example, a study of 1,208 residents of Athens, Greece found that 88% were reporting moderate to severe symptoms of posttraumatic stress in the wake of the Great Recession, with the elderly, women, and those caring for dependents being the hardest hit [55]. Perhaps even more troubling for our purposes, a survey of financial planners in 2009 found that in the months after the Great Recession, 93% reported medium to high levels of posttraumatic stress – including intrusive thoughts, sleep difficulties, waves of strong feelings, and feelings of emotional numbness [56]. The researchers highlighted that this experience corresponded with a mass movement from a buy-and-hold approach in favor of tactical asset management, as planners were left to question their approach to money management.

In more recent history, the COVID-19 pandemic set an entire planet back financially and socially, with long-term implications on the financial, social, and educational outcomes of students around the world. The long-term effects of the COVID-19 pandemic will not be fully realized for years to come. But what we know thus far is that in 2020, the labor market suffered significant setbacks, highlighting income disparities across the globe. In the wake of the COVID-19 pandemic there was a combination of financial trauma and financial reform that may affect economics for generations. As a society as we gain a better sense of the personal and financial cost of COVID-19, planners will have to be sensitive to how their clients interpret and react to this ever-changing world. Such financial flashpoints and traumatic events impact the financial beliefs and biases within individuals, families, and communities. When working with a client, it is critical that planners consider a client's cultural financial experiences as well as their family and personal financial experiences.

Financial flashpoints, whether experienced directly, witnessed, or endured by our ancestors, have a profound impact on the genesis of our relationship with money. In our attempt to survive and thrive, we develop our money beliefs. They do not occur and freeze within a given period of time, but, rather, stay with us. These beliefs, in turn, drive our financial behaviors and lead to predictable financial outcomes. In the next chapter, we continue our focus on understanding a client's financial psychology by exploring the research on money beliefs, common patterns seen in clients, and their impact on financial behaviors and outcomes.

KEY POINTS

- Financial flashpoints are life events associated with money that have a lasting impact on our financial beliefs and behaviors.
- Some financial flashpoints are experienced directly, and others have been experienced by our ancestors, but all have a profound impact on our relationship with money.
- Financial flashpoints include experiences such as growing up rich, growing up poor, stress and trauma, gender, cultural or economic events, and death and divorce.

CFP BOARD LEARNING OBJECTIVES COVERED IN THIS CHAPTER

H.66. Behavioral finance

a. Identify how cognitive biases and heuristics can impact financial decision-making.
b. Describe how a client's psychology, such as their financial comfort zone, socialization, money beliefs, and past financial experiences and behaviors impact their objectives, goals, understanding, decision making, and actions.

CHAPTER 5

Money Beliefs

We all have beliefs about money. Have you ever wondered how two people could live within the same community, generation, socioeconomic group, and even family, and have dramatically different beliefs about money? Each of us spends, saves, and invests differently. Two members of the same family with the same income and upbringing could be different clients with different goals, needs, and behaviors. Many of these differences relate to factors such as culture and environment. Although we all have similar challenges related to our outdated brains, we each have a variety of life experiences that stay with us and impact our daily financial lives.

A young girl sat at the dinner table with her parents one evening. She had heard her friends talking about how much money their parents made and was curious about her own parents. So, she innocently asked her dad how much money he made. Without hesitation, her mother slapped her. Through teeth gritted in anger, the mother said, "We do not ask people how much money they make." The girl was stunned and confused. Later, in her adult life, she understandably felt a great deal of anxiety whenever she talked about money. She avoided the topic of money whenever she could, which led to her being money-avoidant. Because of her negative associations with money and wealth, she sabotaged her financial success. She ignored her bank statements, ran up debt from overspending, financially enabled others, and had trouble sticking to a budget.

Consider the power of these flashpoints. Although there could have been multiple similar incidents as the one just described, the one incident with her mother was so profoundly vivid that it had an impact on her financial life

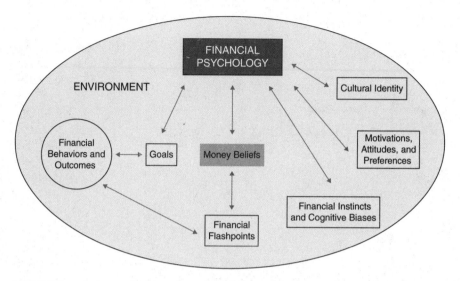

FIGURE 5.1   Klontz-Chaffin Model of Financial Psychology

forever! Although not all of our flashpoints are as clear (or violent) as this one, we all have them. They could be as mundane as how our parents described their spending on a vacation or how we discussed money while playing *Monopoly*. Regardless, they all exist within each of us, as well as in our clients. These financial flashpoints lead to money scripts, or internal conversations that play on repeat in a person's mind due to their adverse, and not so adverse, money experiences early in life (as illustrated in Figure 5.1). It can help financial planners to understand these money scripts so they can understand how to counter them and lead a client to better decisions about their money.

MONEY SCRIPTS

Financial flashpoints, which often occur in childhood, create underlying assumptions and internal conversations about money that are only partially true, incomplete, conflicting, and are subconsciously followed in adulthood [57, pp. 23–24]. These money scripts are often passed down from generation to generation, directly or indirectly, within families and cultures. Money scripts can lead to positive financial behaviors as well as self-destructive ones. Many clients aren't consciously aware of their money scripts. Since money is a taboo topic in our culture, we rarely have the opportunity to become aware of, let alone confront, self-limiting beliefs about money. When a client feels stuck in painful or self-destructive patterns around money, there is likely some unresolved emotional pain or trauma hidden in their past. When this unresolved pain is left unexamined, it can cause a client to live reactively, rather than actively. An effective financial planner is familiar with common money scripts. This allows them to help a client navigate through their subconscious beliefs and make healthy financial decisions.

While the field of psychology has known about the impact of beliefs on emotions and behaviors for decades, only recently has research investigated the impact of beliefs about money on an individual's financial life. To help identify these beliefs, the Klontz Money Script Inventory (KMSI) was developed in 2011 and is used by many financial professionals to measure their clients' money beliefs and attitudes [58, pp. 77–81]. The KMSI (and the newer, more streamlined KSMI-R) is a comprehensive, valid, efficient, and reliable test that can serve as a guide for clients to help them identify money scripts that are helping and/or causing harm to their financial well-being. In the revised version of the test, there are 32 money statements that fall into four categories: (1) money avoidance, (2) money worship (often referred to as money focus when used in a financial planning context), (3) money status, and (4) money vigilance.

Money Avoidance

At the heart of money avoidance is the belief that money is dirty, evil, stressful, and/or makes people greedy. In fact, the money-avoidant may believe that there is virtue in having less money. Most people are familiar with the belief that money is evil, whether it was instilled in them from a religious background, their parents, or their communities. Money-avoidant money scripts associated with the idea that money is bad include beliefs such as:

- "Rich people are greedy."
- "Good people should not care about money."
- "It is not okay to have more than you need."
- "It is hard to be rich and be a good person."
- "Most rich people do not deserve their money."
- "Money corrupts people."
- "There is virtue in living with less money."

When examining this belief, it's easy to see why someone would sabotage their own financial progress [58, pp. 77–81]. If a client believes that having too much money will make them evil or miserable, it makes sense that they would struggle to earn and save.

Money avoidance is often linked to those in helping professions and strong religious backgrounds. In this mindset, people believe that as long as they do what's right with the best intentions, they will be rewarded with "good karma" or abundant blessings from God or the universe. This belief can lead people into a life of righteous poverty and scarcity. It is necessary to do good for others while simultaneously helping oneself. Those who work in social services or religious servitude often adopt this mindset. The belief that being of service, happiness, love, and belonging are more important than money can be a positive one, as long as it doesn't go too far. When a person is so devoted to others that they forget their own needs, this mindset becomes problematic. It can also be a cover for money avoidance or lack of financial responsibility.

Those who avoid money may also think they don't deserve money, illustrated by the money script: "I do not deserve a lot of money when others have less than me." This could be associated with imposter syndrome, or the idea that the client has no right to enjoy their money when others are suffering. This money belief is commonly associated with low self-esteem. Even if someone manages to accumulate wealth while operating within this mindset, they will be impoverished emotionally and spiritually.

Studies show that those with money-avoidant beliefs tend to have lower levels of education, as well as lower income and net worth. Money avoidance can lead to many self-defeating money behaviors, such as hoarding disorder, financial enabling, compulsive buying disorder, workaholism, and financial denial [3]. Young, single adults tend to be money-avoidant. Occupation is also associated with money avoidance, especially among mental health professions [59].

Money Focus

Clients who have money-worshipping tendencies may have beliefs such as:

- "More money will make you happier."
- "There will never be enough money."
- "You can never have enough money."

- "Money would solve all of my problems."
- "Money is power."
- "Money buys freedom."

It's common for people to believe that money brings happiness, peace, security, or whatever it is they're seeking. But usually this "more money" vision is based on an arbitrary, magical number that has very little to do with happiness. Once our essential needs are met, happiness is much less related to the amount of money we have in the bank than many of us think. Instead of lamenting about what they don't have, clients may benefit from shifting their focus toward making what they do have work for them.

Those who grew up economically disadvantaged may look at the life of a wealthy person and wish they could be rich too. They may see money as a magic wand that demands respect, opens doors of opportunity, and makes life more meaningful. In this frame of mind, a person may equate money with success. Just like with other money beliefs, there is partial truth to this one. However, it doesn't consider the whole picture, such as respect being earned by those who work hard, make meaningful achievements, and treat others with respect.

Studies show that the clients who are most vulnerable to these beliefs are typically younger, single, and have lower levels of education, income, and net worth, while having higher levels of revolving credit debt. Those with money-worship beliefs are predicted to be more susceptible to compulsive buying disorder, hoarding disorder, workaholism, financial dependence, financial enabling, and financial denial [56].

Money Status

Those who operate under money status beliefs will equate their self-worth with their net worth. Money status includes beliefs such as:

- "Your self-worth equals your net worth."
- "If something is not considered 'the best' it is not worth buying."
- "People are only as successful as the amount of money they earn."
- "I will not buy something unless it is new (e.g. car, house)."
- "If someone asked me how much I earned, I would probably tell them I earn more than I actually do."

It is a sign of good financial health to believe that we have a right to enjoy and spend our money on ourselves and our loved ones. However, this belief wanders into dangerous territory when it serves as a catalyst for spending beyond one's means. Creating and sticking to budgets and committing to savings can curb this entitlement around overindulgence.

Like the two previous categories, money status beliefs are associated with younger, single people with lower education, income, and net worth. Those with a money status mindset have a greater likelihood of having grown up in a lower socioeconomic class. Money status beliefs are a predictor of compulsive buying disorder, gambling disorder, financial dependence, and financial infidelity (56). Those in the top tiers of wealth are also impacted by these beliefs, indicating that the money status mindset can be a motivator to reach high levels of wealth, since self-worth is equated with net worth [93].

Money Vigilance

Some degree of money vigilance is a good thing. It keeps people from building up high revolving credit debt and can be the catalyst for saving money. However, it can also be the source of shame and secrecy around money. Money vigilance includes beliefs such as:

- "Money should be saved and not spent."
- "It is important to save for a rainy day."
- "You should not tell others how much money you have or make."
- "It is wrong to ask others how much money they have or make."
- "If you cannot pay cash for something, you should not buy it."
- "I would be a nervous wreck if I did not have money saved for an emergency."
- "It is extravagant to spend money on oneself."
- "I would be embarrassed to tell someone how much money I make."
- "It is not polite to talk about money."

Money vigilance is great for your financial health but at its extreme it can cause undue stress and anxiety. There may be a fear of not having enough, even when there is financial solvency.

From the money vigilance category, the belief that there will never be enough money can do a great deal of harm to one's financial life. Ebenezer Scrooge lived according to this belief and found himself in a life of deprivation and loneliness. This mindset can cause constant fear and anxiety around money. It leads people to become workaholics who sacrifice everything else to protect themselves from scarcity, even beyond necessity. Others adopt a "what's the point" attitude. They blow through any extra money or revolving credit as fast as possible before it vanishes, which in turn causes more scarcity.

THE ROLE OF THE FINANCIAL PLANNER

Awareness is an important first step in the process of dismantling harmful or negative beliefs around money. Often, when a person becomes aware of erroneous or misguided money beliefs, they can make modifications to those beliefs and change their behaviors. However, if there are intense emotions attached to those beliefs, money scripts can be difficult to change. Even though the client knows the beliefs are unbalanced, they may not be able to change their behaviors. In some circumstances such individuals may need the assistance of a financial therapist to help unlock their money beliefs. Financial planners can help clients become aware of their money scripts through discussions or using instruments such as the KMSI or KMSI-R. Financial planners who use the KMSI-R in practice have outlined the following four-step framework for administering and reviewing the test as well as delivering and reviewing the results with clients [60].

Step 1: **Administer.** Financial planners can administer the test in the discovery phase of the financial planning process, after trust and rapport have been established, often taking place in the second or third client meeting. They note that it is important for the planner to not just hand the test to the client or send a link without an explanation of why and how the information will be used in the financial planning process. The following is a version of what they suggest: "Our beliefs about money influence our financial decisions, whether we are aware of the connection or not. This assessment is designed to help us learn more about your money scripts. As will all information you share with us, your answers will be confidential. The most useful responses are the ones that come to mind immediately, without censoring yourself. So make sure to respond honestly, and we can talk over the results during a future session."

Step 2: **Analyze.** In this step the planner scores the assessment or reviews the automated scoring. Rather than distinct "personalities," it is common to see elevations in more than one scale. For example, studies have found a strong association between high scores on money avoidance and high scores on money focus [56]. In other words, the people who have the strongest negative associations with money are also the ones who most desperately want to have more money themselves. The analysis of the client should be done objectively, meaning it is important not to attach labels to the client based on the results. We are using this as a tool to help us help our clients. After this analysis of categories, the advisor can dive deeper into the assessment to review extreme scores on individual items.

Step 3: **Clarify.** Assessments are not meant to diagnose or come to a conclusion about the client's financial psychology. Instead they are meant to be starting points for conversation. In this step, financial planners can explore the deeper meanings, and stories behind their clients' responses, using open-ended questions. For example, a planner may comment: "I see you responded to item 5 as 'strongly disagree.' Tell me more about what that means to you."

Step 4: **Incorporate.** The final step is utilizing this newfound information in your work with the client. For example, for a client who scores high on money vigilance and has little experience with investing, you might predict that in times of market downturns they may appreciate you proactively reaching out to them to get in front of their anxiety about losing hard earned money.

Flashpoints at different points in our lives create conscious and subconscious beliefs about money that have a profound impact on our decisions and behaviors, whether as individuals or as clients. Money scripts emerge out of our attempts to make sense of these financial flashpoints. An important step in understanding why people do what they do around money is to recognize, and ultimately evaluate, underlying beliefs and where they came from. In the next chapter, we explore how financial behaviors can have a negative impact on a person's financial outcomes, with a focus on behaviors that are commonly seen in the financial planner's office. We also explore the role of the financial planner when these behaviors are observed. In some cases, the financial planner is uniquely positioned to address them, and in others the planner should look for an appropriate referral. In the accompanying toolkit, you can take the KMSI-R as well as learn more about ways to help clients of different money scripts profiles.

KEY POINTS

- Our money beliefs, created by our financial flashpoints, are often only partially true, incomplete, conflicting, and are typically outside of our conscious awareness.
- A financial planner who is aware of a client's money beliefs can help them navigate some of their assumptions toward meeting their goals.
- For a financial planner to be aware of a client's money beliefs, it can be helpful for them to administer the KMSI, and follow a four-step process that includes: (1) administer, (2) analyze, (3) clarify, and (4) incorporate.

CFP BOARD LEARNING OBJECTIVES COVERED IN THIS CHAPTER

H.66. Behavioral finance

a. Identify how cognitive biases and heuristics can impact financial decision-making.
b. Describe how a client's psychology, such as their financial comfort zone, socialization, money beliefs, and past financial experiences and behaviors impact their objectives, goals, understanding, decision making, and actions.

CHAPTER 6

Financial Behaviors and Outcomes

Thus far, we have focused on all of the factors that impact what we do as related to money. Whether it be evolutionary traits, cultural and environmental factors, or financial flashpoints born out of our own experiences or those of our ancestors, we arrive at a set of beliefs around money that drive our financial behaviors. Unfortunately, in many cases, our responses and behaviors are inconsistent with our own personal goals. There are numerous financial behaviors that can have a significant impact on our clients' financial well-being (see Figure 6.1). In Part III, we introduce strategies and tools that the financial planner can adopt to address many of these financial behaviors, all in helping the client meet their financial and life goals.

Many of our clients have great financial behaviors. For starters, many have acquired sufficient assets that necessitate the assistance of investment advice from a financial planner. Typically, this requires the ability to delay gratification, prioritize future goals over near-term rewards, save, invest, and resist impulses to act irrationally, such as taking excessive risks or falling for get-rich-quick schemes. However, good financial health is not necessarily the norm, and the average American is in terrible financial shape. Financial planners often encounter problematic financial behaviors with clients from all different economic backgrounds. Even if most of their clientele have good financial health, it is not uncommon for clients to have spouses, children, family, or friends who exhibit problematic behaviors, many of which can have a direct or indirect impact on them.

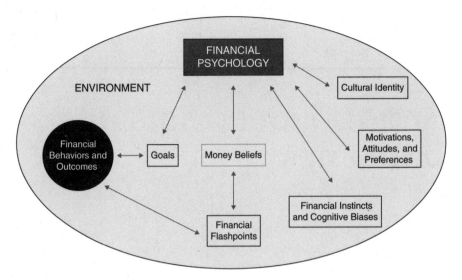

FIGURE 6.1 Klontz-Chaffin Model of Financial Psychology

OVERSPENDING AND UNDERSAVING

In American culture, it is easy to fall into the trap of overspending. Celebrities on social media flaunt their wealth and pop stars sing about their fancy cars and jewelry. There is a strong pull on Americans to spend more than they have, in many cases spending impulsively. But aside from the allure of social media and pop culture, overspending can also result from money disorders such as compulsive buying, gambling, workaholism, and financial enabling. Regardless of the reason, overspending is a serious issue for many people. Consumer debt has become a chronic problem for Americans. As of 2021, Americans owed $807 billion, with the average family owing approximately $6,000 [61]. According to a survey in debt.org, roughly 40% of Americans reported that their credit card debt had a negative effect on their happiness, and one in five people said the stress from credit card debt was harming their health [61].

FINANCIAL DENIAL

People with financial denial try to avoid thinking about money, try to forget about their financial situation, and avoid looking at their bank account. Financial denial is usually in response to some difficult financial situation and since those tend to develop gradually over time, financial denial tends to build as well. Studies have found that financial denial is associated with being younger, less educated, single, and having lower income, lower net worth, higher revolving credit card debt, and self-destructive financial behaviors, including compulsive buying, pathological gambling, compulsive hoarding, workaholism, financial dependence, and financial enabling [62].

FINANCIAL PARALYSIS

There is a paradox of choice, where we value the power and autonomy that come from more options but we can become incapacitated when we try to evaluate all of them. Choosing between options, particularly if they all seem similar, can be cognitively taxing. When a definitive choice is not readily apparent among many, our tendency is to become overwhelmed and take no action. In one of the famous studies related to choice, two different stands contained different types of jam for sale at a grocery store [63]. One of the stands had 24 options and the other had only 6. The stand that had only 6 jams to choose from made far more sales than the one with 24. More options may seem like more freedom but it is actually the opposite and can create financial paralysis in clients if they do not have help from their advisor in walking through limited options. But financial planners can utilize choice architecture, a strategy in which an overwhelming or sometimes confusing number of choices is limited to a small number. In many cases, the financial planner can share the top three choices (being transparent that there are more options) and discuss how clients with similar goals or backgrounds tend to opt for one of them.

FINANCIAL INFIDELITY

Money stress can be hard on marriages. Research shows that money is the main source of marital disagreement in the early years of marriage and fights over money are the leading cause of marital dissatisfaction [64]. According to a survey by CNBC, one in five couples admitted that money is their biggest challenge [65]. While some disagreements about money may occur between spouses from time to time, this behavior can become dysfunctional in some cases. When couples constantly fight over money, keep secrets or lie about money, or one uses it to control and wield power over the other, they are in the territory of financial infidelity. Financial infidelity can not only destroy marriages, but it can also affect future relationships. Situations in which someone lies, keeps secrets, or tries to control their spouse with money inevitably lead to an unhappy marriage and, likely, divorce. After moving on from the dysfunctional relationship, a person may have trouble trusting a new partner when it comes to money, which can lead to money-avoidant behaviors.

FINANCIAL ENMESHMENT

Financial enmeshment occurs when parents share too much information about their finances with their children, or involve them inappropriately in financial matters [66]. Examples of financial enmeshment include:

- A parent relying on a child for emotional support when dealing with financial stress.
- Using children to pass on messages about money between divorced or separated parents.
- Using their child's social security number to open accounts in the parent's name.
- A parent borrowing a child's savings or earnings from babysitting or other teen-appropriate jobs.
- Disparaging a child's other parent in front of them (e.g., "I can't buy you a birthday present because your mom makes me pay so much in child support.").

Financial enmeshment can not only cause a negative relationship with money as the child grows into adulthood, but it can also cause severe psychological pain. While it is important for a parent to teach their children about money, it is inappropriate for a parent to involve children in adult financial matters. Although a parent may feel tempted to lean on their children for emotional venting or support, it is better for them to rely on a trusted adult who has the maturity and emotional capacity to deal with that kind of burden. If a parent is actively taking financial advantage of a child, it may be time for a mental health professional or social worker to step in and offer assistance.

FINANCIAL ENABLING

As parents, it can be difficult to say no to children when they ask for money, even when they are adults and can provide for themselves. Financial enabling is a problematic money behavior that can complicate the parent/child relationship. Of course, there may be times when parents need to help their child through difficult financial situations or emergencies, such as unexpected job loss, medical bills, or a down payment on a home or vehicle. But it ventures into the territory of financial enabling when the adult child is capable of handling their own finances but has become accustomed to their parents bailing them out.

Parental enabling is one of the most common issues financial planners notice among their clients [58, pp. 127–130]. It's an age-old dilemma. Parents don't want to see their children suffer, but too much help can actually prevent them from learning how to become independent and resolve their own problems. It may seem that financially helping an adult child would benefit the child and satisfy a parent's sense of care and responsibility, but constant enabling comes with unintended consequences. It can create a sense of entitlement and dependence in the child, while brewing anger and resentment in the parents. Young adults who have everything handed to them are at risk of losing their creativity, drive, self-respect, and innovation [58, pp. 127–130]. Parents who constantly give their adult children money may lose their retirement savings, which could potentially make them dependent on their adult children in the future.

A good question for parents to ask before giving their adult children money is: "Will this financial support help solve a problem and make the recipient more stable and stronger . . . or . . . will this create an unhealthy dependency, further weakening them and destroying their own ability to help themselves?"

This question can help the giver to discern the difference between necessary financial support and destructive financial enabling.

For those on the giving end of financial enabling, it can be just as destructive as it is for those on the receiving end. Studies show that financial enablers tend to have higher debt in revolving credit accounts and lower net worth. Studies have also found that financial enabling often takes place in individuals who grew up in lower-income households [3]. Many also engage in financial denial and money avoidance, and exhibit financial enmeshment behaviors, often following money worship scripts while being less vigilant with their own finances [3]. Some strategies for clients who are stuck in financial enabling behaviors are as follows [3]:

- *Recognize that financial enabling can do more harm than good.*
  Financial planners have an important role in helping their clients realize the ways the financial enabling can exacerbate financial problems, rather than making them better.

- *Lift the curse of too many options.*

    When a person has too many options, it can create a dizzying loss of a sense of direction and lack of purpose. If financial enabling has left the recipient with too many options or too much unstructured free time, their lives may atrophy. All human beings need to engage in active, gainful pursuits that motivate them to interact with the world, overcome challenges, and achieve goals. These pursuits are essential to a meaningful, fulfilling life.

- *Make a plan and stick to it.*

    If a client doesn't want their dependents to go "cold turkey," they may find it more appealing to make a plan of slowly removing financial support over an agreed-upon time period. It can help to write out an agreement, which both parties may sign, stating the conditions in which financial support will come to an end. This could be a three- or six-month plan to give the recipient time to make arrangements to be self-sufficient. However, if the enabler does not stick to the agreement, it could create the opposite effect. The recipient may not make any serious future attempts to stop the support. This could cause a perpetual cycle that is quite hard to escape: The enabler bails out the recipient, says it's the last time, the recipient doesn't believe them because they've said that many times before, so they continue their problematic money behaviors. Instead, they get into financial trouble again, and the enabler once again bails out the recipient, saying this is the last time. To avoid this cycle, here are some steps a client may take to stick to their agreement to stop the financial support:

    1. Set dates for when the financial contributions will be reduced or stopped.

    2. Learn other ways to provide support, such as contributing to a trade school or career counseling, paying for therapy or coaching, or donating financial planning sessions.

    3. Write and rehearse a script for informing the recipient that the financial support is ending. A therapist may be able to help the client with this. Rehearsing the script before telling the dependent is crucial so that they don't get flustered or waver off track.

    4. Gather a support system that will help the enabler stick to the agreement. It can be difficult to break family patterns. Support, in the form of friends or a support group, can help the giver stay strong and remember the reasons they are doing this in the first place.

5. Enlist the help of other professionals. Sometimes, a financial planner may be able to help a client refrain from financial enabling. Other times, a client may need to reach out to a mental health professional and/or a financial therapist. If a client has tried repeatedly to stop their financial enabling behaviors but keeps falling back into the same pattern, it's likely a sign that they need a therapist to help them.

FINANCIAL DEPENDENCE

On the other side of financial enabling, one usually finds financial dependence. Financial dependence occurs when someone finds themselves relying on the support of others for nonemployed income. This dependency often causes anxiety, anger, or resentment from the fear of being cut off while suppressing their motivation, innovation, passion, creativity, and drive to succeed [3]. Financial dependence and dependent personality disorder share similar characteristics. According to the fifth edition of the *Diagnostic of Statistical Manual of Mental Disorders* (*DSM-5*), a person might exhibit dependent personality disorder in the following ways [67]:

1. Trouble making decisions on their own without an extreme amount of advice and encouragement from others.
2. A strong need for others to assume responsibility for important aspects of their lives.
3. Trouble disagreeing with others for fear of losing approval or appreciation.
4. Difficulty initiating projects or doing things on their own.
5. Tries too hard to get approval, nurturance, or support from others.
6. Feels scared of being alone because they feel helpless and are worried they can't take care of themselves.
7. An urgent need to seek out new relationships when another relationship ends to satisfy their needs for care and support.
8. Unreasonably fearful and preoccupied with the worry that they will be left alone to fend for themselves.

To qualify for a diagnosis of dependent personality disorder, a person must exhibit at least five of the above criteria [58, pp. 127–130]. Financial dependence can present itself in similar ways to dependent personality disorder, and can be just as unhealthy for the dependent as well as for the enabler. Financial dependence can cause increased amounts of parent/child conflict. It's a growing problem, with as much as 60% of parents financially supporting their adult children [58, pp. 127–130]. This can cause financial hardship for the enabling parent, as well as an unhealthy dependence for the adult child.

The parent/child relationship is not the only place where financial dependency can be present. Dependency may occur between siblings or other relatives and can be passed down through generations. Financial dependence may go hand-in-hand with other disorders, such as gambling disorder, compulsive buying disorder, or hoarding disorder [58, pp. 127–130]. Similar to financial enabling, financial dependence is associated with lower income and less education and occurs more often in those who are single [62]. However, it can also occur in beneficiaries of trust funds from wealthy parents. Those struggling with financial dependence are more likely to have money worship and money status scripts [58, pp. 127–130]. Financial dependence can be created by an imbalance of power in a marriage or partnership. Victims of domestic violence might feel compelled to stay in an abusive relationship because they are financially dependent on their abuser. One study showed that 46% of domestic violence victims cited a lack of money as the reason for returning to their abusers after escaping [68].

As with financial enabling, a financially dependent person may benefit from seeking the help of a therapist. Financial planners may need to refer the enabler and the dependent(s) to a mental health professional to explore deeper issues around these money behaviors.

MONEY DISORDERS

Sometimes, money behaviors can become so problematic that they meet the threshold of psychological disorders. Money disorders can occur in those who are poor just as much as in those who are wealthy. Some common elements in these disorders are emotional pain, often a history of trauma, and impairment in one or more areas of their lives, including social, relational, and/or occupational functioning. A financial planner is not qualified to try to address these behaviors in someone who needs this level of psychological help. When a client is dealing with a money disorder, they should be referred to a mental health professional.

As a financial planner, it is likely that you may never encounter the following set of behaviors in your client, because they are often accompanied by denial and a lack of financial planning and/or resources. However, you will likely hear clients report some of these behaviors in family members, children, and/or business partners. As such, it is important that financial planners are aware that these conditions exist and to have some basic information regarding how they manifest and what they can do within the boundaries of their professional competence when they recognize these behaviors.

Gambling Disorder

Gambling can be a fun pastime but like most behaviors, if taken to the extreme, can lead to significant problems. In fact, excessive gambling can become a full-blown clinical addiction. According to the National Center for Responsible Gambling, approximately 1% of the adult population in the United States has a severe gambling problem, with recent research estimating that 6–9% of young people and young adults experience problems with gambling [69]. The *DSM-5* defines gambling disorders as a "persistent and recurrent problematic gambling behavior leading to clinically significant impairment or distress" [70]. The gambling industry understands the psychology of gambling and uses that information to keep people gambling. For instance, the use of poker chips, tokens, or digital credits serves to distance people from the experience of losing actual money. This keeps the reality of the loss out of a person's mind and keeps them at the tables.

Slot machines are designed around the most powerful behavioral reinforcement schedule known to psychology, called the "variable ratio schedule of reinforcement." As discussed in Chapter 2 as it relates to gambler's fallacy, the gambler doesn't know when they will hit or how much they will get, but they know if they keep hitting the button they will eventually win something, relying on that old adage, "you have to play to win." These periodic "wins" keep them gambling longer and longer and eventually losing more and more. It's not only casinos that create an environment for people with gambling disorders to lose their money. Day trading is another siren song for gamblers, luring them into making risky investments. Individuals with gambling disorder will often make promises to themselves and their loved ones to stop, but chronically break these intentions and promises. In its extreme, gambling disorder can lead to criminal behavior, such as theft and embezzlement.

Compulsive Buying Disorder

A person with compulsive buying disorder is similar to a person with gambling disorder, in that they can become addicted to the behavior. Compulsive buyers feel compelled to keep buying merchandise and services, even when those purchases cause negative financial, personal, or occupational consequences [71]. For someone with compulsive buying disorder, excessive purchases are often used as a way to cope with stress, improve their mood, boost their self-esteem, or feel accepted [72]. They often feel shame, guilt, and regret after the purchases, making them rush to soothe themselves with even more purchases. A financial planner rarely has a client who has a compulsive buying disorder. However, a planner may encounter a married couple in which one spouse is a compulsive shopper and the other is asking for help trying to manage the problem. As with all money disorders covered in this section, a financial planner is not qualified to diagnose or treat the condition. Instead, they should look to refer the individual who appears to have difficulty curbing their shopping behaviors to a qualified mental health professional for diagnosis and possible treatment.

Hoarding Disorder

It is not uncommon for those with compulsive buying disorder to also engage in hoarding behaviors. In the *DSM-5*, hoarding disorder is classified under obsessive-compulsive and related disorders [73]. Hoarders feel the need to save items, even if they have no value, often feeling distressed at the idea of parting with them. They accumulate possessions until their belongings fill their homes, stacking up to create fire and safety hazards. They usually need outside intervention to declutter their living spaces, such as the persistent nudge of friends or family members, cleaners, or authorities. In addition to items, it is also possible to hoard money [74]. Planners may come up against compulsive hoarding in clients who feel a strong fear toward spending their money, even if they have a lot of it.

THE ROLE OF THE FINANCIAL PLANNER

In their work with clients and families, financial planners encounter the entire spectrum of financial behaviors. While many clients exhibit prudent financial behaviors that coincide with wealth creation, others engage in behaviors that at minimum, limit and at worse, threaten their financial well-being. The financial planner plays a role in some of these behaviors as a trusted advisor, flagging potential issues in discussions with clients and providing guidance and support.

In the following chapters, we review strategies and techniques drawn from psychology and counseling and how financial planners can adapt and use them within the boundaries of their competence to help facilitate the financial health of their clients. It is equally important for financial planners to know the warning signs of money disorders so they can refer the client to a mental health professional. As discussed earlier, financial planners should never try to diagnose or treat clients with money disorders.

KEY POINTS

- Our financial behaviors are a result of our financial beliefs and are a product of our environment and past experiences.
- Although not equipped to treat or diagnose, the financial planner can highlight problematic financial behaviors to the client and help lead them to better financial decisions.
- Financial planners need to be aware of financial behaviors that could indicate the need for a referral to a mental health professional.

CFP BOARD LEARNING OBJECTIVES COVERED IN THIS CHAPTER

H.66. Behavioral finance

a. Identify how cognitive biases and heuristics can impact financial decision-making.
b. Describe how a client's psychology, such as their financial comfort zone, socialization, money beliefs, and past financial experiences and behaviors impact their objectives, goals, understanding, decision making, and actions.

PART III

PRINCIPLES OF COUNSELING, PSYCHOLOGY, AND COMMUNICATION

In Parts I and II, we explored the client's financial psychology. In Part III, we turn our focus to how financial planners can take this understanding and apply theories and techniques from psychology to help clients improve their lives and meet their goals. As we all know, financial planning is a helping profession and the client should be the primary focus of the work. However, we spend a considerable number of resources, in both time and attention, investing in what we are saying, doing, and even how we look. Perhaps more importantly, we can (knowingly or not) impose our worldview onto our clients or provide the same advice to entirely different families from different environments, money beliefs, and even goals. As our profession continues to mature, we must seek opportunities to know our clients better so that we can maximize our ability to have a positive impact on their financial well-being.

Part III focuses on what it actually means to be client-centered. It opens with a discussion of communication techniques that can be easily implemented by advisors from all types of firms and business models. We then explore techniques advisors can use with clients from solution-focused, cognitive behavioral, and positive psychology approaches. Part III closes with a discussion on how to work effectively with couples and families in

83

conflict around money from a systems perspective. As we have highlighted throughout this book, our goal is not to create therapists out of planners, but rather, to bring some of the insight and techniques from a variety of psychological disciplines to help us be better advisors. We hope that many of these theories of counseling and communication will inspire you and that you will find ways to integrate one or more of the techniques in your current or future work with clients.

CHAPTER 7

Sources of Money Conflict

Martin has been to three different financial planners in the past few years. During each visit, he acknowledges that he spends too much money on shopping, dining out, and other unnecessary luxuries. He asks the planner for help in creating a budget, promising to pay off his credit card debt as soon as he gets his spending in check. Once his debt is paid off, Martin expresses a desire to invest in his retirement and build up a savings account for emergencies. The financial planner shows Martin his options and together, they make a financial plan. Martin starts strong in the first couple of months. He refrains from going out to fancy restaurants and makes higher credit card payments with the money he saves. But inevitably, he falls back into his old behaviors of overspending. His credit card balances go up again, and eventually he winds up right back at square one. Martin's ideal version of himself, someone who is debt-free, careful with his money, and has savings for the future, is not aligned with his actual behaviors. Out of shame, Martin stops communicating with his financial planner. When the credit card bills start piling up again, Martin seeks the help of a new financial planner in the hopes of aligning his real self with his ideal self. The cycle continues.

There are many sources of money conflict. Some are external struggles with others whereas others are internal. In most cases, when people think of sources of money conflict, their mind immediately goes to the married couple battling over finances. That is certainly one major source. However, sources of money conflict also can be with a variety of other people in our lives, such as friends, bosses, and business partners. There can be internal sources of money conflict, such as the struggle Martin experienced in the client story above. This chapter discusses all sources of money conflict and the role of the financial planner when addressing these conflicts. These include:

1. Conflict with oneself
2. Conflict with a spouse
3. Conflict with family
4. Conflict with others (such as business partners, friends, bosses, or business associates)

Each of these conflicts can have an impact on a client's financial and emotional well-being. Unresolved conflicts can lead to destructive financial behaviors that can ruin the client's attempts at reaching their money goals. Examining each source of money conflict can help the planner provide support and guidance that will ultimately benefit the client.

CONFLICT WITH ONESELF

Ideal Self versus Real Self

There can sometimes be a chasm between what we know we should be doing with our money versus what we actually do. Humanistic psychologist Carl Rogers categorized the self into two parts: the ideal self and the real self [75]. The ideal self is the person we wish we could be. This person earns a high income, saves for the future, doesn't have a high amount of revolving debt, sticks to a budget and doesn't overspend, and has healthy, realistic attitudes regarding money. The real self, by contrast, is a normal human being, with subjective money beliefs, and money behaviors that could be modified to improve financial health. Whenever a client's behaviors are not in line with their financial goals, there is an internal money conflict. Everyone has a gap between the desire to follow the well-documented and proven financial best practices that will lead to the successful achievement of goals, and actual financial behaviors. Sometimes this gap is narrow, and sometimes it's wide. Self-actualization occurs when our ideal self matches our real self. The problem isn't a lack of information on how to achieve financial goals. The problem is taking consistent action and controlling problematic money behaviors.

Money Ambivalence

Money scripts, which lead to financial behaviors, may give a planner insight as to why there is a disconnect between a client's goals and a client's actions. Often clients have conflicting money scripts. A common conflict is between money avoidance and money worship, where clients believe that money is bad while simultaneously wanting more of it [3]. This money ambivalence can lead to wild swings in behavior, when clients vacillate between working hard and saving and then spending out of feelings of guilt [4]. Additionally, when a planner understands inherent needs, cognitive biases, and ancestral instincts, they can help a client use those elements to their advantage, such as automatically pulling retirement savings out of a client's paycheck before they have a chance to spend it and then using the client's status quo bias to keep the contributions going.

Client Motivation

Are you reading this chapter because you have a client who is stalled at some stage of your engagement? Maybe they have been delaying major decisions in their estate plan or perhaps they have not returned your calls or emails, so you want to learn more about ways you can "ignite the fire." Perhaps you are reading this chapter because someone told you to (and you have already looked to the end to see how long it is). You can think of motivation as a drive or need that desires some element of change, whether within ourselves or the environment around us [76]. Motivation can be intrinsic and/or extrinsic. Intrinsic motivation is our desire to do or achieve something that is personally important to us. In contrast, extrinsic motivation comes from outside of ourselves, like trying to achieve money or status to impress others or to avoid a punishment or negative consequence. There are a number of techniques from positive psychology that can help the planner discover what is most rewarding to the client – for example, talking about numbers on a spreadsheet and how they can fund experiences that will bring joy and meaning to the life of the client (we explore how financial planners can use positive psychology in their work with clients in Chapter 11).

Financial planners need to understand what motivates their clients, how they started their financial journey, and what they hoped their work efforts would create for themselves and those closest to them. This knowledge not only helps to ensure that the planner is developing, following, and monitoring a plan that is aligned with the client and their goals, but is also vital when things go awry during the planning process. The practitioner can take the client from inaction to action when they become stalled in their decision making or engagement, using a variety of motivational techniques. We discuss some of the most powerful change techniques a planner can implement to help a client overcome resistance to change in Chapter 18.

CONFLICT WITH SPOUSE OR PARTNER

Jennifer comes from a big family. She was raised in a community where everyone shared everything with each other. Her mother would cook big meals and invite the whole neighborhood to her home every Sunday. Her father painted the neighbors' fences and gave money to family members in need. Jennifer's parents, aunts, uncles, and cousins were highly involved in each other's lives, helping with the family businesses, living in the same neighborhood, and going to the same church. For Jennifer's family, it was considered disrespectful to save anything for themselves.

Tom comes from a family of strict savers. He had to wake up early in the morning to work at the donut shop down the street before school to save for his own car. His parents were tight-lipped about money. They believed it was foolish to share or give away money. Tom's parents enjoyed a healthy nest egg when it was time for them to retire. Tom learned how to save money and keep his finances to himself.

When Jennifer and Tom got married, they had no idea that their money beliefs and behaviors were so different. Tom would get upset when Jennifer sent her cousins money. Jennifer couldn't understand why Tom was such a penny-pincher who refused to discuss his finances with her. When they arrived at their financial planner's office, tensions were high. The financial planner was soon able to see that Tom and Jennifer had opposing money beliefs.

Conflicts around money in relationships are common and can be one of the more difficult areas of conflict to be resolved. Studies have identified common sources of conflict in couples to include those that are initiated due to financial stress, problems with communicating around money, power imbalances, and conflicting beliefs about money, based on individual histories and experiences around money [77].

Conflicting Money Beliefs

When spouses have conflicting money scripts, financial conflict is inevitable. When one spouse prefers to save money while the other prefers to spend it, a divide may occur that needs attention. Many times, a couple is married before they realize that they have different financial goals, money scripts, and behaviors. Each partner is coming into the relationship with their own history, family dynamics, career, and beliefs about money. In some cases, people are drawn to partners who have different money scripts and behaviors, perhaps in a subconscious attempt to create a sense of balance or to heal certain parts of themselves. Someone who is money avoidant may seek out a partner who is diligent with money. This balance can be complementary, but it can also be a source of disagreements.

It can help for a planner to externalize the conflict by reframing it as a difference in money scripts rather than something fundamentally wrong with one or both partners or the relationship. By learning about one another's money scripts and past financial experiences, couples can get necessary insights and cultivate empathy for each other. Exercises that help couples explore their money scripts are provided in the accompanying practitioner toolkit.

A Lack of Financial Transparency

Unresolved conflict can lead to problematic money behaviors, including financial infidelity. Acts of financial infidelity can include lies of commission, such as saying something cost less than it did, or lies of omission, such as just not telling a partner about a purchase. With financial infidelity, there is an underlying assumption that the couple has agreed to be open and honest about their spending, so when acts of financial infidelity come to light, it can shake the foundation of trust in the relationship. We explored the topic of financial infidelity further in Chapter 6: Financial Behaviors and Outcomes.

Conflicting Financial Goals

It's not uncommon for members of a coupleship to have different financial goals. In fact, couples are often attracted to each other because of their differences. Since money tends to be a taboo topic, often couples have not sat down and talked about their goals with each other. Ideally, such discussions would happen early in the dating process, around the time couples talk about other important issues, such as career, family, and other such topics. This lack of transparency around goals is another common reason for couples to be in conflict. A skilled financial planner can help facilitate a discussion around goals and work with the couple to develop a win-win solution and integrate it into the financial plan.

Power Imbalances

In 1938, sociologist Willard Waller made the observation that in a romantic relationship, the one who is the least emotionally involved tends to have the most power in the relationship, a phenomenon he called "the principle of least interest" [78]. Subsequent studies have found that when this type of imbalance is common, it tends to be stable over time, and is associated with more conflicts in the relationship [79]. Financial imbalances are also common in relationships, sometimes referred to as the "household CFO," and can lead to conflicts around money. Sometimes they are triggered by gender role issues, levels of financial literacy, level of personal interest in financial matters, and/or in situations where one partner earns more than the other. At times, this can lead to power imbalances in the relationship, where one partner exerts control over the financial behaviors of the other. These power imbalances need to be taken into consideration in the financial planning process for two reasons. The first is that the person with less power is often more vulnerable and can be left ill-equipped to navigate their financial lives in the event of the relationship ending through a breakup, divorce, or death. If one member of the household has no experience managing the financial component of their relationship, they likely have a lower level of financial literacy. Second, the person who has taken on more financial responsibility in the relationship may be feeling unnecessarily high levels of stress, and involving their partner could improve their own relationship with money [80]. It is important to note that not all partners who take on the responsibility of managing the couple's finances are necessarily doing it for the sake of power or control. They may merely have a higher level of financial self-efficacy than their partner and merely feel the responsibility to take on this additional role.

Financial Abuse

At their extreme, power imbalances can set the stage for financial abuse. Financial abuse occurs when one person exercises power over another's financial life, limiting their access to financial resources and stifling their ability to be independent, often in an attempt to keep them dependent and stop them from leaving or ending the relationship [81]. Abusers may also restrict or steal a victim's personal finances. Many victims of financial abuse are not allowed to work, or they are not given full access to money or other resources. If a victim does have limited access to funds, they are usually forced to account for every penny they use.

Where financial abuse is present, it is highly likely that domestic violence might also be occurring. One study showed that financial abuse was involved in 99% of domestic violence cases [82]. Financial abuse is often one of the first signs of domestic abuse or dating violence [82]. Abusive restriction of a spouse's finances is a powerful way to keep the victim trapped in the relationship, as financial insecurity is one of the main reasons abuse survivors return to their abuser [83]. Some ways that financial abusers use money to control their victims are as follows:

- **Exploiting the Victim's Resources**
    This includes:
    - Restricting access to the money their partner has earned or saved
    - Stealing money to use for their own personal benefit
    - Lying about or hiding money
    - Confiscating their partner's paycheck, credit cards, debit cards, and passwords for bank accounts
    - Opening their partner's financial statements
    - Expecting their partner to pay for all bills and expenses
    - Borrowing money with no intention of paying it back
    - Threatening to tell officials that the victim is abusing assistance or cheating on their taxes [83]

- **Job Interference**
    This includes:
    - Pressuring their partner to quit their job
    - Using children as an excuse for wanting their partner to leave their job
    - Belittling the victim about their choice of career
    - Dictating where their partner may work
    - Sabotaging work assignments and responsibilities
    - Taking the victim's transportation or car keys so they can't get to work
    - Harassing their victim at work with excessive phone calls, text messages, and spontaneous visits [83]

- **Controlling the Finances**
  This includes:
- Hiding shared assets and resources
- Criticizing and instilling doubt in the victim every time they make a financial decision
- Unilaterally making significant financial decisions
- Refusing to work together with shared finances
- Refusing to contribute financially
- Giving the victim a restricted allowance and monitoring their spending
- Double standards for spending on things like clothing, haircuts, or entertainment
- Withholding money as a form of control
- Forcing their partner to sign forms and documents without explanation
- Refusing to pay child support or using child support as a way to stalk or belittle the other parent
- Engaging in abusive litigation to force the victim to miss work and drain them of their time, energy, and financial resources [83]

A financial planner won't always see the direct signs of financial abuse, but may see hints of it. When efforts to engage a partner are thwarted repeatedly, issues of power imbalance are worthy of consideration. If a financial planner suspects there is financial abuse and/or domestic violence occurring, they should not try to intervene directly or even discuss it with the clients. If you suspect that one of your clients is experiencing financial abuse, call the domestic violence hotline at 800-799-7233 and consider enlisting the help of a trauma-informed mental health professional.

Planners find success in bridging the money conflicts between couples by hitting the pause button on the current argument and focusing on an open, honest, supportive dialogue about their money beliefs. More details on helping couples is provided in Chapter 12: Working with Couples and Families, and throughout the toolkit.

CONFLICT WITH FAMILY

After working together to understand their conflicting money scripts, Jennifer and Tom decided that the best course of action would be to meet in the middle. Tom agreed to be more open about money, and allow for a percentage of spending and sharing. Jennifer agreed to curb her sharing instincts and limit the amount of money she was giving to her family and spending on big family gatherings. While this arrangement worked well for Tom and Jennifer's marriage, it caused a rift in Jennifer's family. They were baffled by Jennifer's sudden change of heart and felt she was disconnecting from the family. Not only was Jennifer grappling with her ancestral instinct to share with the herd, but she was also up against a lifetime of financial conditioning. On the other hand, Tom's family expressed concern that he seemed to be spending more money. They made comments about his family vacations and expressed judgment about Jennifer's family.

Family conflicts can arise from a variety of financial behaviors, such as financial enmeshment, financial dependence, a difference in socioeconomic status among family members, shared culture, and using money to control other family members. In Jennifer's case, she had to become comfortable with the notion that she was allowed to save money while her family shared their resources. In Tom's case, he had to adapt to spending and giving more than he was used to contributing. One way for a planner to frame this would be to tap into that hardwired drive in Jennifer to give and the learned drive in Tom to save, introducing the idea that they could help their communities even more if they were in a happy, financially stable relationship. In the instance that giving to family becomes problematic, it can help curb the sharing instinct by contributing to a charity that has meaning for the giver. We discuss some of the most common areas of family conflicts around money in the following sections.

Sharing Instinct

Conflict with family can carry a great deal of weight. We are hardwired to share with those we love in their times of need, causing us to experience pain watching others suffer [84]. Jennifer may feel stuck between trying to please her family and trying to protect her marriage, which is why she must find a balance between the shared culture in which she was raised and the desire to save for her own family's future. Although she might understand why she needs to save to be financially successful, it can be hard to break the ingrained money behaviors of family.

Financial Enabling and Financial Dependence

The "dance" between the financial enabler and financially dependent is a common source of money conflict financial planners will see in working with clients. Financial enabling is any type of financial help that hurts the financial well-being of the giver and/or creates financial dependence in the recipient. Both of these conditions can create emotional, financial, and relational problems. Financial planners are in a unique position to help clients develop a plan to reduce the negative impact of these behavioral patterns. We explore the topics of financial enabling, financial dependence, and how financial planners can help in Chapter 6 on money behaviors and outcomes.

Financial Enmeshment

Financial enmeshment is a blurring of boundaries around money, often between those of a parent and child [58]. It is a violation of the parent–child hierarchy and can have a negative impact on the family system. With children, common examples include sharing too much financial information around household financial stressors, talking disparagingly about one's partner's financial contributions, fighting about money in front of the kids, or having children pass along financial information to other adults, such as in the case of divorce or even answering calls from creditors. In adulthood, financial enmeshment can lead to adult children feeling like they can never become financially independent with regard to their decision making. We discuss financial enmeshment in more detail in Chapter 6 on money behaviors.

Elder Financial Abuse

The financial exploitation of elders is the most prevalent form of elder abuse, with an estimated 4.7% of the elderly being victims at some point in their lives. Forms of elder abuse include: (a) having money or property stolen, (b) being forced or misled into surrendering rights (such as being forced to change a will), (c) having their identity stolen, (d) receiving inadequate contributions toward household expenses, and (e) being left broke or destitute with inadequate assistance from family [85]. Sometimes elder financial abuse can be perpetrated by family members, friends, or even caregivers. Sadly, the perpetrators are the people closest to them.

Some of the most common signs of elder financial abuse are large amounts of money missing from the elder's bank accounts, or an abrupt increase in a client's credit card balance. Financial planners should exercise a higher level of vigilance if they suspect that there are significant changes to the client's account or if there are changes in the mood of their client. Like with so much of our work, asking questions and knowing our clients from the beginning is valuable, and in this case can be a powerful tool in detecting any changes that might lead to elder financial abuse.

If a financial planner suspects that elder financial abuse is occurring, the Consumer Financial Protection Bureau recommends the following: (1) report the incident to Adult Protective Services (APS) in the state in which the alleged abuse occurred, (2) if the individual appears to be at imminent risk of physical harm, call 911, and (3) make a report of the financial abuse to their local district attorney's office [86].

CONFLICT WITH OTHERS

When Javier and Max started a construction business together, they thought they were a perfect match as partners. Javier was a skilled bookkeeper, savvy businessperson, and effective negotiator. Max knew everything about construction. He had been building and woodworking with his father since he was a young child. They didn't realize until three years later that they had opposing ideas about the finances of the business. Javier thought Max was overspending on expensive tools and materials, while Max asserted that the tools decreased his work time, opening him up to take more clients and thus increase profits. From a financial psychology perspective, this is a conflict between a spender and a saver. If Max and Javier don't have an open dialogue about their differences in money beliefs, their business partnership could be in jeopardy.

Business Partners

When people go into business together, they rarely anticipate that they may have two completely different sets of money scripts. Similar to a marriage, a business partnership requires open communication, teamwork, and empathy. Before starting a business, potential partners would benefit from learning about their own and their partner's money beliefs and discussing how they want to handle money in the business. This will allow each person to see if they are truly compatible and enable them to have empathy for the other's point of view. They may decide to do a quarterly check-in to make sure both parties are still working toward the same financial goals, reassess the budget and business costs, discuss owners' draw increases or decreases, savings, investments in equipment or labor, and projections for the next quarter. If individual circumstances come up, such as marriage, divorce, having a baby, loss of a spouse, disability, or other life events that could affect the finances of the business, both partners should discuss the potential impact so they can be prepared. The lines of communication are like blood flow to the business. When the flow is cut off, the business won't be able to thrive.

Employees and Employers

Employees and employers can also benefit from understanding money beliefs and behaviors from an objective point of view. When an employee asks for a raise, it would help them to know their boss's money beliefs before negotiating. If the boss is a penny-pincher who loves a good deal, the employee may leverage that by listing out all the ways the employee adds value to or saves money for the company. Similarly, if a boss wants to reduce turnover and keep loyal employees happy, they could make an effort to learn their employee's "financial love language." Certain employees may value flexibility, while others may prefer an increase in benefits. Some staff members may just want the cold hard cash in the form of raises and bonuses. Bosses who have top-notch, long-term employees have taken the time to learn about their employees' values and goals and make decisions accordingly.

Friends

Loaning money to friends can be dangerous. There is a shift in the dynamics of a friendship when one lends money to the other. Suddenly, the lending party has become a loan officer instead of a friend [87]. If someone gives a friend a loan, they should be comfortable with never getting their money back. If a friend has prioritized other bills and expenses overpaying back the loan, it could cause problems in the relationship. They may start to avoid the friend they owe, which could lead to resentment on the lending friend's part. If someone loans a friend money, it could ruin the relationship. However, if they don't loan the money, it could also potentially ruin the relationship. It's a delicate situation. It is important to have a plan in place for repayment before money changes hands. This will allow each party to understand the expectations and reduce the likelihood of avoidance or resentment. The lender may benefit from taking time to think about it before giving a substantial loan. The lender may want to find out if the friend has good money habits before giving the loan.

Whenever money is involved in a relationship, the potential exists for money conflicts. If a planner is helping clients deal with money conflicts, it can be helpful to be familiar with the sources of those conflicts. One of the most effective ways in which a planner can address a money conflict is to ask questions to get to the source of the issue, which in many cases involves the individuals' money beliefs. This approach can take the personal and sometimes emotional elements out of the issue and reframe the issue. Planners should be sure to listen, get clear on the issues, help when possible, or refer clients to a therapist or other professional when necessary.

KEY POINTS

- There are four types of sources of money conflict: conflict with one-self, conflict with a spouse, conflict with family, or conflict with others (such as business partners, friends, bosses, or business associates).
- Financial planners can work to better understand the source of these money conflicts by asking questions of the client and, in most cases, getting to the source of the issue, which is usually the individuals' money beliefs.
- Financial planners should always try to help when it comes to issues of money conflict, but should refer a client to a therapist when appropriate.

CFP BOARD LEARNING OBJECTIVES COVERED IN THIS CHAPTER

H.67. Sources of money conflict

a. Identify a client's motivation for achieving their financial goals.
b. Explain to the client the consequences of a lack of transparency with a spouse or family when making financial decisions.
c. Identify areas of potential financial conflict between a spouse and/ or family.
d. Communicate the importance of agreeing on financial goals and objectives with a spouse and/or family.
e. Identify situations in which money may be used as a means of undue influence, control, or abuse in relationships (e.g., power imbalances, financial abuse, and financial enabling).

CHAPTER 8

The Principles of Effective Communication

To be an effective financial planner, you need to first establish a relationship built on trust, honesty, and credibility. Building this foundation of trust with the client helps facilitate lasting change in financial beliefs and behaviors. There are several psychological techniques a facilitator can utilize when they are developing a fulfilling relationship from which the client can benefit, even in times of financial uncertainty and volatility. Savvy financial planners know that the best way to help their clients is by creating a supportive environment to encourage change, rather than forcing change.

BEING PRESENT

It is crucial that planners learn to be fully present with their client to build trust. This includes limiting distractions and discussing and, perhaps more importantly, listening to and responding to the client's speech and nonverbal communication. Following the client's timeline and agenda will reap far more benefits than trying to force the client to take action based on the planner's terms. This requires training and practice.

It's a common misconception among financial planners to believe they are only providing value to a client when they are telling them what to do,

99

whether it is giving specific investment advice, designing financial plans, or helping clients with goal setting. But the most value comes from taking the time to listen to the client. Clients who have planners who truly listen to them feel understood, safe, and more at ease. With proper education, financial planners can develop skills in exquisite listening, motivational interviewing, verbal and nonverbal communication, active listening, and following the client's lead.

COMMUNICATION SKILLS TO ESTABLISH RAPPORT

To be an effective financial planner, it's important for the planner to first establish rapport with the client. According to Dictionary.com, rapport is defined as "a close and harmonious relationship in which the people or groups concerned understand each other's feelings or ideas and communicate well." There are a variety of verbal and nonverbal techniques that can help establish a sense of rapport. The following sections highlight some of the key verbal and nonverbal strategies a financial planner can employ to establish rapport.

Verbal Strategies: Active Listening

Human beings are terrible listeners. Typically in a discussion with someone we are paying more attention to what we want to say next than what the other person is saying. That's what makes skilled listening such a powerful experience. It is rare that someone is putting their focus on truly listening and trying to understand what we are saying. Being in the presence of someone who is a skilled listener can feel exquisite. Often, we will look for opportunities to be in that person's presence again because it feels so good. As opposed to sitting back and listening with minimal effort to what a speaker is saying, active listening requires focus and participation. An active listener will employ many of the following tools to stay engaged with the speaker and make sure they understand everything that is being conveyed. Here are some verbal tools for active listening.

Reflection

Reflection involves verifying and clarifying what was truly conveyed, rather than what the listener thinks they heard. A planner can reflect back to the client what they are hearing periodically throughout the conversation, watching for verbal and nonverbal cues for the right moment to interject. As the word implies, reflection is a way of "throwing back" to the client what they have given you. It is a powerful technique to establish rapport and an impactful intervention on its own. Often, when we hear our thoughts returned to us by a skilled listener we will immediately start to modify them. When we are in the midst of making a difficult decision or feeling stuck around a choice, having our words reflected back to us can be a powerful motivating force.

The content of what is being reflected is up to the financial planner, and this is where a clear understanding of the goal and an intimate knowledge of human psychology and motivation is so important. When a client is talking, there are multiple areas a financial planner could target for a reflection. For example, the financial planner could reflect back the content of what is being said ("So you are saying you are ready to take action on this"), and/or the emotional experience that is being conveyed by the client ("So this is a very exciting time for you"). What the planner chooses to reflect should be dependent on their goal for the conversation.

Perhaps more importantly, for a client who is stuck or feeling ambivalent about taking action, the financial planner could reflect one or both sides of the internal conflict. For example, if a client is talking about the pros and cons of meeting with an estate planning attorney, the financial planner could reflect back one of three things:

1. Arguments in favor of not taking action right now:
   "So you're saying you're worried this could cause a fight with your spouse."
2. Arguments in favor of taking action right now:
   "So you recognize this is an important thing to do."
3. Or reflect both sides of the argument:
   "So on the one hand you recognize this is an important thing to do, but on the other hand you're worried this could cause a fight with your spouse."

Reflection also gives the client the opportunity to confirm whether the message received was the one intended. If the planner's perception matches the client's intended message, the conversation may continue with both parties in agreement about what was said and heard [58, p. 17]. If the message the planner heard doesn't match what the client was trying to say, reflection gives them both a chance to clarify before the conversation goes too far in the wrong direction. Some example reflection phrases include:

> "If I've heard you correctly, you feel concerned about losing the assets you have now, and would like to do what you can to protect them. Is that right?"
>
> "What I'm hearing is that you want to make sure you have enough retirement funds to travel when you get older, is that accurate?"
>
> "So, you want to make sure your money is invested with as minimal risk as possible, correct?"

By repeating the client's statements back to them, the client can hear their message interpreted by the planner and provide further clarification or key bits of information. The client's follow-up statements have important information that will either correct or elaborate on what the planner has heard [58, p. 17]. Reflective listening can help a planner track and follow a client's train of thought while staying in the moment rather than thinking of their own replies. This useful skill will help clients feel heard and understood and will ensure that planners gather the right information to help the client in the best ways possible. It's a powerful method of building and maintaining client/planner trust and ensuring a positive experience for both parties.

Paraphrasing

As a financial planner tracks the client with reflective listening, they can use paraphrasing or summarizing to bring together different aspects of a client's story to form a cohesive message. It is not uncommon for a client to go from one thought to another in a stream of consciousness during meetings. Paraphrasing brings together all of the most important aspects of the conversation and weeds out the unnecessary parts. Dr. William Miller, who founded the concept of motivational interviewing, compares paraphrasing to picking flowers and handing a bouquet back to the client, with the flowers representing the client's statements that support positive change [88]. The client tells the planner their story, the planner picks the parts of the story that are crucial to the client's progression toward positive change, then presents those parts of the story back to the client in summary form. Paraphrasing may sound like this:

> *Planner:*   *So let me see if I understand. You are concerned that you are overspending. You don't have a savings plan for*

emergencies, so you find yourself spending unplanned
money on unforeseen circumstances. And while you are
following your plan pretty well, you tend to overspend on
things like clothing and eating out. It sounds like you're
becoming more aware that you shop when you're stressed
out, which leaves you feeling anxious, guilty, and even
more stressed than you initially felt. Is that right?

Client: *That pretty much sums it up, yeah.*

Planner: *So, tell me where you would like to start.*

Paraphrasing helps the client see what's important to them distilled down into manageable summaries, which helps them get to the heart of their problems so they are better able to see solutions.

Open-Ended Invitations versus Closed-Ended Questions

Active listening advocates encourage the listener to ask open-ended invitations rather than closed-ended questions when engaged with a speaker. An open-ended prompt invites the speaker to expand the conversation. A closed-ended question shuts the conversation down and invites a "yes" or "no" or one-word response. For example:

Closed-ended question:

Financial planner: "What's your ideal retirement age?"
Client: "60."

Open-ended invitation:

Financial Planner: "Tell me more about your ideal retirement."
Client: "Hmmm, let's see. I think I would like to stop
                     working around 60 and perhaps move to a
                     warmer climate . . ."

Notice that in this example we are not using an open-ended question, but rather an open-ended prompt. It turns out that good listeners ask very few questions, if any at all. Surprisingly, the very act of asking someone a question, regardless of what the question is, can have a negative impact and cause some resistance [89]. A client may start to feel nervous or defensive when asked direct questions – especially about finances. A sentence with a question mark on the end has been shown to increase stress and, in some cases, make the client shut down. Instead, it is more effective to lead with statements that invite the client to talk about what's on their mind.

As we all know, the topic of money creates a high amount of stress and anxiety for many. The last thing a planner wants to do is make a client feel as if they're back in school trying to give their teacher the "correct" answer to a question. There is a simple way to avoid this feeling by turning questions into statements.

Staying in "statement mode" will help the client feel like they are in a conversation, rather than making the client feel like they are being interrogated or pressured to conform with what they think the planner wants to hear. A planner may begin a meeting with an open-ended invitation instead. This invitation should encourage the client to discuss what is most prominently on their minds. For example:

Instead of: "What brings you here today?," try:

"I'd like to know what brings you here today."

Or: "Tell me the most pressing item on your agenda that you want to make sure we cover today."

Or: "Tell me what we need to discuss that's come up since our last visit."

After the client shares, the planner can practice active listening, reading verbal and nonverbal cues while the client is speaking, to use reflective listening responses, and then paraphrase what they've just heard.

Instead of: "What did you mean by (fill in the blank)?," try:

"Tell me more about (fill in the blank)."

Or: "I'm curious about (fill in the blank)."

Or: "Say more about (fill in the blank)."

When the client feels more relaxed, it will be easier for them to open up, making the meeting more effective. Open-ended invitations can set the tone for a productive meeting. When making follow-up statements inviting the client to share more, it's important to remain calm, relaxed, and conversational. In addition to these tools, the planner may move the conversation forward with open-ended invitations to explore options and solutions. It can be helpful to frame these invitations in a way that elicits more detailed answers. Here are some Miller and Rollnick examples of open-ended invitations [89]:

When inviting the client to elaborate:

"Tell me how that feels/affects your life."

"Tell me how you're coping with that."

"Explain for me how that's a problem for you."

"Tell me what makes you concerned about that."

"Tell me more."

When exploring the pros and cons of doing things differently:

"Tell me what will happen in the long run if there is no change."

"Tell me the best results you can imagine if you make changes."

"Tell me the worst thing that could happen if you don't do things differently."

"Tell me how things would be different if you are successful in changing things."

When regarding the past:

"Tell me the differences between how it used to be and how it is now."

"Tell me about a time in your history when things were better and what made that time different than the way it is now."

"Tell me how this lack of change has kept you from moving forward in your life."

When looking toward the future:

"Tell me how you hope it will be different in the future if you make changes."

"Tell me how you'd like things to turn out for you ten years from now."

"Tell me what your life will look like in five or ten years if things stay the same."

Nonverbal Strategies

In addition to verbal cues, people communicate with their bodies, eyes, and facial expressions. Active listening involves taking in a person's verbal as well as nonverbal cues. The words a person speaks only account for about 7% of their actual communication, while tone of voice is 38% and body language is 55% (when considering context and other circumstances) [90]. When a planner is sitting down with a client (whether in person or in a video conference), it's important that they notice their visible nonverbal cues, such as their posture, facial expressions, gesturing, how they are sitting (are their arms crossed or are they more relaxed?), and where they are looking (down toward the floor or making eye contact). Additionally, financial planners should monitor a client's vocal pitch, tone, and speed to gauge how they are feeling. For instance, a client's voice may wander into a higher pitch, and they may speak faster than usual if they are feeling nervous [91]. Active listening tools can help a planner read the client's verbal and nonverbal cues so they stay on the same page throughout the meeting.

One effective approach to keep the client at ease during the meeting is to use the S.O.F.T.E.N. method [92].

S – *Smile*, especially when welcoming the client, but also throughout the meeting.

O – *Open* posture. A planner should refrain from crossing their arms or closing themselves off physically to the client. Come out from behind the desk when greeting the client. Avoid any postures or obstacles that serve to create emotional distance.

F – *Forward* leaning. Leaning in while the client is talking will show that the planner is interested and engaged.

T – *Touch*. Small, appropriate touch that fits the planner's personality and the client's level of comfort can be meaningful. Warm handshakes or pats on the back can help the client feel at ease, as long as the contact doesn't go too far. Most clients would prefer not to get a big bear hug from their financial planner. Another touch that goes a long way is familiarity, such as remembering the names of the client's family and other details.

E – *Eye* contact is a valuable cue to let the client know the planner is invested in the client and what they are saying, as long as it's culturally appropriate.

N – *Nod*. Validating the client with nods and brief acknowledgments, such as a quick "uh-huh" can let them know the planner is paying attention to what they are saying.

Financial planners can subtly mirror their client's posture, tone of voice, rate of speech, and other nonverbal behaviors to help them get a sense of belonging. Friends mirror each other naturally and subconsciously all the time.

Pacing

It is not just what we communicate, but also the speed at which we communicate it. The planner must constantly use vigilance in determining the appropriate speed at which they use both verbal and nonverbal gestures with their clients. In the initial stages of the engagement, mirroring the client's pace – in terms of the speed at which they talk and even some of their nonverbal gestures – can help establish rapport. Throughout your communication with a client, the financial planner should check in to determine whether the client is engaged and understanding all aspects of your conversation. The planner should regularly pause in their verbal communication and ask if the content "makes sense" or if they have any questions. Speeding through the presentation of a financial plan without the client fully grasping it is nothing short of a waste of time. It is a conversation and by determining the pace that is most comfortable for the client, you can make the most of both your time and theirs.

Nonviolent Communication

Nonviolent communication is a method designed to increase empathy [105]. It is not designed to end dissent, but rather, to deepen the understanding and emotional connection between the parties in a conversation. Once empathy is offered, effective communication and knowledge sharing is more likely to be achieved. Nonviolent communication is built upon the premise that most conflict between individuals relates to some element of miscommunication about some aspect of human needs.

There are four components of nonviolent communication:

1. Observations are what we see, hear, and touch that are separated from our interpretations or even attach meaning to them.
2. Feelings are emotional reactions that are free of labels or thoughts, and are merely indicators of whether our needs are being met.
3. Universal human needs include sustenance, safety, love, understanding/empathy, creativity, recreation, sense of belonging, autonomy, and meaning.
4. "No" is an acceptable answer. Requests are literally just that, and saying "no" to a request should not be seen as a negative outcome in a relationship.

Nonviolent communication has evolved as a process rather than a list of steps. The focus is on intent, desiring to listen to the other person in the conversation, engaging in meaningful conversations with others, and connecting in an authentic way.

EFFECTIVE COMMUNICATION TECHNIQUES IN PRACTICE

Roberta was the kind of client who might make some financial planners question their choice of profession [58, p. 17]. She was a single woman with no children or siblings. While she wasn't a Certified Financial Planner®, she knew just enough to be dangerous. She would question every purchase, constantly compare her portfolio performance to those with other financial planners, and exercise hypervigilance regarding every variation in her investment returns. To top it all off, she would often question whether her financial planner's fees were worth it!

Roberta's financial planner, Luis, would spend hours with Roberta, going through reports with her and trying to explain every nuanced detail about her rate of returns. Finally, Luis tried something different at one of their meetings. He had prepared a detailed investment update, as well as a persuasive report on why he was using a certain commodities mutual fund. Wiping the sweat from his brow, he worried that it was about to be another one of those trying, hours-long meetings with Roberta.

This time, however, Luis opened the meeting differently than usual. He started with a question: "So, what is at the top of your agenda that you want to be sure we cover today?"

Roberta told Luis about her reluctance to sell the family ranch that her grandparents had homesteaded. Her eyes lit up as she talked about its rich history and her memories growing up there. Instead of steering the conversation toward his own report and agenda, he decided to listen intently and let her speak. Occasionally, he would sum up what he was hearing her say and ask Roberta, "Is this right?"

Roberta would affirm that Luis was right and continue. She shared with Luis that the ranch was a place that made her feel grounded. Luis validated her feelings by saying it made perfect sense that she would feel grounded there, both emotionally and literally. They filled the three-hour meeting almost entirely with the discussion of the ranch. Roberta came to the decision that she wasn't going to sell the ranch. They spent the final 10 minutes of the meeting going over investment returns. Roberta agreed to keep the mutual fund she had previously questioned. By the end of the session, Luis and Roberta had not gone over any detailed reports, nor did they have their usual conversation about whether the planner's fee was justified.

Luis was certain that Roberta would think the whole meeting was a huge waste of time. But as Roberta was headed for the door, she turned and said, "Wow, we sure covered a lot of ground today. This is one of the best meetings we've ever had. Thanks!" [92] Since that meeting, Roberta has become one of Luis's favorite clients. Luis earned Roberta's trust by letting her take the lead and by practicing exquisite listening, which allowed their relationship to blossom.

Exquisite listening involves an intense curiosity and deep exploration of what a client is communicating. It's not just hearing their words, it's about reading their cues and diving deeper for profound truths and meaning behind the spoken words [58, p. 17]. The Latin origins of the word "exquisite" mean "to seek" and "search out thoroughly." When practicing exquisite listening, the listener immerses themselves in the present moment, eliminating all distractions, including their own inner dialogue.

With exquisite listening, the listener becomes consumed by the listening process. They will ask open-ended questions and seek clarification and expansion. The listener invites the speaker to go deeper into their subjective experience. This type of deep listening facilitates a process of discovery for the client [92]. When practicing exquisite listening, the planner needs to be alert for cues. They respond to the client in ways that allow them to understand their subconscious money scripts and subsequent behaviors. The listener will find opportunities to direct the conversation in a way that fosters an awareness so they may consider new options and solutions to becoming financially healthy. The secret to exquisite listening is letting go of our own agenda so we can be fully present with the client and their needs.

Exquisite Listening Techniques and Strategies

There are specific techniques and strategies that help financial planners to build skills in exquisite listening. Using these techniques and strategies, a planner will be able to build a productive, satisfying, and mutually beneficial relationship with their clients [58, p. 17]. What follows is a specific conversational script that can help planners become better listeners.

The Flow Process

The flow process is a seven-step protocol developed by Dr. Ted Klontz and Dr. Brad Klontz, designed to facilitate optimal listening. It helps financial planners to know when to talk, what to say, and how to focus on the client's cues. Here are the steps of the flow process:

1. **Start with an invitation.**

   A good start to a conversation with a client could sound something like, "Before we start on my agenda, I am curious about what's concerning you most right now."

2. **Listen with focused attention.**

   To listen without distraction, the planner must put aside their own agenda. It may help for them to physically move their papers and files or computer to the side of the desk to clear space for the incoming information from the client. This can help both the client and the planner shift gears so they can be fully attuned to the client's concerns and questions. It helps the client feel heard when the planner uses reinforcing verbal and nonverbal behaviors to encourage continued talk by the client, such as appropriate eye contact, nodding the head, and verbal validation, such as "uh-huh" or "yes."

3. **Summarize.**

   When planners are attuned to their clients they will be able to read the client's cues that signal when they are ready to pause for processing. When the client's energy drops, that's the perfect time for the planner to step in with a quick summary of what they've just heard. Energy changes, such as a lowering of the voice as their sentence trails off or an expectant pause, are cues to the planner to begin the process of summarizing what they've said. The summaries should be short and succinct, sounding something like, "So if I'm understanding you correctly, you're most concerned about your financial stability right now."

4. **Ask for what you have missed.**

   After providing a summary, the financial planner follows up with a prompt to test the accuracy and scope of the summary. This process could include saying something like, "Tell me if I've got the full picture." Or "Let me know if I'm missing anything." Statements like these usually have the effect of an increase in the client's energy and further disclosures regarding the topic at hand. If the planner notices an increase in energy, it is best to continue to listen. It is important to note that even if the financial planner provides a comprehensive and accurate summary, the client may say something like: "No, that's not it." In many circumstances, this is not a reflection of a poor summarization, but rather of the client becoming clearer about what they mean. As such, the financial planner would simply respond with something like: "Okay, please say more."

5. **Notice drops in the client's energy and repeat Steps 3 and 4.**

In the flow process the financial planner will continue to listen, summarize, and check in on the accuracy of the summary. If Steps 3 and 4 do not bring the energy back up in the client, then it's likely that the conversation is coming to a natural conclusion. It is then time to move on to Step 6.

6. **Identify an overarching word, idea, phrase, or concept that captures the essence of what the client is saying.**

In Step 6, the planner may pick one element from the client's disclosure and invite the client to give more information on that. This may sound like, "Based on what you are saying, I get the sense that *financial stability* is important to you. Tell me more about what *financial stability* means to you."

7. **Close with a grand summary.**

After the planner has gone through the entire flow process and feels like they have sufficiently captured the client's concerns, they should summarize what they've heard in three or four sentences. Then, they can check in to see if they've missed anything. If there is more, the planner should listen intently and then summarize what they've heard.

The flow process makes clients feel like the most important person in the world to the planner. And in that moment, the client *should* be the most important person to them. Making the client feel heard meets two basic psychological needs: the need for human connection and the need to belong. Feeling fully understood fosters a deep connection and makes the client feel valued and respected. Each moment of the exchange should reinforce the client's psychological needs. The flow process is a powerful technique that significantly increases effectiveness for financial planners and their clients.

When a planner practices the tools and methods listed in this chapter, they will be well on their way to forming trusted bonds with their clients, making their meetings powerful and effective. Exquisite listening strategies, such as the flow process, motivational interviewing, reading verbal and nonverbal cues, reflective listening, paraphrasing, open-ended invitations, and the S.O.F.T.E.N. method, when practiced and used regularly, can serve to facilitate a good relationship between client and planner.

KEY POINTS

- To be an effective financial planner, you must establish a relationship built on trust.
- Planners can use a variety of verbal strategies, including active listening, reflecting, paraphrasing, and using open-ended invitations.
- Nonverbal strategies are also helpful in building rapport, including maintaining an open posture, nodding, and effective pacing.

CFP BOARD LEARNING OBJECTIVES COVERED IN THIS CHAPTER

H.69. General principles of effective communication

a. Assess the components of communications, including verbal and nonverbal communications.
b. Apply active listening skills when communicating with clients.
c. Select appropriate counseling and communication techniques for use with individual clients.

CHAPTER 9

Solution-Focused Techniques in Financial Planning

Take a moment to consider this unusual question:

Tonight, while you're sleeping, a miracle happens and your biggest financial concerns are now solved. What would be the first signs you would notice in your life? What would other people notice? How would your thinking change? What would you be doing differently? How would it feel?

During the discovery process, financial planners learn about a client's past financial experiences because in order to help someone get to where they want to go, it is useful to know how they got to where they are now. The biases, life experiences, and habits that led to a client's financial situation need to be recognized and accounted for in order to move forward. While there are often changes that need to be made, there is also great benefit in focusing on what the client has been doing that has been successful, with an emphasis on reinforcing those efforts and looking to do more of the same. This is where solution-focused techniques in financial planning come in.

Solution-focused therapy (SFT) is an approach to counseling that draws a client's attention toward utilizing their positive characteristics, strengths, skills, and assets to set and work toward goals for the future. Instead of focusing on what hasn't worked in the past, the solution-focused approach highlights the possibilities of the future. SFT has been used in a variety of fields, including marriage and family therapy, health care, education, social work, child welfare, substance abuse, domestic violence, criminal justice, policy evaluation, and business. It can also be used in the field of financial planning [93]. Dr. Kristy Archuleta at the University of Georgia is credited with integrating SFT theory and techniques into financial planning.

Solution-focused techniques are built upon the following assumptions in SFT about human psychology and change [94]. They include:

1. If it's not broken, don't fix it.
2. If it works, do more of it.
3. If it's not working, do something different.
4. Small steps can lead to big changes.
5. No problems happen all the time; there are always exceptions that can be utilized.

THE CLIENT HAS THE POWER

Rather than focusing on a client's problems, SFT operates under the assumption that clients *want* to make changes in their lives and that they are fully capable of making these changes. If a client is sitting in your office, it's most likely because they want to find solutions to their financial well-being or they have concrete goals for their lives. Solution-focused therapists may encourage clients to develop effective solutions by helping them find methods that have worked in their past in addressing similar problems. The SFT approach has clients review their history for examples of how they overcame difficulties in the past. Instead of building an action plan from scratch, a financial planner using an SFT framework would look to build on what's already working in the client's life and expand on those solutions. Using SFT in discovery sessions could reduce client anxiety in the short term, likely because the client feels a bit more control over their financial destiny [95].

FINANCIAL SELF-EFFICACY

Change can be difficult, so SFT invites clients to go slow and make small, lasting changes. This helps clients be gentle with themselves while gathering proof that these small changes are working. When clients see that those changes are making a difference in their lives, they are more inclined to continue making small changes toward their goals in the future. In essence, the advisor is helping build financial self-efficacy. Self-efficacy refers to an individual's belief in their ability to execute the behaviors necessary to produce specific performance achievements in a variety of contexts [96]. Advisors can help build their client's financial self-efficacy by focusing on positive behaviors and celebrating victories, whether large or small. In many regards, the advisor is like the spotter helping the weightlifter at the gym, supporting the lifter to make sure nothing goes wrong (like a dropped weight), but also offering positive feedback to encourage the lifter to follow through and succeed.

A FOCUS ON SOLUTIONS, *NOT* PROBLEMS

Rather than focusing on what is holding them back and getting in the way of their goals, SFT asks the client to look for alternatives to their current behavior. The advisor works with the client to help the client identify strategies that will lead them to achieve their goals [93]. Conversely, traditional forms of counseling tend to focus on the problem rather than the solution. This leads to rigid thinking and a negative emotional experience, and can cause clients to have difficulty recognizing alternatives. In SFT, the client is asked to identify and talk about the times in their life when the problem wasn't present. For example, if a client is dealing with a stressful financial situation, the planner may ask for them to talk about a time when they weren't so stressed. Then the financial planner would spend time helping the client identify the attitudes, behaviors, and conditions that were in place to allow them to be more at peace with their financial circumstances. Once the client can locate the time in which they didn't have the problem, they can identify the things in their environment and the behaviors that were present. Then the client can work to recreate those circumstances.

Focusing on our strengths, rather than our weaknesses, can be harder than it seems. Most people can think of a long list of their weaknesses, but struggle to create a long list of strengths and opportunities. SFT invites people to think of the positive behaviors and situations of the past and then pinpoint the circumstances that made those behaviors and situations positive. Reflecting on the positive aspects of the past, or how they overcame difficulties of the past, can help them develop strategies they could use again to overcome their current challenges. SFT brings clients to the fundamental truth about themselves: that they already possess the skills, assets, abilities, wisdom, and talent to overcome obstacles. They just need to remember those qualities and put them to use in the present, rather than dwelling on the problems and negativity of the past. SFT is an effective way to help clients take small, calculated steps toward achieving their goals.

SOLUTION-FOCUSED TECHNIQUES FOR THE FINANCIAL PLANNER

There is some preliminary evidence to suggest that solution-focused techniques may be beneficial to clients in a financial planning context. For example, Dr. Kristy Archuleta and her team found that following a solution-focused financial goal-setting session, participants reported lower levels of financial anxiety [95]. This can be beneficial, as studies have linked high levels of financial anxiety to being less likely to seek the help of a financial planner, and lower levels of financial anxiety to being more likely to seek financial planning advice [97]. What follows are some of the key solution-focused techniques financial planners can use to help their clients implement change and achieve positive outcomes.

Recognizing and Affirming Client Change

Even before the first session, the client has already taken the first step of scheduling an appointment, which can lead to change. This is important and should be acknowledged. Let's face it: Many people avoid addressing their financial lives and never schedule an appointment for help, which should be celebrated. You can't help a client if they never become a client in the first place. The planner may ask the client about any changes, big or small, that have occurred since they made the appointment [93].

It can also be helpful to ask the client what happened that led them to seek out financial planning services, reinforcing their motivation to take action. This can help the client see that change is not only possible, it is already happening.

Discussing Past Attempts at Change

Reviewing what actions the client has taken in the past can help the planner understand what the client has tried before, what has worked, and what hasn't worked. The planner can make a note of what's been successful for the client in the past, even if they were minor victories, and expand on those victories to create present-day solutions [93]. The planner can also avoid rehashing strategies that have already met with failure. Within a solution-focused framework, the planner develops a collaborative relationship instead of dictating a course of action, which includes encouraging the client to do more of what's worked before. It is important to note that the financial planner views the client as the expert on issues related to the client's life, and it is up to the client to ultimately decide what works and what doesn't [93]. A solution-focused planner will refrain from presenting themselves as "the expert" and instead follow a more client-centered approach. Rather than being an expert who dictates what a client should do next, the planner becomes a guide, helping the client find solutions that work best for their individual needs based on their unique strengths and positive attributes.

Using the "Miracle Question"

The miracle question is the essence of SFT, and lends itself exceptionally well to a financial planning context. It is designed to help the client create an image of what their life would look like if a miracle occurred that magically solved all of their problems. An example of the miracle question in the financial planning context is illustrated at the beginning of this chapter.

After the client paints the picture of what life would look like, the planner can ask follow-up questions to help them understand the positive changes the miracle would make in the client's life [93]. An important follow-up question would be, "How would you know that the miracle occurred?" The solution-focused approach should direct the client to answers based on the process of change, such as "I would feel relieved," or "I would give it some thought before I made a trade." The client should be directed away from content, such as "All of my debt is wiped out." The advisor can help the client get more specific by asking questions such as, "What would it look like if you thought about making a trade before you clicked the button?" The client's answers to these questions can lead them to specific and meaningful solutions that can be used to solve their financial concerns in the present [93]. Other examples of follow-up questions are:

- "What is the first thing you notice after the miracle occurs?"
- "How do you know that things are different?"
- "What would you be doing differently with your finances?"
- "How would you know things are improving?"
- "What would your family and friends notice about the differences in your life?"
- "How would your feelings be different around your financial life?"
- "What else would be different?"

Developing Goals

After exploring the miracle question, the planner can use the client's responses to help develop short-term, intermediate, and long-term financial goals. When shaping these goals, the focus should be on the changes the client wants to see now and in the future [93]. It is important that the goals be concrete, measurable, and achievable. Focusing on the goals and how they fit with the client's values and sense of meaning and purpose, rather than on the problem, can keep clients motivated. The planner and client then have a "North Star" by which to direct their efforts.

Use Scaling Questions

In a solution-focused framework, scaling questions can be used to assess a client's progress toward their goals and keep them on track. Since the planner relies on the client's perspective to gauge their progress, these questions help the client and planner visualize their path toward their goals. Scaling questions may be used in follow-ups to the miracle question as well. Some examples of scaling questions include:

- "On a scale of 0 to 10, with 0 being 'not at all' and 10 being 'perfectly,' how would you rate the way you are managing your money?"
- "On a scale of 0 to 10, with 0 being 'how you felt when you made your first appointment' and 10 being 'how you will feel when you've met all your financial goals,' how would you rate your concerns and anxiety right now?"
- "On a scale of 0 to 10, with 0 being 'completely hopeless' and 10 being 'full of hope,' how hopeful are you that you will achieve your financial goals?" [93]

When the client moves up on the scale, the planner could highlight that progress and explore the things that brought on the improvement [93]. If a client regresses on the scale, the planner could work with the client to explore what happened, always keeping the client's positive attributes in mind. Some examples of these explorations are:

- "You said you are a 3 on the scale. What kept you from being a 2 or a 1?"
- "You say you are a 0 on the scale. What could you do to move up half a point?" [93]

These questions keep the client's attention on positive improvements, rather than negative events and behaviors. The planner can help the client realize that their situation could be worse, or that they have the skills and strengths to make even a small improvement with solution-focused scaling questions. The client's answers to these positive, solution-focused questions will reveal positive aspects of their behavior and circumstances. Those positive behaviors are what hold the potential for reaching a solution.

Don't Be Afraid to Give Compliments

A well-placed, meaningful, and sincere compliment can work wonders in increasing a client's motivation and stamina. Congratulating a client's mindset and habits that have brought them business and/or financial success can make them feel seen and appreciated. Complimenting their efforts in the face of difficulties helps them see how far they've come and how capable they are. A compliment such as "Wow! It's impressive that you were able to make that much progress on your estate planning since we last met." It's important to remember that compliments help when the client is regressing as well as progressing. If the client says they slipped from a 5 to a 3 on a scaling question, the planner may acknowledge that the client was able to keep themselves from slipping to a 2 or a 1. When the planner reframes it from defeat to perseverance, the client will be able to focus on the skills and abilities they possess that kept them from regressing further. Compliments should always shine a light on the things a client is doing that are working [93].

LEAD WITH CURIOSITY

Solution-focused techniques work best when the planner takes a nonjudgmental, unassuming, collaborative, and curious stance when talking with the client. This stance creates an environment of genuine interest, positivity, and support. It can be challenging for a financial planner to work with clients in this way, given that they've been trained to gather data, analyze that data, and give recommendations based on the data. But the SFT approach can turn those recommendations into suggestions. This is more of a client-led approach, which makes it more successful because people tend to follow through on something when it's their idea.

KEY POINTS

- Solution-focused therapy (SFT) is an approach to counseling that draws a client's attention toward utilizing their positive characteristics, strengths, skills, and assets to set and work toward goals for the future.
- Using a solution-focused approach in financial planning can empower the client to make the changes they want in their life in meeting their personal goals by focusing on their strengths as well as past successes.
- The major assumptions of a solution-focused financial planning approach include: If it's not broken, don't fix it; if it works, do more of it; if it's not working, do something different; small steps can lead to big changes; no problems happen all the time; there are always exceptions that can be utilized.

CFP BOARD LEARNING OBJECTIVES COVERED IN THIS CHAPTER

H.68. Principles of counseling

1. Explain the applications of counseling theory to financial planning practice.
2. Demonstrate how a planner can develop a relationship of honesty and trust in client interaction.
3. Select appropriate counseling and communication techniques for use with individual clients.

CHAPTER 10

Cognitive Behavioral Approaches in Financial Planning

If you are ever perplexed about the motivation for someone to do something, being familiar with cognitive behavioral therapy (CBT) can help. CBT is an approach to counseling that operates under the theory that our thoughts, feelings, body responses, and behaviors are all connected. It asserts that what happens to us shapes our thoughts, those thoughts affect our emotions, and those emotions drive our behaviors. While planners are not therapists, it is helpful for them to understand the psychology behind their clients' biases and behaviors so they can help clients make good financial decisions.

CBT has been shown to be helpful in treating money disorders, such as compulsive buying disorder, hoarding disorder, and gambling disorder. However, components of CBT can easily be adapted and used by financial planners in their work with clients to help increase a client's confidence around challenging financial situations and to help modify limiting financial beliefs that lead to self-defeating behaviors. Financial difficulties are an indicator that there are underlying beliefs about money that could benefit from further exploration. For example, studies have shown that money scripts, including money status, money avoidance, and money worship scripts are significant predictors of problematic money behaviors, higher credit card debt, lower income, and lower net worth [3, pp. 33–43]. CBT uses a variety of techniques that can identify and correct self-defeating beliefs and can be applied in financial planning.

121

CBT has several core principles that can help us make sense of human behavior [98]. These principles apply directly to understanding behaviors a financial planner will encounter in their work with clients: (1) problems in a client's life are based, in part, on inaccurate or unhelpful ways of thinking; (2) problems in a client's life are based, in part, on learned behaviors that are unhelpful or self-destructive; and (3) clients can learn better ways of coping with life's challenges, leading to better emotional experiences and outcomes.

CBT offers a helpful model for giving planners a glimpse into the reasons for a client's behaviors. It is a model of human psychology that includes four key elements:

1. The Situation

    Clients often seek the help of a financial planner after experiencing some type of change in their lives, such as a career transition, getting married or divorced, having a child, inheriting money, or nearing retirement. From the CBT perspective, the situation is typically viewed as neutral. In other words, whether the individual interprets a situation as exciting or stressful, or both, is directly related to their thoughts about the situation. In the CBT model, a client's behaviors emerge from the meaning they place on the situation and their emotional responses to the meaning they have ascribed.

2. Automatic Thoughts

    Our thoughts are the intermediary between a situation and our emotional and behavioral response to it. A situation on its own is not necessarily good or bad until we assign meaning to it. Therefore, two people having the exact same experience could have dramatically different reactions. For example, when the stock market drops some people get scared and sell, while others get excited and buy. The same event leads to dramatically different emotions and responses. Often our thoughts arise instantly and have a profound impact on our experiences. They typically occur without conscious deliberation, and are thus automatic. When they are based on inaccurate information, or an unhelpful way of looking at a situation, they can lead to problems. One of the primary goals of CBT is to help clients become aware of their automatic thoughts so they have the opportunity to evaluate them and change them if they are deemed to be inaccurate or unhelpful.

    Sometimes automatic thoughts emerge in a pattern of systematic errors in thinking, referred to in CBT as *cognitive distortions* [99]. These can include patterns such as: (a) dichotomous thinking, where we think in a polarized, all-or-nothing, either-or way; (b) selective abstraction, where we focus on a detail and ignore the broader context; (c) personalization, where we mistakenly attribute external events to ourselves; and (d) overgeneralization, where we have a tendency to draw general conclusions about ourselves, other people, or the world based on a single event.

3. Emotional Response

René Descartes said, "I think; therefore I am." But in the psychology world, CBT asserts, "I think; therefore I feel" [100]. Thoughts drive emotions. Let's try an experiment: Take a moment right now to make yourself feel as excited as possible but here's the catch – try to get excited while keeping your mind blank. How did you do? Chances are it was tough to dive deep into that emotion. Now try it again, but this time think of something you are looking forward to. Perhaps it's an upcoming vacation, or your plans for Friday night. Close your eyes and picture it. Now try to make yourself feel as excited as possible. Did that feel different? When an emotion is tied to a thought, it is stronger and lasts longer.

4. Behaviors

The seemingly craziest financial behaviors will make perfect sense when we understand the situation, a client's thoughts about the scenario, and their emotional response to those thoughts. A financial planner can help clients deconstruct situations, such as investing mistakes in the past, and help them examine their thoughts and feelings to make sense of their behaviors. This can be done quite easily within a financial planning context, by simple but strategic conversation. These conversations can help the client and the planner better understand the reasons behind the client doing what they do around money – for better or for worse. Increasing self-awareness is an important step in developing a healthier relationship with money.

THE COGNITIVE MODEL IN PRACTICE

The cognitive model just described can help financial planners make sense of their client's behaviors. For example, let's say that Joe's partner is mad at him because Joe didn't disclose the cost of a mountain bike he purchased. Joe asserts that he hasn't done anything "wrong," because his partner knew about the purchase ahead of time. However, Joe was honest in admitting that he purposely didn't tell his partner about the cost of the bike. Joe's lack of upfront disclosure has caused tension and mistrust in their relationship. But if Joe didn't do any-thing wrong, as he asserts, why did he choose to keep the spending a secret?

In analyzing his behavior, the pattern became clear. Joe grew up in a household where his parents fought about money – a lot. His father, in par-ticular, was very controlling and he would often hear his father yell at his mother for a purchase she made. Here are the elements of the cognitive model and how they apply to Joe:

1. *The situation:* Joe bought a mountain bike but hid the actual cost from his partner.
2. *Automatic thoughts:* "If I tell my partner how much it costs they will get upset and yell at me" but "I will *not* be controlled!"
3. *Emotional response:* Fear and anger.
4. *Behavior:* Bought the bike and hid the cost from my partner.

Whether or not a financial planner has this discussion overtly with a cli-ent or couple, Joe's behaviors make perfect sense when viewed through the cognitive model. In the next section we explore CBT techniques that can be adapted for use in the financial planning relationship. This information is provided in two sections: (1) addressing a client's thoughts, and (2) address-ing a client's behaviors.

COGNITIVE BEHAVIORAL TECHNIQUES FOR FINANCIAL PLANNERS

Within a CBT framework, a financial planner will look for opportunities to influence a client's thinking and behavioral patterns. This section begins with an overview of Socratic questioning – an overarching conversational technique that can be seamlessly integrated into the financial planner–client relationship. We then explore additional cognitive behavioral techniques that can be used to help financial planning clients improve their financial lives and tackle common money-related problems.

Socratic Questioning

Socratic questioning, named after the teaching method of the Greek phi-losopher Socrates, is a conversational technique that helps clients answer their own questions [99]. It is used to explore ideas and to shed light on and evaluate the helpfulness of automatic thoughts or help a client navigate a challenging life situation. What follows are examples of Socratic questions that a financial planner might use with a client, based on the planner's goal:

Goal 1: Clarifying thinking: "Why do you say that?" "Could you explain further?"

Goal 2: Challenging assumptions: "Is that true in every case?"

Goal 3: Evaluating evidence: "Is there any reason to doubt that might be the case?"

Goal 4: Exploring alternative viewpoints: "What would be the counter-argument to that point?"

Goal 5: Thinking through implications: "So if _____ happened, what would be the likely result?"

Goal 6: Question the question itself: "Why do you think that question is so important?"

Addressing Client's Thoughts

At the level of thinking, cognitive behavioral techniques aim to help clients: (1) identify beliefs that may be inaccurate and lead to problems, (2) gain insights into the motivations and behaviors of themselves and others, (3) use problem-solving skills to tackle problems, and (4) enhance self-confidence [98]. CBT pioneers Aaron Beck and Albert Ellis introduced techniques to restructure cognitive distortions that cause problematic behaviors. Although not therapists by any means, financial planners can use some of these techniques to help clients reassess unhelpful beliefs that stand in the way of healthy financial behaviors. This approach can help people create a mindset that allows them to challenge harmful beliefs and develop proactive strategies and behaviors to address, resolve, and improve their financial circumstances. The following three steps often used in a cognitive restructuring intervention can be adapted for use by financial planners to help address a client's thoughts.

Cognitive Restructuring

Step 1: **Identify Self-Limiting Beliefs.** When a client is talking about a problem, a skilled financial planner will notice that the client has some assumptions about money, themselves, and others that are not entirely accurate [101]. For example, money scripts have a profound impact on a client's financial outcomes, and many of these beliefs about money are distorted versions of the truth. Increasing a client's awareness of their beliefs can be achieved through a variety of strategies, including: (a) asking questions about their upbringing around money, (b) asking specific questions about their opinions around investing, giving money to others, and so on, or (c) using a formal assessment of their beliefs, such as the Klontz Money Script Inventory (KMSI) [62]. Financial planners who are operating in a financial coaching capacity could go even further by having the client keep a log of automatic thoughts around money. We present some of these specific tools (e.g., the Money Script Log) in the toolkit. With these types of exercises the client keeps a journal of their automatic thoughts to keep track of both useful and harmful beliefs that emerge in their financial lives and the planner or coach can help them evaluate the usefulness and accuracy of those beliefs.

Step 2: **Challenge Self-Limiting Beliefs.** Harmful exaggerations may happen when a person overgeneralizes, magnifies, or minimizes importance, or puts an unhelpful label on something. For instance, if a person misses a bill payment, they may overgeneralize and believe that they are always bad with money. It is important to test the validity of these beliefs and point out that just because a person missed one payment but paid all their other bills on time, it means they made a mistake, but not that they are "bad with money." Here are a few steps to test the validity of beliefs:

a. Define and quantify terms around the belief. For instance, help the client define what "financial success" means to them.

b. Examine evidence supporting and contradicting the belief using deductive and inductive reasoning. Deductive reasoning looks at factual evidence, whereas inductive reasoning looks at probable evidence. For instance, a client may believe that the worst will happen, but the probability of the worst-case scenario is slim, making it unlikely to happen. If the client is unsure whether the belief is helpful or harmful, they may benefit from writing a list of pros and cons.

c. Another approach is to test the assumption in a real-life situation. For instance, a person may believe that financial planners only work with wealthy people.

Step 3: **Create Replacement Beliefs.** When unhelpful thoughts are identified as a hindrance to a person's financial life, alternative thoughts can be created to shift the person to a more positive and helpful mindset. This can look like different interpretations of the events that cause the harmful belief. For example, if two people pass each other in the street and don't say hello, a potentially inaccurate thought might be that one person doesn't like the other. But a valid replacement thought could be that they were busy and had other things on their minds. This can help a person decrease negative self-talk and increase positive thoughts, which will lead to behavior that supports improvement and success.

In a financial coaching or financial therapy context, the Klontz Money Script Log can help clients identify, challenge, and change problematic money scripts. It helps clients examine their thoughts, emotions, and subconscious thinking patterns about money. Clients are encouraged to identify specific financial situations that cause them distress, then identify the emotions and ask themselves, "What money-related thoughts are going through my head right now?" After they identify the situation and underlying feeling that occur based on that scenario, the clients are invited to pinpoint the automatic money script that accompanies the emotion. Then they are asked to create an alternative, more useful money script that will lead to a better behavioral response. This tool is explored further in the toolkit.

Addressing Client's Behaviors

Changing behavior can be challenging. For some, change brings discomfort, so they avoid it. As we discussed earlier, we are hard-wired to seek what is familiar and comfortable. We can take gradual steps – breaking a goal down from large tasks into small, easy-to-accomplish goals so we can become more comfortable – or we can dive right in and make the change. On the level of behavior, CBT targets two areas: (1) facing one's fears and concerns versus avoiding them, and (2) using role-playing to prepare for challenging conversations with others [98].

Facing One's Fears

The American Psychological Association's "Stress in America™" survey consistently identifies money as a top source of stress in the lives of Americans. Humans are naturally wired to seek pleasure and avoid pain. As such, trying to avoid thinking about one's finances is a logical coping strategy. However, this type of avoidance, often referred to as financial denial, is associated with lower income, lower net worth, and higher credit card debt [3].

From a CBT perspective, avoiding a situation not only makes the situation worse, but the act of avoidance can also become the primary problem. The only way to conquer a fear is to face it. In CBT, helping a client face their fears is referred to as "exposure." This exposure could be to a real-life scenario or an imagined stimulus through talking about it. For instance, a wealthy person who tends to hoard money may be asked to imagine spending money on something indulgent, like a fancy dinner. As their anxiety wanes from imagining the experience, they may be ready to try this out in real life. Exposure strategies can help desensitize a person to the stress and anxiety they may be feeling when making a change. The therapist or planner can ask the client scaling questions to gauge their level of discomfort and monitor their progress. Here are several ways a financial planner can use exposure techniques with clients to help lower their anxieties and fears around money.

1. **Conversations About Finances:** Talking with clients about money can be an intervention in itself. Often new clients worry that a planner will judge them or laugh at them if they reveal their actual financial circumstances. Just talking to a supportive financial planner can help ease a client's fears around money.

2. **Cognitive Flooding:** This technique is based on the assumption that if a client remains in the presence of the feared stimulus long enough, their fears and anxieties will dissipate. For example, if a client is fearful of what might happen in the market, rather than reassuring the client, the planner could facilitate a discussion, in detail, of what *would* happen if the stock market crashed.

3. **Stress Inoculation:** An exercise the authors have often used with clients is the "Worst-Case Scenario" (included in the toolkit). Rather than dismissing a client's fears as being invalid, the planner will ask the client to talk about the feared scenario in detail and dive deeper and deeper. For example, if a client fears the negative response of a friend or family member for the client's refusal to give or loan them money, the planner would repeatedly ask, "Then what would happen?" Often, this discussion arrives at a client thinking through the consequences in detail, which are often not as bad as they initially feared. This exercise, with instructions, is explained in greater detail in the toolkit.

Role-Playing

Financial planners have a unique expertise and skill set. They are frequently exposed to difficult financial situations and have a lot of experience to draw from. Conversely, clients often feel alone in their thoughts and circumstances. Many feel like they are facing unique problems that are actually quite common, but most people don't talk about. One of these areas is that of challenging conversations around money. For example, how do you say "no" to a request for money from a friend, family member, or adult child, or how do you ask your boss for a raise? In these situations, the financial planner can help the client practice effective ways of communicating through role-playing the situation. Typically the helper in this scenario would take the role of the client and model the strategy. This allows the client to come up with all their anticipated and feared concerns around what the other person may say. The role-playing exercise can then shift to the client taking on the role of themselves in the presentation and rehearsing their responses.

Through these approaches and techniques, the planner has the ability to help clients make good decisions that are consistent with their short- and long-term goals. First and foremost, the planner needs to always remember that their own reactions to a life event are not necessarily going to be the same as the client's reaction to the exact same life event. There is real benefit to the life experience of the planner, particularly in showing empathy and exercising active listening. However, the most important realization of any planner is that the worldview, experiences, biases, and any other thought, feeling, and emotion that the client brings is based on their lived experience and, frankly, all the other variables that are outlined throughout this book. Beyond that realization, it is important to note that none of this information or the techniques that are part of this book is designed to educate financial planners to become therapists by any means. Rather, this information is designed to help planners better identify the sources of the biases and behaviors that impact a client meeting their short- and long-term financial goals. We provide more information on the role of the financial planner later in this book.

KEY POINTS

- Cognitive behavioral therapy can help us make sense of even the least logical financial behaviors.

- Cognitive behavioral therapy has four key elements to human psychology: the situation, automatic thoughts, emotional response, and behaviors.
- Financial planners can use cognitive behavioral approaches such as Socratic questioning, cognitive restructuring, and role-playing to help clients identify and challenge unhelpful money beliefs.

CFP BOARD LEARNING OBJECTIVES COVERED IN THIS CHAPTER

H.68. Principles of counseling

a. Explain the applications of counseling theory to financial planning practice.
b. Demonstrate how a planner can develop a relationship of honesty and trust in client interaction.
c. Select appropriate counseling and communication techniques for use with individual clients.

11

Positive Psychology in Financial Planning

What brings you the most joy? Is it your work? Is it helping clients navigate their financial lives and achieve their goals? Or does your joy come from something completely unrelated to work? Perhaps you volunteer with a charity, mentor students or younger professionals, or serve as a leader at your place of worship? Or maybe it's all the above?

We all have things that fulfill us, challenge us, help us feel like we are part of something bigger than ourselves, and help us feel like we are making a difference. Like the title suggests, positive psychology focuses on the positive parts of a person's life, and has great strategies for helping clients recognize their strengths and use their assets, be they money, time, or knowledge, toward the activities and experiences that provide them happiness. Positive psychology applied to financial planning is an emerging area of interest in the field, and many aspects can be seamlessly integrated into financial planning to the client's benefit. In this chapter we introduce the field of positive psychology and how it can help enhance a client's financial life and overall well-being.

AN INFUSION OF OPTIMISM

Theo sat down for his first discovery session with his new financial planner, Bobbie. After talking through his financial situation, goals, and how his family and partner were connected to those goals, Bobbie asked Theo to imagine his best possible future self in terms of his work, his relationship, his family, and his health. After Theo provided a general overview of some of these areas, Bobbie asked Theo to think about exactly what his life would look like once he achieved the ideal version of each – specifically, what would he be doing, who would he be with, where he would be located, and how would he feel?

Bobbie was leading Theo through a positive psychology exercise designed to help him to think about his most important goals and about what life would be like once he met those goals. This process is known as a *systematic optimism intervention*, a positive psychology technique. It takes the financial goal discussion to another level. Not only does the conversation result in a positive emotional experience for the client but getting a clear image of one's goals can increase emotional engagement in the goal, which can, in turn, have a dramatic impact on increasing a client's motivation to reach their financial goals. For example, in an intervention that included spending time naming goals, visualizing having achieved them, creating a visual representation of their goals, and connecting their goals to their deepest held values, participants in one study reported a 73% increase in savings as percentage of income [102].

Positive psychology is one of the newest and most exciting areas of study in psychology. Instead of focusing on abnormal behavior like many schools of thought do, positive psychology explores avenues to help people live happy and prosperous lives. Positive psychology is less a field of psychology and more a category describing areas of study that are more "positive" and less problem focused. This includes many areas of importance to financial planning, including well-being, happiness, flow, coping, problem solving, goal setting, gratitude, altruism, positive responses to loss, pursuit of meaningfulness, social support, and relationship connection [103].

Positive psychology in financial planning can help clients get beyond the numbers and focus on the real intrinsic value that money can bring. Sarah Adebado, PhD, CFP® from Texas Tech University and Martin Seay, PhD, CFP® of Kansas State University are credited with being the first to apply positive psychology to financial planning. They argue that a positive psychology approach to financial planning moves from traditional financial planning that is needs-focused to a more strength-focused approach, where resources are used as a tool to optimize well-being [104].

Think about Theo. As the years go by, he could easily become distracted by the numbers in his accounts, focusing on achieving arbitrary benchmarks. He could spend decades building his consulting business, where one goal bleeds into another and another. His financial planner can be instrumental in helping him think through what it takes to succeed financially but what is all the work for? What will make Theo the happiest? A financial planner using positive psychology can help answer that question. As discussed, this book is not designed to create therapists, but there is real benefit in financial planners knowing the value of some simple yet powerful positive psychology techniques that can help their clients experience deeper levels of psychological well-being through their financial success.

THE THREE LEVELS OF POSITIVE PSYCHOLOGY

There are three levels of study within the field of positive psychology: subjective, individual, and group. A client's financial life impacts all these levels, and as such, financial planners are uniquely positioned to help clients optimize their functioning in all three. The first is the *subjective level*, where the emphasis is on feelings of happiness, optimism, and overall well-being within an individual's daily life. The focus here is on feeling good as opposed to doing good. The second level is the *individual level*, with an emphasis on elements such as love, forgiveness, and courage. At this level, there is a focus on the attributes that make up a life well-lived and a positive and productive individual. The third level is the *group level*, where the emphasis is on positive interaction with the larger community, including altruism and social responsibility – essentially, how an individual participates and contributes to their environment as a neighbor or citizen. A good financial plan seeks to enhance a client's experience in all these domains: increasing financial satisfaction, enhancing one's quality of life, and maximizing one's potential to make a positive impact on one's family and community at large.

Dr. Martin Seligman, the founder of positive psychology, developed the PERMA model to identify the areas that can help us define happiness and achieve a greater level of overall well-being [105]. With this model in mind, financial planners can help clients make positive impacts on the subjective, individual, and group levels. What follows is a review of the PERMA model. Each area includes some ideas on how a financial planner might have a positive impact on a client's life by making sure the financial plan takes all these areas into account, using the example of Theo and Bobbie introduced earlier.

Positive Emotions

Positive emotions can go beyond happiness and include joy, compassion, love, pride, and gratitude. Positive emotions can counter the effects of negative emotions and promote resilience, which is our ability to respond or bounce back from challenges [106]. Activities that elicit such responses could be a vacation, spending time with people one cares about, hobbies, or aesthetic experiences such as appreciating visual art or listening to music.

Theo's response to Bobbie's questions could be that he enjoys visiting each of the major baseball stadiums around the country with his nephews. They have a goal to visit each of them before his nephews go off to college. His planner, Bobbie, can help ensure that money is set aside for these trips each summer and follow up with Theo on how the trips are going.

Engagement

The activities you seek after a stressful period to "reset" yourself can range from exercise to hobbies, volunteering, or even working. Essentially, engagement is a state of "flow," where we lose our self-consciousness and become completely immersed in an activity or experience, losing track of time and ourselves in these activities [107]. Notably, excessive unstructured free time can have a negative impact on flow, which is a well-known potential negative consequence of the financial enabling/financial dependence dynamic. Specifically, children growing up knowing they do not need to work to support themselves can lead to a lack of opportunities to immerse themselves in challenging activities, which can lead to a lack of drive, motivation, and increased feelings of depression and frustration [108].

Bobbie and Theo discussed his work and how it challenges him mentally and spiritually, where the mental component is the strategy, along with the day-to-day engagement with his employees and the broader marketplace. He sees his work as fueling him spiritually since he views himself as a model to those he hires, working to provide a good living wage as well as a place where people want to be for 40 hours a week.

Positive Relationships

Human beings are social creatures, and the quality of our relationships are very important. These relationships can be with partners, family, friends, co-workers, and our neighbors and community in general. We can build stronger relationships with those around us by playing an active role in our communities, by joining a church or synagogue or nonprofit, or even our local gym, working to regularly engage and communicate with those we value in our lives. Many opportunities for positive social contact are built into a career. For clients who are nearing retirement, financial planners can offer tremendous value around predicting the loss of incidental social connections and help clients take the need for connection into consideration as they develop a financial plan post-retirement.

Meaning

It is a natural human quality to search for meaning and purpose in our lives. We want our lives to have worth, whether to those closest to us or to our communities and society. Each of us individually determines what meaning looks like. It could be volunteering, teaching others, or finding ways to serve our families or communities. A good financial plan looks to incorporate elements of meaning for clients, which could include allocating time and resources to spend with one's loved ones and making sure to incorporate meaningful bequests as part of a client's estate plan.

Accomplishment

Accomplishments are activities and achievements that are more long-term and require some element of perseverance. They tend to be intrinsic and goal-based, including more long-term plans, such as fitness goals (running a marathon or achieving an ideal weight), a promotion that brings greater impact, or graduating with an advanced degree [109].

THE ROLE OF THE FINANCIAL PLANNER

The planner can use positive psychology in their practice by working to focus the client's plans toward the items that are part of PERMA. Conversations that ask the client to reflect on the items, activities, and people that bring them the most joy can be a great way to help the client think beyond the numbers of the financial plan and lead them to more overall happiness. What follows are two positive psychology exercises that can be adapted and used in a financial planning context: (1) the Three Good Things exercise, and (2) the Gratitude Exercise.

The Three Good Things Exercise

In this exercise, each night for a week clients write down three things that went well for them during the day while reflecting on why they went well. This is one of the few psychology techniques that have been studied in a personal finance context. Dr. Sarah Asebedo and her colleagues studied this technique in a group of 993 participants. They found that when compared to a control group, the Three Good Things Exercise led to significant and enduring increases in both feelings of happiness and financial satisfaction [110].

The Gratitude Exercise

Gratitude is a positive emotion associated with positive psychology, and often emerges when we consider the positive impact others have had on our lives. The Gratitude Exercise is a Positive Psychology technique that provides an opportunity for a client to get in touch with and express gratitude to someone who has impacted our lives in a meaningful way [109]. Financial planners encounter opportunities to help clients recognize and experience gratitude as they begin to understand their story. In addition, they often have the opportunity to work with several generations within a family or family business, and can encourage the expression of gratitude among family members [104]. In a financial planning or financial coaching context, the gratitude exercise could be formalized with the following instructions:

1. Reflect on a person who made a positive contribution to your life.
2. Write a thoughtful, clear, and brief letter to the person (approximately 300 words).
3. Describe their contribution, how it impacted you at the time, and what it means to you today.
4. Reach out to the person and arrange a call or visit.
5. During the meeting, read the letter and spend time talking about the event and your relationship to the person.

Financial planners can use positive psychology in a way that helps their clients take inventory of the parts of their life that are bringing them the most fulfillment. Asking someone to articulate the facets of one's life that bring joy (or even challenge) is no easy undertaking, so it requires patience and perhaps multiple attempts in order to identify each. The rewards for both the client and the planner are immense, helping guide the client toward dedicating their time and resources to what provides them the most meaning while helping the financial planner develop a deeper relationship with their client. Once the client has identified all the areas of their life that are the most rewarding, the planner can help the client determine if they are spending their resources across all these areas evenly, essentially helping the client use their money (and time and effort) toward achieving happiness and fulfillment.

KEY POINTS

- Positive psychology is a growing area of psychology that explores avenues to help people live happy and prosperous lives.
- Positive psychology focuses on several areas of importance to financial planning, including well-being, happiness, goal-setting, the pursuit of meaning, and healthy relationships.
- Planners can use positive psychology in their practice by building into the financial plan the client's pursuit of happiness and meaning.

CFP BOARD LEARNING OBJECTIVES COVERED IN THIS CHAPTER

H.68. Principles of counseling

a. Explain the applications of counseling theory to financial planning practice.
b. Demonstrate how a planner can develop a relationship of honesty and trust in client interaction.
c. Select appropriate counseling and communication techniques for use with individual clients.

CHAPTER 12

Working with Couples and Families: A Systems Perspective

In the mental health field, there are professionals who are trained as specialists to work with couples and families. In the financial planning field, no such training exists, even though a large percentage of a planner's client base is couples and families. As previously discussed, a planner is not only dealing with a client's current relationship, but also the influence of a client's past, present, and possibly future relationships. Working with couples and families is different than working with individuals.

There are tools a planner can use to improve their effectiveness in working with couples and families to address financial disagreements. These tools not only help planners identify and solve financial issues, but they can also help a planner recognize when it is inappropriate to continue working with family members and refer them to a mental health professional. It can be rewarding to help couples achieve financial health for themselves as well as each other.

THE SELF-AWARE FINANCIAL PLANNER

For a planner to be neutral and effective in their work with couples and families, they must cultivate a strong sense of self-awareness. If a planner does not exercise self-awareness with regard to their own financial psychology, they run the risk of subconsciously choosing sides with one individual over the other within the couple. Remaining neutral when a couple is in the midst of a struggle can be challenging. But taking sides will only alienate one partner, disempower them, and further inflame the conflict. Even with the best of intentions, picking a side will backfire. Instead, the focus should be on compromise and resolution.

If a financial planner has their own unresolved issues, they could potentially be triggered by the struggles of their clients. If a client scenario reminds the planner of their mother's old penny-pinching habits, for instance, the planner may feel triggered or tempted to work out unresolved issues through the client. When planners identify too closely or transfer their own feelings to a client, it can be detrimental to all involved. In the mental health field, this is known as "countertransference" [111]. Countertransference commonly occurs subconsciously. Financial planners can avoid countertransference by understanding and identifying their own triggers, money scripts, and histories. Self-awareness around these issues can help a planner realize when they are having reactions and take control of their reactions. One telltale sign that a planner may be experiencing countertransference is if they start to see one partner as being right or without fault and the other partner as wrong or the one to blame. If these thoughts and feelings come up, a planner may need to reexamine their own past experiences, triggers, and money beliefs. An effective financial planner must separate their own emotions from the couple's issues.

In addition to addressing their own financial psychology, it is important for a planner to maintain healthy boundaries with couples. When dealing with something as personal as couples' finances, it can be easy for boundary lines to get blurred. Professional boundaries must be maintained and monitored to make sure a healthy detachment is kept so that the planner may be able to objectively assist couples in their financial decisions.

MAINTAINING NEUTRALITY

A financial planner can maintain neutrality by viewing a couple as one entity rather than two separate individuals. If a planner prefers, they can discuss this approach with the couple at the first meeting to establish a precedent. Some financial planners prefer to establish neutrality over the course of several sessions, rather than to say they won't take sides at the initial meeting to avoid coming off as confrontational. Maintaining neutrality in an environment where one partner is looking for advocacy or validation can be challenging. Sometimes clients come to a financial planner with the intention of having a professional who agrees with them.

Maria, a financial planner, met with Anne and Jacob to help them diversify their investments. In an earlier phone call for which Anne was not present, Jacob asked about selling their large home, since their children were grown and had moved out. Later, at a meeting with Jacob and Anne, Maria revisited the conversation she had with Jacob about selling their home. Anne was clearly distraught at finding out that Jacob had previously discussed such a big decision in her absence. Anne left the meeting and later fired Maria because she felt excluded from the conversation about her financial future.

Maria learned that all conversations regarding a couple's finances should include both parties. All communication should include both members of the partnership and input from both sides. Maria may have been able to help her clients by scheduling phone calls only when both parties are present and to include both of them in all correspondence. When processing this event with her own financial therapist, she learned how to handle the situation differently in the future.

Another valuable way to maintain neutrality is to view couples as equal partners, regardless of their individual net worth or earnings. A good approach to working with couples is assuming that each party shares equal responsibility for both their challenges and successes. In other words, it is important for them to each take 100% responsibility for their 50% of the relationship. This concept asserts that both parties are equally responsible for working toward solutions to conflict and for taking actions to honor mutual agreements.

TRANSFERENCE VERSUS COUNTERTRANSFERENCE

From the couple's perspective, one or both partners may become overidentified with the planner, or they may reject the planner. This is called "transference," which occurs when a client subconsciously overidentifies with the planner or transfers their emotions onto them. As is the case with countertransference, transference clients react to the planner due to some unresolved issues in their past, which they are subconsciously trying to resolve. Both countertransference and transference usually occur outside the realm of awareness for planners and clients alike. To make matters even more complicated, sometimes two members of a client couple may be reacting with transference in opposite ways. One partner may overidentify with the planner, while the other is rejecting the planner. Clients who are having strong reactions to a financial planner may be hearing communication from the planner as if they are coming from an influential character in their past, such as a critical father or overbearing mother. This can make clients hypersensitive to what they perceive as judgment from the planner.

Financial planners can reduce the risk of transference by asking clients about their past experiences with financial planners. This is a good opportunity for a planner to use their exquisite listening skills to gain a full understanding of a client's views and avoid misunderstandings throughout the client–planner relationship.

COUPLE CONFLICT

The top source of discord in the early years of marriage is money [112]. Financial conflict between newlyweds can be a predictor of divorce [113]. Financial issues can become a boxing ring for a couple to fight through their unresolved problems of the past in a subconscious desire to heal. When a planner meets with a couple they are also meeting with their unresolved issues from the past. If a couple is going to succeed in meeting mutual financial goals, they will need to get past those unresolved issues.

Sometimes, the best a couple can do is to accept their unresolvable differences, compromise, and learn to manage them. Instead of trying to change one another, which is highly unlikely to work, couples would benefit from acknowledging each other's differences with empathy. For instance, if one spouse is a giver and the other is a saver, they may agree to set aside a certain dollar amount each month for the giver to donate, satisfying their charitable tendencies while taking care to make sure they are still meeting their own financial needs.

In reality, money conflicts are actually conflicting money scripts, since each individual has their own family history, past experiences, careers, and interpretations of events. When a couple can take an open look at their money scripts, as well as each other's, it opens the door for understanding and empathy. It is from this place that resolution is possible.

FINANCIAL INFIDELITY

As described in Chapter 6, financial infidelity occurs when one or both partners lie or keep secrets about money, or use money to try and control their partner. It affects a large number of couples. Forty percent of people admit that they have deceived their spouses about money, such as lying about purchases or hiding accounts [114]. Financial infidelity occurs whenever a partner or spouse is being secretive about money, whether they are saving, giving, spending, borrowing, investing, gambling, or earning additional income without their partner knowing. This kind of secretive behavior around money can lead to instability in the relationship. Their partners may have trouble trusting them, not just in regard to money, but in other areas as well. Financial planners should monitor situations in which financial infidelity is present, since it can destroy relationships. If they're not careful, planners can find themselves stuck in the middle of the destruction.

FINANCIAL ABUSE

Beads of sweat formed on Allen's forehead as the couple in front of him started to argue. While Allen was a seasoned financial planner, the topic at hand seemed to be outside his professional realm. The conversation about the couple's financial transparency was escalating into a heated exchange. Corrine had just discovered that Bob had a secret savings account and had been hiding money from her over their entire seven-year marriage. During that time, they shared a car, which Bob took with him to work every day, leaving Corrine home with two small children and no way to get around. She was not allowed to work, nor access their joint checking account. Instead, she was given a credit card with a limited balance for spending, which was tightly controlled and monitored by Bob. In a private phone call in the past, Corrine had hinted to Allen that she was experiencing depression. She said that her therapist suggested she get a babysitter for a few days per week so Corrine could do something she enjoyed outside the home, such as take a painting class. But when she asked Bob, he insisted that they didn't have the money and couldn't afford to hire a babysitter. Later, Corrine found out that Bob had a bank account in his name only with over $50,000 in it. Corrine was devastated. Bob was indignant and claimed that the reason he hid money was because Corrine was frivolous and impulsive.

Allen recognized Bob's behavior as not only financial infidelity, but also financial abuse and control. From his studies in financial psychology, he also knew that this extent of financial control could be a warning sign of possible domestic violence, either currently or in the future. He understood that it would be inappropriate to probe or involve himself in this matter, given that it was outside his area of expertise and it might put Corrine in danger after they left the office. Even though he was worried about how they would respond, Bob knew he couldn't ethically work with the couple in a safe and effective way, so he referred them to a couple's therapist who was skilled at working through domestic violence.

Since abuse thrives in the shadows, it can be challenging to recognize it. It can happen to anyone, at any socioeconomic status, race, or education level. Financial planners are in a unique position to notice possible indicators of domestic violence, as money is often used to control victims. It can be dangerous for a financial planner to dig too deep or intervene in cases where domestic violence may be present, as it puts the victim at risk for escalated abuse once they leave the planner's office. The best thing for a planner to do if they suspect domestic violence is to limit their work with the couple to exterior matters, like portfolio options or investment solutions. Planners should consult with a mental health professional about the specifics of a situation to determine what else, if anything, they should do. We discuss the role of the financial planner as it relates to all elements of financial psychology in Chapter 20.

STRATEGIES FOR HELPING COUPLES RESOLVE FINANCIAL CONFLICTS

Since financial health ties into the well-being of relationships, it can be helpful to take a collaborative approach that considers the individual within a larger system. The systems theory approach takes into account the larger systems surrounding an individual, such as family, friends, community, and their environment [93, p. 122]. From a therapy perspective, it is necessary to examine all aspects of the system that influence a person's life, rather than just the individual in isolation.

Relational Financial Therapy

Financial planners and family therapists have collaborated to develop an experimental approach called *relational financial therapy* (RFT) [93, p. 122]. It has been found to be effective in reducing conflict and stress as well as increasing satisfaction within the financial planning process. This suggests that there may be some benefit to integrating aspects of financial planning with techniques associated with couples therapy. Financial issues are often interrelated with other issues, and it is important to consider the bigger picture of a person's family, environment, and community. The collaborative approach allows professionals to use their specific expertise to work with clients in addressing each part of their system. In practice, a financial planner may work in conjunction with a family therapist, a financial coach, or employ couples-informed techniques themselves to help a family find financial solutions and resolve conflicts. In collaborative and integrated approaches, it is always important to stay within one's own boundaries of competence and professional limits. *A financial planner should never give mental health advice, and a therapist should never give financial advice.*

TOOLS FOR RESOLVING CONFLICT IN COUPLES AND FAMILIES

A financial planner who has mastered the basics of effective communication will have a solid foundation from which to help individual clients as well as couples and families. When a planner is dealing with financial conflict between spouses, the best things they can do are to listen, reflect back what they've heard, and work to understand the points of view of both parties.

Active Listening

A planner should listen to both partners with their full attention, taking into account their nonverbal cues as well as their tone and body language. After hearing both sides, the planner may reflect back what they've just heard from each partner, clarifying what was said so that both spouses can get clear on the issues so they can work toward an effective solution. In a couples and family context, such active listening meets several goals. Not only does it help establish rapport and allow the speaker to feel understood, it also helps the other family members understand the speaker's position. Perhaps most importantly, it models healthy communication for the couple and the family.

Planners must remain neutral, taking caution not to label one partner as right or wrong. It can be common for one partner to try and label the other partner as "the problem," citing their overspending, undersaving, workaholism, or their habit of making unilateral money decisions. But it is important for the financial planner to remember that both parties are responsible for their collective financial situation. Even if an issue seems to be all the fault of one partner, the other partner may be adding to the problems by trying to control their spouse, or by enabling, avoiding, or inflaming the situation. For instance, if one spouse controls all of the money, but the other spouse has given up that control because they believe they are bad with money, then the responsibility to change the situation lies with both of them. One partner will need to relinquish some control over the family finances, while the other will need to take more responsibility with managing their money.

Identify Conflicting Money Scripts

For couples, self-awareness and self-reflection can help them learn more about each other, gain insight, and cultivate empathy. If one partner is anxious about money because he grew up poor and often went to bed hungry, their spouse may be able to see that the penny-pinching wasn't a result of them being cheap, but is tied to a childhood need for survival. Identifying conflicting money scripts can help couples make sense of financial behaviors they didn't previously understand. They may also gain insight into their own money scripts so they can take responsibility for changing their beliefs, and, therefore, their behaviors. Financial planners can help bring awareness to couples' money scripts through asking questions about their financial flash-point experiences and resulting beliefs, or using tools such as the Klontz Money Script Inventory (KMSI). We present a case study of conflicting money scripts in the toolkit, along with step-by-step instructions for how the financial planner can help couples negotiate solutions, while also honoring the unique needs and perspectives of both.

Money Agreements and Compromises

Establishing limits around money can sometimes bring couples closer together. For instance, if a couple makes specific agreements and establishes boundaries in areas that are known to cause conflict, they may be able to enjoy a closer, more relaxed, healthier relationship. A planner can suggest that couples put their agreements in writing, to solidify their commitment to a joint approach. Some agreements that can help resolve common conflicts are:

- **Establishing spending/giving limits**
     When one partner spends or gives more money away than the other partner is comfortable with, it can cause conflict. A planner may encourage a couple to draft an agreement in which each person

identifies a spending/giving limit. The couple may reassess this limit as needed, either monthly, quarterly, or yearly. If one partner wants to go over the spending/giving limit, the other partner has the right to veto that request. Each partner should have equal spending and veto power, which will empower both of them, especially if one spouse is the primary breadwinner [111].

- **Establishing debt limits**

  A couple can avoid confusion and conflict if they decide together how much debt they are comfortable with carrying. It might be helpful for them to agree not to exceed that limit without discussing it with their partner and, perhaps, their planner. The couple may also set goals for paying off debt and put those goals in writing. This will allow both partners to feel in control of their debt, while encouraging communication and collaboration.

- **Unique couple agreements**

  Sometimes, a couple may have a situation completely unique to them. For instance, if one spouse has a disability and is living off of settlement money, their partner may agree to never touch that account and may even sign a prenuptial agreement so that the disabled partner can rely on that money. Couple-specific agreements can help partners address their unique challenges and needs.

SEPARATE OR COMBINED FINANCES

When working with newly formed couples, a financial planner may encourage them to determine whether they would like to combine their finances or keep them separate. Neither decision is "right" or "wrong." It just depends on what is best for the couple. Some couples may want to have their own individual accounts and also share a joint account for paying mutual expenses, such as utility bills and rent. Planners can assist new couples in making lists of their income sources and expenses, and determine their approach to combining their finances, or keeping them separate. For couples who earn widely different incomes, it may be beneficial for them to contribute to bills and expenses from a percentage of their income, rather than equal dollar amounts [111]. For instance, if one partner makes $100,000 per year, and the other partner makes $60,000 per year, they may each contribute 30% of their income to mutual bills, meaning one would pay $33,000 each year and the other would pay $18,000 each year. This can bring equality to the relationship, empowering both parties to feel they are contributing.

In second marriages, it can be helpful for couples to allocate which assets and expenses are individual and which are mutual. If there are stepchildren involved, a financial management plan can ensure that the children's needs are met, while allowing the couple to make their own financial plans for the future. Deciding which assets will be passed down to which children can eliminate future arguments among siblings or stepsiblings. Whether it's a first, second, or third marriage, creating a financial plan is crucial to minimizing conflict and helping families achieve financial well-being.

SCENARIO PLANNING

Couples can help themselves by having a plan to handle unexpected financial situations. They may have a Plan A, which is their plan if everything goes the way they expect. But they should also develop a Plan B, and even a Plan C [111]. For instance, in Plan A, both partners have full-time, well-paying jobs. They will have a Plan B in case one of them is laid off or has to take a pay cut due to a recession, for example. In Plan C, they may consider what they would do if one of them was ill or disabled and unable to work for an extended period of time. Planners can help clients use scenario planning by introducing it as a normal part of financial planning.

MONITORING

Couples and planners might want to consider checking in regularly to discuss the things that are working well and the things that could be improved. During these check-ins, clients can review their financial agreements with their planner to see if they need to be revised. They can also discuss any life changes to see if their scenario planning needs to be updated. Clients can also have important events, such as a career transition or an inheritance due to the death of a family member. Staying engaged with clients through the seasons of life can help them stay on the right track for financial health.

KEY POINTS

- Working with couples and families is different than working with individuals and brings with it unique challenges as well as opportunities.

- To be effective and maintain neutrality, financial planners need to understand the impact of transference and countertransference in their work with couples and families.
- Tools to help couples resolve financial conflicts include active listening, identifying conflicting money scripts, and helping the couple or family arrive at money agreements and compromises.

CFP BOARD LEARNING OBJECTIVES COVERED IN THIS CHAPTER

H.67. Sources of money conflict

a. Identify a client's motivation for achieving their financial goals.

b. Explain to the client the consequences of a lack of transparency with the spouse or family when making financial decisions.

c. Identify areas of potential financial conflict between the spouse and/or family.

d. Communicate the importance of agreeing on financial goals and objectives with the spouse and/or family.

e. Identify situations in which money may be used as a means of undue influence, control, or abuse in relationships (e.g., power imbalances, financial abuse, and financial enabling).

H.68. Principles of counseling

a. Explain the applications of counseling theory to financial planning practice.

b. Demonstrate how a planner can develop a relationship of honesty and trust in client interaction.

c. Select appropriate counseling and communication techniques for use with individual clients.

PART IV

CLIENT AND PLANNER ATTITUDES, VALUES, AND BIASES

In the previous sections, we examined the client's financial psychology and techniques to help the planner use that knowledge to better serve their clients. We now turn to client attitudes, values, and other types of biases that impact the financial planning process. From the client perspective, we dive deep into cultural competence, risk tolerance, preferred learning styles, and what motivates our clients to achieve (or not achieve) their goals. We explore the fundamental reasons clients bring the lens they do into our practice: what deters them, what motivates their behavior, and what draws them toward working with a financial planner.

From the advisor perspective, we focus on how today's planner can be more culturally competent and better able to serve each client regardless of background or experience. We once again challenge you to reflect on your own biases and how they can complement, or perhaps work against, your ability to build relationships with clients who may differ from you. We spent a considerable amount of time on this topic attempting to first bring value to you, the advisor. That is what this book is all about!

Most importantly, we wanted our chapter on multicultural competence in financial planning to offer a space for you to reflect on your own background and experiences, and ultimately, the ways in which you can be more effective. We hope this chapter can help you and your firm establish deeper relationships with existing clients while attracting a new and diverse clientele.

We then shift our focus to your client's financial risk tolerance, preferred learning styles, and values and goals, with a focus on specific techniques to better serve your clients. Our intention was to explore these topics with a focus on how a financial planner can use this information in their day-to-day work with clients.

CHAPTER 13

Multicultural Competence in Financial Planning: Understanding Your Client's Cultural Identity

A woman and her husband sat in front of their financial planner in awkward silence. They were in conflict around their approach to money and had come to the financial planner for advice. The woman described herself as "thrifty" and "frugal" and wanted to save as much money as possible. In contrast, whenever they got money, her husband wanted to spend it on items of varying necessity. In fact, he had a garage full of items that he wasn't using but still thought were of value. The planner hypothesized that the husband was an overspender, and that he was maybe even struggling with a hoarding disorder. The conflict between the husband and wife was evident in their meeting with the planner. The planner agreed with the wife and, in a kind and professional manner, suggested that the husband's mindset around money was unreasonable, recommending that he stop "overspending" and save more money. The husband left the meeting feeling disrespected, while his wife felt vindicated that a professional took "her side" in their ongoing financial conflict.

Sounds simple, right? But there is much more to the story. Since the financial planner didn't consider the cultural background of the clients, he missed an opportunity to help them come to a deeper understanding of their cultural identities and how they factored into their relationship [115]. It turns out that the woman was raised in a Midwestern, White community, where she was taught the importance of independence, savings, and frugality. In contrast, the husband was raised in South America, growing up in a world of economic insecurity and rising interest rates. It turns out that his approach to spending did *not* stem from a lack of financial literacy or some type of spending disorder. His desire to immediately buy things to have the option of selling them later made perfect sense given his experiences around money. He grew up in a country in which inflation was such a problem that the only practical approach was to use the money right away, assuming the currency would drop in value while the value of goods would only increase. So, in the context of his experiences, his desire to spend as quickly as possible made perfect sense. But instead of exploring the "why" behind his behaviors, working with the couple to come up with a plan to address his concerns in a multiculturally competent manner, the White, Midwestern financial planner agreed with the wife, attacking the husband's desire to spend without understanding the context. There was a disconnect not only between the couple, but also now one between the couple and the planner, as he was not working to better understand the mindset of his clients. The implications of such a meeting could be disastrous, both with regard to the relationship of the planner to the husband and within the marriage itself.

THE MULTICULTURALLY COMPETENT FINANCIAL PLANNER

The purpose of this chapter is to equip financial planners with a multicultural mindset so they can be more effective in their work with clients. As we have discussed throughout this book, clients come from diverse backgrounds, perspectives, and sets of experiences that can have profound impacts on the financial planning process and the client–planner relationship. Although the financial planning workforce needs to be more representative of the broader population in the United States, that is not the focus of this chapter. We do not attempt to address each segment of the population and how they *should* be served. Rather, we explore the specific ways that planners can be more effective in working with their clients through a better understanding of their own worldview and experiences, and a focus on areas of cultural identity and majority/minority group status, all of which affect the client–planner relationship and the financial planning process.

SELF-AWARENESS AROUND MAJORITY AND MINORITY STATUS

Financial planners should consider examining the ways they are influenced by their own cultural identity and their minority and majority status across some important categories within that culture. The better a financial planner understands their own cultural identity, the more they will become aware of the biases and assumptions that can impact their work with clients. Becoming aware of how our own life experiences differ from those of others will help increase our empathy and effectiveness.

We are all vulnerable to biases that grow out of our own personal stories, experiences, family dynamics, and socialization. Additionally, human beings have an innate tendency to categorize things and generalize, which can contribute to erroneous or even harmful assumptions about people whose cultural identity differs from their own. Majority group members – as defined by historical power and influence in the culture, rather than just numbers – may have difficulty noticing their own biases because the values of their dominant culture are widely held and strongly reinforced. This is often referred to as "majority group privilege."

Meanwhile, a member of a minority group may be reminded of those differences daily. For example, regarding socioeconomic class, those with lower income can be considered a minority group. They have less access to resources and less power in the culture than other socioeconomic groups. Their minority status increases their conscious awareness of how their socioeconomic status impacts their lives every day, recognizing how others aren't experiencing the same food insecurity, lack of access to good education, stable housing, and so forth. Conversely, someone who is upper-middle class is likely to not have a daily appreciation of the benefits that their socioeconomic status confers. Their majority group status gives them the privilege to not have to be concerned about many of these stressors.

When we are members of the majority group within a culture, such power differences can be difficult to see. It's like asking a fish to describe water when that fish has never been on land. However, those who have minority group status in one or more areas are frequently made aware of how their experiences, opportunities, and concerns differ from the majority group. There are many aspects to majority group benefits and minority group challenges across a variety of categories within a culture. Race and gender quickly come to mind, but there are other aspects of majority/minority group status that can have a profound impact on a client's financial life.

RECOGNIZING MAJORITY GROUP PRIVILEGE AND MINORITY GROUP DISADVANTAGE

Being born in the United States at this time in history comes with an "invisible knapsack" of unearned privilege, where even the poorest among us have a quality of life that would be unimaginable to the poorest around the world – let alone throughout history. This, of course, is very difficult to grasp and acknowledge [116]. But the fact is, you did nothing to "earn" the privilege of being born at this time in U.S. history. It is no different than people who were born during the thousands of years of difficult periods on this planet. It just happens. Your special position, therefore, is not "fair" or "just." It is just a mere accident of birth. Perhaps some credit can be given to your parents or grandparents, but that has nothing to do with you, even as you reap many advantages as a result.

The word "privilege," as a noun, is defined by the Oxford Language Dictionary as: "a special right, advantage, or immunity granted or available only to a particular person or group." In every culture, there are elements of privilege built in, which are unearned but offer benefits of the dominant culture and majority group.

For example, you are likely to enjoy some special advantages in the United States if you are middle-class or higher, able-bodied, male, heterosexual, English-speaking, Christian, White, and/or come from a home with loving and involved parents. Being a member of the majority group in any of these areas comes with special advantages. They are not advantages inherent to themselves, but only in the context of the social structures in our country. For example, if you were a Christian in a primarily Muslim country, you'd likely feel marginalized or, at times, disadvantaged because the culture isn't oriented around Christian holidays, or doesn't extend the same cultural benefits to minority groups, and so on. Majority group status within every culture yields special unearned advantages and yet, those advantages can be challenging to see unless you view them from the perspective of the minority group.

Consider the example of able-bodiedness. From the perspective of someone who needs to use a wheelchair, being able to get to the second floor of a building without the need for an elevator is a special advantage available only to able-bodied individuals. With an elevator, getting to the second floor may no longer represent a "special advantage" that "excludes" someone who uses a wheelchair from accessing the second floor. In a similar fashion, people who are living at the poverty level are very aware of their minority status and the special advantages that money gives others.

The benefits of becoming aware of our invisible special advantages are many. If a financial planner can acknowledge the areas in which their majority status gives them special advantages, it will be much easier for them to be sensitive to the experiences of clients from diverse backgrounds. In turn, they can dramatically increase the effectiveness of the financial planning process with clients by building this awareness into their work with clients.

CULTURAL HUMILITY

The concept of cultural humility was developed to help physicians deliver culturally competent care. It approaches multicultural work from two orientations: (1) intrapersonal – developing an awareness of one's limitations to truly understand someone else's background and views, and (2) interpersonal – adopting a stance toward clients built on a foundation of openness and respect in attempting to understand the client's worldview [117]. Robinson, Masters, and Ansani identified the five Rs of cultural humility that provide a great framework for financial planners who are dedicated to providing services in a multiculturally competent manner [118]:

1. **Reflection:** Approach every encounter with humility and understanding, with an openness to learning from the client instead of just teaching.
2. **Respect:** Treat every client with the utmost respect and a dedication to preserving their dignity.
3. **Regard:** Hold every client in the highest regard while not allowing unconscious biases to interfere in the planner's interactions.
4. **Relevance:** Apply cultural humility in every encounter with our clients.
5. **Resilience:** Embody the practice of cultural humility to enhance personal resilience and compassion toward our clients.

TEN AREAS OF CULTURE AND MAJORITY/MINORITY STATUS THAT IMPACT FINANCIAL PLANNING

For a planner to facilitate an awareness of their own culture, as well as the culture of others, the ADDRESSING acronym is a great place to start. This model was developed by Dr. Pamela A. Hays [119] and first applied to the area of financial planning in 2015 [115]. The ADDRESSING is an acronym, which stands for:

A: Age and generational influences

D: Developmental disabilities

D: Disabilities that are acquired

R: Religion and spiritual orientation

E: Ethnic and racial identity

S: Socioeconomic status

S: Sexual orientation

I: Indigenous heritage

N: National origin

G: Gender

Clients and planners will fall into either a majority or minority category in each of these areas. In the areas in which they represent minority groups, they are likely to experience unique challenges that majority group members do not face. The following categories are drawn from the work of Dr. Pamela Hays [120], who has also helped apply this model to working with people around personal finances [115]. It is a good idea for a planner to think about where in these categories they fall as well as where a client falls. This will help planners increase their awareness of the influence culture has on the thoughts, decisions, behaviors, values, and opportunities they and their clients experience.

Age and Generational Influences

Our age and generation have a significant impact on some of our experiences and the social expectations placed on us. Social movements of and influences on our generation help shape our worldview and experiences. In addition, there are often biases against older and younger individuals. Age discrimination has been such a concern in the United States that the Age Discrimination Act of 1975 was set in place to prohibit it in terms of employment. However, age discrimination can work in the other direction too. For example, younger financial planners are often viewed by clients as being less competent. Having a youthful appearance can be a major disadvantage in situations where someone wants to display competence and confidence. This happens because the younger a person looks, the more likely they are to elicit subconscious caretaking responses in others.

As a workaround for younger-looking financial planners, the following research-based psychological tactics have been suggested: (a) bringing in an older-looking planner in the early stages of the relationship, (b) talking about and prominently displaying accomplishments, such as news articles, degrees, and certifications, (c) exuding confidence and reducing anxiety, because fear changes facial muscles and elicits caretaking responses in others, (d) expressing passion, which acts as an indicator of trustworthiness, and even (e) wearing glasses, which studies have found increase one's perceived trustworthiness and intelligence [121].

Developmental or Acquired Disability

In our earlier example, able-bodiedness is a majority group advantage. If you or someone you love has a disability, it can have a profound impact on your daily experiences and your opportunities. It is important to note that not all disabilities are visible. Nonvisible disabilities include things like mental health challenges, learning disabilities, and chronic pain. As with many areas of diversity, these conditions are not necessarily noticeable and many clients won't bring them up unless prompted. However, they can be very important to the financial planning process. As such, a financial planner could simply ask during the discovery process: "Are there any disability-related concerns for you and your family we should take into account in the financial planning process?"

Religion and Spirituality

A client's religious beliefs can be deeply entwined with decisions around money. It can be a primary motivator, the core of meaning and purpose in their lives, and have significant implications on their cash flow (e.g., tithing) and estate planning (e.g., bequests). Majority group status in this area is recognized as the degree to which the culture centers around traditions and holidays associated with one's religion. In the United States, the majority religious culture is that of Christianity, as evidenced by established holidays and a legal system based on a Judeo-Christian framework. In more homogenous areas of the country, it can be easy to assume that if someone looks like you, they share similar religious values. However, this could very well not be the case. An important component of multicultural competence is to not make assumptions and to simply ask. For example, the financial planner could ask: "Do you identify with a religion or spiritual practice that could have an impact on the financial planning process?"

Ethnic and Racial Identity

When we think about cultural identity the first thing that comes to mind for many is that of ethnic and racial identity. An individual in the majority race will often be immersed in a culture that was built upon the foundation of their ancestors' values and traditions. For example, they are likely to share similar phenotypic characteristics (e.g., skin color) and cultural beliefs and values (e.g., individualism vs. collectivism) as many of the leaders, media personalities, and business leaders in their culture. An important goal for the multiculturally competent financial planner is to be aware that the lived experience of others, based on phenotype alone, is likely to be quite different than their own in many areas. How their experiences differ will not be known, nor should they be assumed, only that they are likely to be different.

A critical goal is for the financial planner to not inadvertently overlay their own cultural values and lived experiences onto the client. This is especially challenging when the financial planner has not yet come to terms with their own majority group status and its impacts in comparison to those with a minority group status. It is also challenging when the financial planner isn't aware of their own cultural values and how they differ from those of others, and/or has a lack of experience working with people from diverse backgrounds. When in the majority group, it is easy to just assume that "that's just how it is" or that "this is how it's supposed to be done," without recognizing that many of the ways we look at finances, work, and family are just manifestations of our specific cultural biases.

In interacting with clients, it is critical that financial planners not inadvertently downplay or make excuses when clients talk about their experiences around discrimination or other sensitive topics. This is usually done with the best of intentions, such as when a planner might say: "Oh, I am sure that they didn't mean it like that," when a client reveals that they felt mistreated by someone based on race. This type of negating is a red flag for the client that the financial planner doesn't understand their reality, often due to an unintended lack of awareness stemming from the financial planner's majority group status. Instead, if a client trusts a financial planner enough to talk about their experiences in this area, the financial planner should take it as a sign that a deeper rapport has been established, seeking to understand rather than trying to challenge the client's perceptions or beliefs about what happened or why. It can be very difficult for a majority culture member to understand the extent of a minority group member's challenges, partially because of their own feelings of sadness, guilt, anger, and/or horror that may emerge when confronted with a client's experience. In an attempt to not experience these negative emotions, it is natural for a majority group member to downplay the experiences of others, either out loud or silently.

In working with a diverse clientele, it is important to have some general hypotheses about cultural differences around money. For example, it is important for the planner to know where their client falls on the continuum of individualism, which focuses on the needs and goals of the individual, and collectivism, which focuses on the needs and goals of the community overall. For many clients, it is not just about one or the other, but rather a delicate and evolving interplay between balancing the needs of the individual with that of their family, friends, and community. This helps planners make recommendations with their clients' cultural identity in mind, instead of asking them to go against their families and communities, or dishonor traditions. Such cultural values are an important driver of motivation and can be critical factors in the financial planning process. When these values come to light, it is important to build them into the financial plan. However, it is also important to not assume that the client sitting in front of you has any particular set of values or that they are manifested in the same way that people who share the same racial features and/or ethnic identity may manifest them. It is important to approach all clients as unique individuals.

Socioeconomic Status

As we discussed earlier in the book, a client's socioeconomic status, especially in childhood, can have a profound impact on their beliefs about money and their financial behaviors. Many of our hardest-working, most money-vigilant clients developed their approach to work and money in an effort to escape financial struggle. Socioeconomic status is a great example of how majority status has advantages that can be out of the members' conscious awareness, while minority status and its challenges can be a daily struggle for those who hold them. Being middle class or above comes with special advantages. There are many things you don't need to worry about, including food, clothing, and shelter. In fact, you could likely go days, months, or even years not worrying about where you will get your next meal or how you will be able to pay your rent. If you grew up as middle class or above, chances are you were much less conscious of day-to-day challenges around money. In contrast, if you grew up poor, chances are you knew you were poor. In addition to possibly developing a scarcity mindset and anxiety about not having enough money, you were likely also acutely aware that there were experiences others were having on which you were missing out.

Sexual Orientation

Financial planner Joe felt like the meeting with Steve was going well, at least at first. There seemed to be a good rapport and he felt like he was going to be of great help to Steve. But then things took a turn for the worst. Steve was talking about his ideal retirement and his plans to buy a house in Hawaii. Joe asked Steve if his wife was on board with the plan. That's when things got uncomfortable. Steve paused, shifted in his seat, and then told Joe that he had a husband, not a wife.

Being heterosexual in our culture also comes with some invisible advantages. For many heterosexuals, it is not even something they think about. In contrast, for example, gay clientele are likely to have been acutely aware of their minority status for their entire life. To illustrate the point, if you are a heterosexual, consider the following: What was it like for you when you revealed your sexual orientation to your parents? How long did you wait until you told them? Did you hide it from them? Were you worried they would be angry or that they would reject you? Did you let your friends know first before you told your family? If you are a heterosexual, you never had to think twice about any of these issues – a great example of majority group privilege. Recognizing your own journey, and the assumptions that emanate from that journey, can help the multiculturally competent financial planner avoid awkward conversations with clients (who may become former clients) like Joe's conversation with Steve.

Indigenous Heritage

Clients with an indigenous heritage, such as those who belong to a Native tribe or nation, such as Native Hawaiian, First Nations, Alaska Native, or

Native American, often present unique financial planning perspectives and needs. Many members of such groups have endured significant trauma both individually and collectively over time. Clients who are connected to their indigenous heritage may also have a unique set of values, concerns, and goals important to the financial planning process. In some cases, this could include a deep sense of duty and connection to their community.

National Origin

A client born in the United States with English-speaking parents is at a huge advantage in our culture. In contrast, those who immigrated to the United States and/or speak English as a second language face unique challenges. Even if a client didn't immigrate in their lifetime, many are aware of the stories of struggle, hardship, and prejudices their parents, grandparents, and/or great-grandparents endured in their attempts to integrate into the majority culture of the United States. In the financial planning process, it is important to be sensitive to how a client's nationality impacts their financial lives with respect to both challenges and opportunities. When working with immigrants, it is important for the financial planner to be aware of the concepts of *assimilation* and *acculturation* and their impact on the financial planning process. A client who has assimilated may have adapted and integrated into the majority culture in many ways. Their level of acculturation refers to the degree to which they have maintained aspects of their previous culture. To avoid making mistakes when it comes to the financial planning process, the key for financial planners is to maintain *cultural humility*. The best strategy is rather simple – approach all clients with an open and curious mind and ask about their values and goals, avoiding any assumptions about how much their client identifies with the majority culture.

Gender

Historically, girls have been raised with different experiences, values, and exposure to money, which has had devastating consequences for women. These consequences include more problems around money, less income in adulthood, and more financial vulnerability in old age [122]. Studies have found that families equip boys with more opportunities to learn about money than they do with girls, and boys are more likely to be included in conversations around family finances than girls, who are more likely to be excluded [50]. How we are socialized around gender can impact not just our finances but also our relationships. Women who go against traditional gender norms often experience negative social and relational consequences. For example, women who earn more than their male partners tend to report feeling less connection with their partners, more disapproval around their partner not meeting their expectations, and are more likely to use blame language in talking about their relationship around money [49].

Financial planning has been traditionally a male profession geared toward males. In fact, studies have shown that as many as 87% of women who are looking for a financial planner say they were unable to find one with whom they could connect [123]. Meanwhile, it is estimated that by 2030, approximately 75% of the wealth in the United States will be influenced by women [124].

Multicultural competence in financial planning requires financial planners to modify their approach to better serve female clients, and financial psychology can help. To provide more effective services to women, Lindsey Larrabee, CPWA®, FBS®, and Dr. Brad Klontz, CFP® recommend that financial planners do the following [125]: (a) focus on using better listening skills – such as reflective listening – to help establish trust, help the client feel fully understood, and explore her thoughts and feelings; (b) adopt a collaborative rather than expert–client approach that includes opportunities for ongoing financial education; and (c) create a financial plan that aligns with the client's needs, values, and goals, which include positive emotions, healthy relationships, and the pursuit of meaning.

Humans are complex, and effective client–planner relationships require planners to meet clients where they are with regard to their life experiences, financial behaviors, or their life journey. Although clients bring with them a unique cultural identity across many domains, the approach to being a multiculturally competent financial planner is simple: Recognize your own worldview, approach others with cultural humility, and be unassuming, vigilant, and responsive to the worldview and lived experiences of your client. By taking this thoughtful approach and using sound judgment, financial planners can effectively serve and positively impact a diverse group of clients from a variety of backgrounds.

KEY POINTS

- Financial planners need to develop a multicultural mindset to optimize their effectiveness in their work with clients.
- The financial planner needs to recognize their own as well as their client's majority/minority status in the areas of cultural identity to be more client-centered.

- Financial planners should approach client interactions with cultural humility, recognizing their own biases, embracing learning, and adopting a stance built on openness and respect in attempting to understand the client's worldview.

CFP BOARD LEARNING OBJECTIVES COVERED IN THIS CHAPTER

H.65. Client and planner attitudes, values, biases

a. Analyze a client's degree of risk tolerance and loss aversion and ensure recommendations are consistent with a client's risk propensity, attitudes, composure (e.g., past behaviors during market corrections), capacity, knowledge, and needs.

b. Explain how a client's psychology, background, preferred learning style, and values (socially conscious investor, etc.) impact the financial planning process.

c. Explain how a client's values, including cultural and religious values, and attitudes may impact their goals and the financial planning process.

CHAPTER 14

Financial Risk Tolerance

Gwen is 70 years old and close to retirement. As she thinks about the years ahead, she wants to receive as much income from her investments as possible while still maintaining her principal. She has a lot of traveling and activities in front of her. Her annuity, pension, and social security cover about 60% of what she is planning to spend, while the other 40% comes from a "bucket" that she fills from her portfolio. Gwen keeps several years of living expenses in that bucket in case of market downturns or other unforeseen financial issues. She remembers her older sister retiring immediately before the Great Recession and how she had to take a part-time job to alleviate her concerns about living through her retirement. Given that Gwen is now nearing retirement, she is not an aggressive investor. She has a three-year cushion in the event of market volatility. Ryan, her financial advisor, talks with Gwen about the historical returns of the market, stating that she has more than enough in her savings to weather any financial downturn and recommends investing a bit more. He also talks with her about what happened with her older sister a decade prior and works to develop a portfolio that alleviates her concerns and gives her confidence that she is on the right path heading into retirement.

RISK TOLERANCE

Risk tolerance is commonly defined as "the degree of variability in investment returns that an investor is willing to withstand in their financial planning" [126]. Gauging a client's risk tolerance can help a planner recommend

167

investments that align with that degree of tolerance. For example, it is not likely that Gwen will be comfortable investing in unpredictable or turbulent stocks given how close she is to retirement. On the other hand, a person in their 40s with decades of employment ahead of them could adopt a more aggressive strategy and may be willing to take chances on higher-reward investments that are not as stable.

Risk tolerance is a "multidimensional, fluid construct affected by many factors" [127]. For example, experts agree that there is often a gap between what clients report as their risk tolerance and their actual real-world tolerance. Often, clients don't realize their emotional capacity to withstand market fluctuations until they are facing one in real-time. There is also fluidity in client risk tolerance not only related to life events, but even throughout the days in a given week. For example, researchers in the UK found that risk tolerance tends to start with a peak on Mondays and decrease to its lowest level on Thursdays, with a bit of an increase on Fridays [128]. They hypothesize that this has more to do with mood throughout the week, with a sour midweek mood, and heightened levels of excitement as the weekend nears. This is not information to build client portfolios around, but it illustrates how environmental factors can have a profound impact on a client's risk tolerance, creating fluidity.

Standard risk tolerance assessments tend to fall short when measuring clients' behavioral aspects as well as current real-world circumstances. As Ron Sages, PhD, at the University of Georgia, pointed out, "When reality hits, as it did in 2008, behavioral facets of risk, which go far beyond self-reporting of one's willingness to accept risk, are much more important to a client's bottom line" [127]. He remembered a married couple in their early 60s who were on the verge of retirement. In the market crash of 2008, the value of their portfolio dropped significantly, causing them to panic. Despite Sages' recommendation to ride it out, the couple decided to move to a more conservative portfolio. They were worried that their retirement assets were going to evaporate right before they needed them. Their fear resulted in them selling equities at the wrong time, locking in their loss. "They had an anchor point and when their portfolio dipped below that mark, they saw it as a financial catastrophe," Sages recalled. In this case, their self-reported risk tolerance wasn't the only factor at play. Age, liquidity needs, and the time horizon for investments also can also affect a client's ability to ride out market volatility or even a crash.

Clients don't live in graphs, surveys, and charts. They are a product of their histories, experiences, cultures, beliefs, values, and resilience. Assessing risk on paper is one thing but assessing risk through a tangible exercise can reveal things that even the client may not know about themselves.

Risk Propensity

A client's past experiences impact their present risk propensity. A person's risk-taking propensity is defined as the "tendency to choose options with a lower probability of success but greater rewards" [138]. An individual's willingness to take on risks will have an impact on their decision making when there is risk and uncertainty. Before making recommendations to clients, financial planners must acknowledge that for most people, the pain of loss is twice as intense as the joy of a gain [129].

Risk Perception

Risk perception is a subjective judgment about the make-up and severity of a certain risk. A client's perception of risk may be based on several factors, including past experiences, current mood and circumstances, conditions of the current market, and recent portfolio performance. For example, people tend to be more confident when overall market performance increases (a product of recency bias, as discussed in Chapter 2). However, when market performance decreases, people become less willing to take risks. A person who experienced severe losses in the past may have a post-traumatic reaction and not be as thrilled to take big risks in the present. Environment plays a significant factor as well. Dr. Ross Otto analyzed two years of lottery purchases in 174 New York City neighborhoods and found that ticket purchases increased following unexpected (and unrelated) positive events, including wins by local sports teams (who were not expected to win) and unusually sunny days [130].

Risk Composure

Perhaps the best predictor of a person's tolerance for risk is how they've behaved in the past when faced with financial loss. Risk composure refers to a person's previous reactions to experiencing loss. If they stood firm and were able to ride out the storm during a downturn in the past, chances are they can do it again in the future. But if they bought when prices were high and sold in a panic when prices dropped, they are likely to repeat that same behavior, regardless of their scores on a standardized risk tolerance questionnaire. A financial planner can ask a client how they responded to an investment loss in the past, particularly during a period of market volatility. As we discussed in earlier chapters, this conversation can remind the client that they have been down this road before and that there is no need to panic.

Risk Capacity

A couple close to retirement does not have the same risk capacity as a 25-year-old with many decades of earning potential on the horizon. Risk capacity refers to the level of risk a person can take based on personal circumstances, such as age, investment time, and other factors [131]. While risk tolerance is about a person's individual level of comfort and how they emotionally respond to potential loss, risk capacity is about a person's current circumstances, which determine how much risk they can safely manage. Gwen had a high level of risk capacity, but a low risk tolerance, given her savings while nearing retirement age. In contrast, some clients may have a low capacity and high risk tolerance, in which case, advisors need to be clear with them about the consequences of high-risk investments.

Risk Attitudes

Risk attitude, or appetite, describes an investor's natural inclination to take risks when choosing investments in reaching their financial goal. Risk attitudes are generally developed subconsciously and are influenced by perceptions of situational factors like familiarity and manageability [132]. Individuals can fall within the spectrum of being extremely risk-averse, where they focus solely on potential threats, to those who see risk as exciting, where they focus solely on the reward [133].

Risk Knowledge

An individual's level of familiarity and knowledge around risk is referred to as risk literacy. Risk literacy refers to an individual's ability to comprehend statistical probabilities and to use that knowledge to make informed decisions related to risk [134]. In other words, it describes someone's ability to make good decisions based on an understanding of risk [135].

EMOTIONS, FOMO, AND RISK TOLERANCE

Every experienced financial planner has received a call from a client saying something like, "I see the market is up 12% but I am only getting 7%. What are we doing here?" Clients see market returns or hear of high investment returns from others and want in. In these cases, the client is experiencing

FOMO, fear of missing out. FOMO can cause an investor to take risks that they otherwise would not take as they do not want to miss out on a return that they think others are getting. An advisor needs to take the time to talk with their client and remind them that their investment portfolio should be consistent with their risk tolerance and that they should only make changes to their portfolio if there are significant life events that warrant such changes. Conversely, a client may panic during market downturns and want to make dramatic changes to their portfolio. It is up to the financial planner to talk about the historic tendencies of the market and tell the client to be patient. In many cases, the financial planner's most beneficial trait is their ability to help their clients "see the forest" and not focus on "the trees."

DEVELOPMENT, HISTORY, AND FAMILY

Gwen's story illustrates how a person's history can impact their financial decisions in the present. Thinking about her older sister's challenges as she entered retirement during the Great Recession had a profound impact on Gwen's level of risk tolerance. Similarly, for someone who learned not to trust the market in the aftermath of the Great Depression, investing large amounts of money in the stock market may not seem very appealing. Conversely, a person who experienced the economic growth of the 1990s may not be resistant to investing in the market. As we have discussed throughout the book, it can be helpful for a planner to understand a client's past, the circumstances of their generation, and their family beliefs and behaviors around money and then use that understanding to help their client see the longer-term and how the market has historically performed over the past several decades.

LOSS AVERSION

Loss aversion was identified in Chapter 2 as a common cognitive bias. How can planners help clients to overcome this bias as it relates to investing? Loss aversion is deeply ingrained in most human beings. Psychologists Daniel Kahneman and Amos Tversky showed this by demonstrating that even something as basic as a coin toss can activate our aversion to loss. If people stand to lose $10 dollars in a coin toss, they want the amount they stand to win to be higher. "People want more than twenty dollars before it is acceptable. And now I've been doing the same thing with executives or very rich people, asking about tossing a coin and losing $10,000 if it's tails. And they want $20,000 before they'll take the gamble" [136].

Financial planners often grapple with a client's aversion to losing when they suggest that it's time to make changes to investments. When presented with a choice, due to our hard-wired status quo bias, often clients may avoid making a decision. It's like the old saying, the devil they know is better than the devil they don't. Studies have found lower levels of loss aversion in clients who have higher levels of income and net worth, which suggests that exploring a client's loss aversion may be important if the client would like to increase their income and net worth [4].

To help clients overcome their aversion to loss without being stuck in indecision, Carl Richards, financial planner and author of *The Behavior Gap,* suggests an exercise called the Overnight Test [136]. If a person is struggling to let go of a declining stock recommended by a family member, Richards suggests that the person imagines going to bed and overnight someone replacing the declining stock with cash. The next morning, the person may buy the stock back for the same price or use that cash to invest in a well-designed portfolio. Richards observed that most people wouldn't buy the stock again. This is one way to work around a client's aversion to loss when holding on to certain investments that are limiting the potential of their portfolio.

As we have discussed throughout this book, the financial planner should work to better understand the client's background, including life experiences, money scripts, behaviors, and familial circumstances to be better equipped to understand the client's level of risk tolerance. There are several valuable tools that the financial planner can use to better assess a client's risk tolerance and to develop a financial plan that is consistent with the client's ability and willingness to take on risk. As with any element of financial planning, emotions can play a pivotal role as clients see the market fortunes of others and want to be part of that success. FOMO can cause a client to take on more risk than they are comfortable with. Like alleviating panic during market downturns, it is up to the financial planner to talk with their client when they are experiencing FOMO to remind them of both historic rates of return as well as all of the environmental and personal reasons that drive their risk tolerance.

ASSESSING A CLIENT'S RISK TOLERANCE

Financial planners have a standard practice of assessing their clients' risk tolerance before making recommendations or designing client portfolios. The set of survey questions that comprise a risk tolerance questionnaire

(RTQ) are designed to build a client's investment profile based on the risk that is associated with investments. The risk tolerance score, in addition to the client's income needs, assets, goals, age, and desired rate of return, helps planners decide which investment category is best for them, whether that's aggressive growth, growth and income, balanced income, or something else. *It is important for financial advisors to make sure they are using a risk tolerance questionnaire that has been shown in research to be both valid and reliable* (we discuss important considerations for assessment in financial planning in Chapter 18). While a research-based risk tolerance assessment tool is helpful, it doesn't factor in many of the more complex aspects of human psychology explored above. Michael Kitces, CFP®, suggests that a good risk tolerance questionnaire can not only help match a client to an appropriate investment portfolio but can also help advisors manage their clients' expectations and flag clients who may be prone to overreact in a market correction [137]. While standardized risk tolerance questionnaires are useful, sometimes they are not always great predictors of a client's actual risk-related behaviors in times of market volatility.

Use Numbers, Not Percentages

As discussed in Chapter 1, many of our behaviors are driven by our emotions rather than logic, and when we become emotionally charged, we become rationally challenged. Presenting a Monte Carlo analysis to a client, showing probabilities of market upsides and downsides, may be interesting, but the advisor using just percentages may lead to an inaccurate assessment of a client's true risk tolerance. The more specificity and concrete information the planner can provide, the more likely they are to get a reliable response from the client. For example, asking a client if they are okay with accepting the probability of a +/- 30% gain or loss in their $1,000,000 portfolio is one thing. But turning those percentages into concrete dollar amounts is likely to elicit a very different emotional response: "Are you okay with us putting you in a portfolio that has a historical potential upside of $300,000 in a good year, which would have you at $1,300,000, but also a potential downside of $300,000 in a bad year, which would put you at $700,000?"

The Trash Can Test

One way to help a person understand their true risk tolerance is to conduct an experiential exercise to help them visualize a loss and see how it feels. To demonstrate a 20% possible future loss in a $1 million portfolio, for example, the advisor could hold a stack of 10 one-dollar bills, pretending each bill represents $100,000. In the visual demonstration, the advisor would ask the person to throw two-dollar bills in the trash can and check in to see how comfortable they are with this simulated loss. Instead of looking at percentages on a page, this exercise brings a person closer to the actual emotional experience of losing actual money [129]. The advisor can follow up with questions that are designed to intensify the experiences and inoculate the person from making bad decisions in the midst of a market downturn. For example, the advisor might ask:

- "Are you SURE you would be okay opening your statement and seeing that your $1,000,000 investment is now worth $800,000?"
- "Are you SURE you wouldn't call me and ask me to go to cash?"

If the client can't answer in a wholeheartedly affirmative way, the advisor could then ask the client how much money they *would* be okay losing in a market correction. The trash can test can help a client familiarize themselves with their risk tolerance and decide whether it's possible to sit with the discomfort of loss without resorting to knee-jerk reactions that can cause an even bigger loss. If losing that 20% in the trash can was unbearable, a more conservative portfolio may be the wisest path.

Understanding risk tolerance can help clients avoid potentially costly emotional reactions like selling when investments are down instead of riding out the uncomfortable feelings associated with the risk. If clients can resist selling when the market falls, instead of waiting for it to rebound, which it has always historically done, they won't be throwing that money in the trash. It all comes down to the tolerance level of the client. For a financial plan, and ultimately a financial planner, to be most effective, they need to have a deep understanding of their client's risk tolerance so they can develop a strategy that accommodates their individual comfort zone and mitigates potential investment mistakes.

KEY POINTS

- Risk tolerance is a multidimensional factor that takes into account a client's history, attitude, and overall capacity to take risks.
- Financial planners need to assess their client's risk tolerance using valid and reliable risk tolerance questionnaires (RTQs) to help match clients to portfolios and manage client expectations.

- While standardized RTQs are useful, they do not always predict a client's actual response during market volatility. Planners can use a variety of tools to help bring to life the potential consequences of changes in their portfolios.

CFP BOARD LEARNING OBJECTIVES COVERED IN THIS CHAPTER

H.65. Client and planner attitudes, values, biases

a. Analyze a client's degree of risk tolerance and loss aversion and ensure recommendations are consistent with a client's risk propensity, attitudes, composure (e.g., past behaviors during market corrections), capacity, knowledge, and needs.

b. Explain how a client's psychology, background, preferred learning style, and values (socially conscious investor, etc.) impact the financial planning process.

c. Explain how a client's values, including cultural and religious values, and attitudes may impact their goals and the financial planning process.

CHAPTER 15

Client-Preferred Learning Styles: Getting and Keeping Your Client's Attention

Have you ever been in a doctor's office when the doctor began discussing the diagnosis of a new disease? There are a great number of details that can be difficult to grasp. It can seem as if the physician is throwing all kinds of information at you all at once, while you're still trying to make sense of the illness itself. You have so many questions, and the doctor may or may not be answering them. *Did they just say what I think they said? What is the nature of the malady? What is the treatment? What do I have to do during the treatment? What is the prognosis?* Your physician is probably sharing many of these details with you in that moment, but you are missing them due to stress and/or just plain information overload. Similarly, you may have parents or grandparents who depart from the doctor's office and cannot remember key points related to their care. You find yourself repeating the same question: "What did the doctor say?" The experience of information overload is so common that researchers found that only 14% of medical information was remembered by patients when it was shared only verbally.

The same holds true when it comes to financial planning. Like medicine, our profession is full of complicated jargon and data that can be overwhelming to our clients, particularly while they may be feeling financial stress. We

177

can find ourselves talking too slowly with some clients and talking too fast with others. Perhaps most importantly, we must determine the best avenue to convey key information. Will we have it via discussion or would it be better to present several charts and graphs? What is the ideal cognitive and emotional experience we want the client to be having while we are talking through these key points? Understanding the fundamentals of attention and client learning styles can be helpful for planners to determine the best avenue to communicate with their clients, focusing their attention on what is important and getting the very most out of the limited time that you have with them.

WHAT IS A PREFERRED LEARNING STYLE?

Our preferred learning style is the way that we learn best [139]. We all learn differently based not only on how information is presented, but also by how we respond or behave while learning is taking place. Given the brief time we have with our clients, we need to present information in such a way that will help them better grasp the important concepts. Not all human beings process information the same way. Learning styles are the different ways in which we focus on, store, and recall new and complex information. When a client isn't tracking the planner's presentation, or they are interrupting to ask questions, or they sit quietly, eyes glazing over, completely checked out because they are overwhelmed by the information, the planner needs to deviate from what they are doing.

Imagine you have a toolbox beside you as each client enters your office. Each client has specific needs that require specific tools. They will have different learning styles, biases, money scripts, and worldviews. The financial planner pays attention to the unique needs of the client in front of them, opens their toolbox, and pulls out the appropriate tools to make the planning session engaging, effective, and satisfying for both client and planner. In this section we review seven categories of client preferred learning styles that we think are important to financial planning: visual, auditory, reading/writing, logical, kinesthetic, social, and solitary.

1. Visual

Visual learners prefer charts, graphics, maps, images, and colors to receive and communicate information and ideas. Some signs that a person may be a visual learner include:

- Their thoughts wander during verbal conversations.
- They are visually observant, but miss things that are said verbally.

- They enjoy reading and intensely focus while reading.
- They find charts, graphs, and diagrams helpful in remembering information.
- They desire to *see* directions rather than *hear* them.

A planner who is in tune with their client will look for signs of a visual preferred learning style. They may notice a client's eyes wander when the planner is talking without giving them something to look at. Vigilance is key on the part of the planner to notice where a client's attention is going during the presentation, and the eyes can be a powerful clue as to where the client's attention is focused. The planner needs to be paying attention to how the client is processing information. Some ways a planner may check in with the client are:

- Asking the client, "Does that make sense?"
- Asking the client if they have any questions.
- Pausing in silence for the client to process the information that was just presented.

These check-ins will help the planner find areas that the client may have missed or where they might need more details. A client will give verbal and nonverbal cues to let the planner know if they are understanding the information. Attention is a finite resource; we only have a certain amount we can give. That is true for both planner and client. The client may need breaks in the presentation to process what they've learned. Likewise, the planner should be as prepared as possible, so they can focus some of their attention away from the presentation and onto the client to make sure that what they are presenting is landing with the client. Some clients may be able to digest more information than others. The focus should be on getting the client to grasp a few points well, rather than making it through a full list with very little client comprehension.

2. Auditory

Auditory learners prefer to receive information through listening and hearing. Some signs that a person is an auditory learner include:

- They like to talk.
- They prefer spoken directions to written directions.
- They prefer audio books to reading.

A person with an auditory preferred learning style may need to discuss the information before they can fully understand it. The planner should note that talking it out can be an important part of the client's learning process. During discussions, it is imperative that the planner listen more than they talk. Financial planners may feel the urge to talk about what they know, their qualifications, and their own experiences, but clients are typically less interested in hearing the planner talk than the planner may assume. Clients are often more interested in having a financial planner who will listen to their stories with empathy and interest. For an auditory learner, listening to an overly talkative planner can be frustrating when what they really need is to verbalize the information so they can make sure they are understanding it. It is important to note that in medicine, when patients only receive verbal communication, they tend to have trouble remembering the actual details of that information later, so often, verbal communication should have some visual component as well to maximize retention [140].

3. Reading/Writing

Some clients prefer to learn information by reading notes, handouts, or textbooks. Reading/writing learners also benefit by rewriting notes and rereading those notes silently again and again. Some signs that a person learns best from reading/writing include:

- They prefer to review materials ahead of time.
- They write a lot.
- They tend to review their planner's advice on the web and compare.

Reading/writing is a more active approach to learning than some of the other preferred learning styles. Active learning can be more effective than passive learning. Many clients with this preferred learning style may want to see written materials before the financial planning meeting. In some cases, a client may rewrite some of the material. They may highlight, scribble notes on the handouts, and even highlight what they're writing. Reading/writing learners often spend time researching the best options and reading the advice of other experts. A planner who understands that the client prefers reading and writing to process information may have materials for them such as notepads and pens. Even if the client isn't actively taking notes, they may like to doodle while they are listening to keep their brain active and engaged. Even if the client leaves the notes behind, the element of active writing can be a helpful part of their learning process.

4. Logical

Logical learners prefer to use reason and logic to process information. Some signs of a logical preferred learning style include:

- They learn through inquiry.
- They may interrupt multiple times with questions or to complete the planner's sentence.

Since logical learners process information through inquiry, they're going to be asking a lot of questions. They may even be asking about the exact thing the planner just clarified. But reasoning is part of their assimilation of information. The logical client may interrupt a planner, or even complete their sentences. They are not doing this to be rude. Rather, they're engaging by posing questions and being interactive. This learning style may require a bit more patience when it comes to the financial planning domain, because planners may be spending more time with logical learning clients. It may seem like a redundant process, but if the planner thinks of this in terms of accommodating the client, the extra effort will be easier to accept.

5. Kinesthetic

Kinesthetic learners prefer physical activity while they are taking in new ideas and information. Some signs of a kinesthetic learner include:

- They enjoy movement.
- They have a tendency to fidget.
- They pace while on the phone.

It may be helpful for kinesthetic learners to take walks with their spouses when discussing their finances. Financial planners may want to have a squish ball or tray of fidget toys handy in their office, in case a kinesthetic learner wants to fiddle with something in their hands when they are discussing important topics. This can help the client stay engaged while satisfying the part of their brain that needs to be active to process information. Providing swivel chairs can also be a helpful solution to clients who prefer to be on the move in the planner's office. For clients who prefer the outdoors, a planner may schedule a session on the golf course.

Dr. John Grable, of the University of Georgia, suggests that clients are psychologically influenced by the physical environment where the client and financial planner meet. Planners who use a more therapeutic office arrangement, with flexible seating and client accommodations, such as notepads, pens, and fidget toys, are able to get the client to share more openly and experience less stress, as opposed to the more traditional financial office arrangement, with heavy furniture that is difficult to move, a cold, bare desk, and a separation of client and planner, usually by a big desk or conference table [141]. The financial planning setting can have a significant impact on a client's ability to process information and their willingness to explore their beliefs, attitudes, and behaviors. While some clients may prefer to talk on the phone and others want to hit a few holes at the golf course, it is important for kinesthetic learners to have freedom of movement.

6. Social versus Solitary Learners

Social learners may want to learn from a group or discuss things with others before they make decisions. In contrast, a solitary learner may want to discuss financial options privately with their spouse so they can process the information on their own.

A MULTIFACETED APPROACH

Perhaps the best approach is when planners use a multifaceted approach of providing information to clients. A planner may even ask a client directly how they prefer to receive and share information. It is important for the planner to check in with the client to see if their learning preferences have changed, or if there are circumstances in their lives that are making it more challenging for them to process information (such as the death of a friend or family member). If a client is feeling overwhelmed or depressed, a change of scenery may be in order. The planner may ask the client if they would like to take a walk and get some sunlight and fresh air during the meeting.

Individuals may display multiple learning styles. Planners should cater to as many learning styles as possible, even before they understand a particular client's learning style. It is important for planners to check in with their clients to make sure they are receiving the information the planner is presenting. It's better for the planner to listen more than they talk and allow the client time to fully process everything that's being presented. Planners are best able to help their clients when they view the relationship as a partnership.

TALK LESS; LISTEN MORE

No matter our profession or how much experience we have, we should always be aware of how much we are talking versus listening. It is important to make the distinction between talking *with* someone, instead of talking *at* them. A useful guideline for planners is the seven-minute rule. In terms of the elements of attention, a planner should not keep talking for more than seven minutes at a time before pausing and checking in with the client and inviting responses, discussion, or feedback. If a planner is presenting something complex or stressful, even seven minutes might be too much. The more complex or stressful a topic, the less time should go by before a planner checks in to make sure the client is comfortable with and following the presentation. Our conversations and presentations are a partnership with our clients, requiring us to act as facilitators relative to client learning and action toward reaching their financial goals.

KEY POINTS

- The financial planning profession is full of complicated jargon and data that can be overwhelming to our clients.
- Understanding a client's preferred learning style will help focus a client's attention and facilitate retention of important content.
- Although there are key preferred learning styles, the most effective approach is multifaceted, where planners provide information to clients through a variety of modes.

CFP BOARD LEARNING OBJECTIVES COVERED IN THIS CHAPTER

H.65. Client and planner attitudes, values, biases

a. Analyze a client's degree of risk tolerance and loss aversion and ensure recommendations are consistent with a client's risk propensity, attitudes, composure (e.g., past behaviors during market corrections), capacity, knowledge, and needs.

b. Explain how a client's psychology, background, preferred learning style, and values (socially conscious investor, etc.) impact the financial planning process.

c. Explain how a client's values, including cultural and religious values, and attitudes may impact their goals and the financial planning process.

CHAPTER 16

Client Values and Goals

What motivates you? What gets you out of bed and inspires you to do all the things you do on a normal day? It could be working to provide food and shelter for your family. Perhaps it is the search for love and affection from others. Some are driven to excel in a very specific area, one in which they have been studying and working for decades. Every human behavior can be explained by a basic set of basic needs. Those needs motivate our behaviors and some are more indispensable than others. Our fundamental physiological needs, such as food, water, and rest, can dominate our behavior if they are not being met. For example, children who suffer from hunger have an impossible time learning, as they are singularly focused on their lack of food. This is known as a scarcity mindset. As financial planners, we work on the front line of an individual's thoughts, feelings, and behaviors as they relate to their values and goals. We may be the only person who has ever asked someone, "What are your goals for the future?" or "What does success look like for you?" If we can better understand what motivates human behavior and how we establish goals (for ourselves and others), we can help clients identify and achieve their own goals.

MASLOW'S HIERARCHY OF NEEDS

To get a glimpse inside the client's mind, it is helpful for a planner to be familiar with the concept of universal human needs. Psychologist Abraham Maslow developed a well-known theory of motivation called *Maslow's*

185

hierarchy of needs. Maslow's theory posits that our behaviors are motivated by hierarchical levels of human needs, represented by a five-tier pyramid, in which our basic needs are at the base of the pyramid and our more complex needs are at the top [142]. The hierarchy of needs in order of ascension are: (1) physiological needs (food and clothing), (2) safety needs (job security, financial security, health), (3) love and belonging needs (family, friends), (4) esteem needs (status, recognition, feelings of accomplishment), and (5) self-actualization (achieving one's full potential).

The bottom four tiers of the hierarchy of needs are commonly referred to as deficiency needs, while the top tier is related to growth or being needs [142]. Deficiency needs motivate people when those needs go unmet. The longer a person is deprived of deficiency needs, the stronger the motivation is to fulfill those needs. For instance, the longer someone goes without water, the thirstier they will become. As the bottom four tiers of needs are met, the motivation to meet these needs decreases. We are less motivated to get food if we just ate a big meal. By contrast, for the top-tier need, motivation levels increase as self-actualization needs are met. For instance, when we see results from exercising, we are motivated to continue. Maslow asserted that most of our behaviors are motivated by "several, or all of our basic human needs simultaneously rather than by only one of them" [142]. Most people want to fulfill all their needs and reach the level of self-actualization. However, unexpected life events can disrupt our ability to meet certain needs. Divorce, financial crises, job loss, or a death in the family can result in a fluctuation between the levels of the hierarchy. Maslow also pointed out that the order of needs in the pyramid could be flexible based on a person's values. For instance, a person may place the need for love higher than the need for esteem or safety [142].

THREE UNIVERSAL HUMAN NEEDS: SELF-DETERMINATION THEORY

In the decades since Maslow developed his hierarchy, researchers have further explored the concept of innate human needs. Self-determination theory suggests that we are motivated to grow and change based on three innate psychological needs: (1) competence, (2) connection, and (3) autonomy. *Competence* refers to the learning and mastery of new skills. People are more likely to stick to their goals when they believe they have the skills they need to accomplish those goals [143]. Financial planners not only help people identify their goals, but they can also actually help clients build the confidence needed to reach their financial goals. By drawing on their experiences and inside knowledge of other successful clients, planners can remind an unsure client that they can achieve mastery over their financial lives, especially when facing challenging life events that might otherwise hamper their ability to reach their goals.

Connection refers to our innate desire to feel close and connected to others [143]. The need for connection can be traced all the way back to our tribal ancestors when connection was integral to our physical survival. This desire for connection can have both positive and negative effects on our clients' behavior. If a client feels disconnected from others, they may make spending decisions that go against their financial plan in an attempt to join a certain group or have the same experiences as the group they are attempting to belong to. Contrarily, feeling a sense of connectedness to one's family can motivate a client to make prudent financial decisions that take their family member's financial well-being into consideration.

Autonomy is our essential human need to feel in control of our lives, behaviors, and goals [143]. Knowing that the actions we take will influence the outcome of our lives plays an important role in feeling self-determined. If people don't see any results from their efforts, they are less likely to feel motivated to continue their course of action. Financial planners can help clients meet their need for autonomy by giving the client a sense of control over their financial lives while taking care not to force them into financial decisions.

Self-determination theory suggests that the need for growth motivates behavior. Human beings need to overcome challenges, have new experiences, and learn skills to build a cohesive sense of self [144]. Intrinsic motivation is an important factor in self-determination. People can be temporarily motivated by external benefits (extrinsic motivation), such as bonuses, awards, and prizes. But lasting motivation is rooted in internal rewards, such as gaining knowledge or independence, growing into a capable human being, or becoming strong and confident.

MAKING SENSE OF CLIENT NEEDS IN FINANCIAL PLANNING

Human needs are dynamic, not static. In our day-to-day lives, things will change, making some needs more important than others. Human needs are like a lava lamp – our various needs float to the surface, constantly in motion.

When a need floats to the top, it gets our attention, and, ideally, that need is met. After the need is met, the urge to fulfill that need subsides for a time, until it needs to be fulfilled again, in which case it will float back to the surface. For example, if a person is hungry, the need for safety and security may float up to the top. But after eating a big meal, that need will sink down to make room for other needs. There will always be human needs to meet. There are rare moments when everything is perfect, but that's not the general condition of the human experience.

In addition to shifting in a client's day-to-day life, financial planners may also see their client's focus around specific needs shift over time. For example, younger clients may be more focused on making more money so that they can attempt to fulfill their *safety needs* related to financial security. Midlife clients may be more focused on *love and belonging needs* and how they can use their resources to deepen their experiences of connection with family and friends. Other clients may prioritize *esteem needs* and/or *self-actualization needs* and look for ways to broaden their impact or leave a legacy. Human needs drive client motivation and are the foundation for the establishment of goals. Financial planners need to understand their clients' needs and values to get a sense of the best way to interact with them and motivate them to make healthy financial decisions.

HUMAN NEEDS AND SELF-DESTRUCTIVE FINANCIAL BEHAVIORS

In financial planning, it can seem baffling when a client is exhibiting self-sabotaging behaviors. For example, if a client says they want to save more money but keeps buying expensive handbags they can't afford, a planner may be confused by this behavior. However, if the planner examines this behavior through the lens of basic human needs, they may be able to see that the client is buying these bags out of a *need to belong* to a specific community. A client who is undercharging for their services could also be led by a need to belong to another community. They may instinctually worry that if they charge what they're worth, their community will reject them, which spells certain death in the prehistoric, tribal, need-based mind. The planner may be able to help a client satisfy their need to belong in a healthier way, such as suggesting they join a social club or an entrepreneur support group. Sometimes many of our needs are being triggered simultaneously, so it can be hard to determine which one to satisfy first. A planner's job is to ask questions, exhibit empathy, and get creative in guiding the client to ways they can meet their needs.

RESPONDING WITHOUT JUDGMENT

Instead of operating from a pathology model, which is to assert that something is wrong with someone and needs to be fixed, a planner can frame challenges as a normal human tendency to try to satisfy unmet and unidentified needs. Early in the client–planner relationship, a planner may show the client a list of basic human needs (see the toolkit for an exercise that can be used with clients), but it's important not to call out these needs as they are being triggered. A planner may understand the basic need that is coming up, but it's more helpful to show empathy and guide the client toward a solution of meeting that need than to challenge it. *The professional goal is to respond to the needs rather than react to the behaviors.* Planners should try to look past the behaviors that seem to go against the client's stated financial goals and instead, try to understand what needs aren't being met. Rather than confronting the client about their behaviors, a skilled financial planner "checks their judgment" and gets curious by asking themselves: "What human need is my client attempting to get met by this behavior?" Then the planner can strategize from a nonjudgmental place about how to address those needs. The planner doesn't even have to guess correctly what need is crying out to be met. The key is that if the planner is focused on the need, they're not focusing on the behavior. They're looking beyond the behavior to see what really matters and to work with the client to get their needs met in a way that is congruent with their overarching values and financial goals.

DOES YOUR CLIENT BELIEVE THAT THEY HAVE THE ABILITY TO REACH THEIR GOALS?

One of the most effective strategies in setting and achieving big goals is surrounding yourself with people who have already achieved them. Not only can they share tips and strategies, but they can provide something even more important: a success mindset. Their assumption is that attaining the goal is not only possible, but is a logical, natural outcome that corresponds with a particular mindset and pattern of behavior. The highest achievers assume that they can reach their goals and take responsibility for the outcome. In psychological terms, they have an *internal locus of control* and *high self-efficacy*.

Locus of Control

An individual's locus can be categorized as internal or external. An internal locus of control means that the individual perceives themselves to have a great deal of personal control over components of their lives and tends to be held more accountable for both their behavior as well as outcomes related to their work and personal lives. Individuals with an external locus of control tend to perceive that outside forces impact their behavior and outcomes. Dr. Sarah Stanley Fallaw, president of DataPoints, explored the impact of locus of control and financial success [145]. She found that financial success is positively correlated with internal locus of control regardless of age or income. This can be explained by behavior, where people with an internal locus of control see their behavior, in this case their saving and investing, as contributing factors to their financial success. Contrarily, those with an external locus of control could see outside factors like not making enough money or having too many expenses thrust upon them. One study of over 1,000 financial planning clients found that a group of wealthier clients (e.g., median net worth of $2.2 million) had significantly higher levels of internal locus of control compared to a group of mass affluent clients (e.g., median net worth of $500,000) [4]. A multitude of studies have found that an internal locus of control is associated with higher income, higher wealth, higher rates of reemployment after a job loss, and better spending control [16].

Our ability to make decisions for ourselves and manage our own lives is crucial to our psychological health and mental well-being. Having a sense of control plays a key role in our levels of motivation. As human beings, we tend to feel more motivated to take action or change our behavior when we believe that our actions will have an impact on the outcome [144].

In a landmark study, nursing home residents were assigned to two groups: One was told they could arrange the furniture in their rooms any way they liked, visit with whomever, and were given a plant that they were responsible for watering and caring for. The second group was told that the staff would completely take care of them as well as their new plant. Eighteen months later, the group that had more autonomy (and responsibility for caring for the plant) had greater outcomes and a lower death rate than the group that had less control [146]. Feeling as if we are in control can mobilize us to take action and set impactful goals that we can ultimately meet. For financial planners, if we can help create a sense of personal control and mastery in our clients, their behaviors will likely follow.

Goal Incongruence

The best goals are the ones for which the client experiences congruence with the goals of their workplace or organization, and that are in harmony with those of their partner and/or family. To maximize the possibility of achieving a goal, it works best when that goal is also congruent with one's closely held, subconscious, implicit motivation. For example, if a client has set an arbitrary goal of making $1,000,000 a year, but what they really want is to feel a sense of financial security and connection to others, that disconnect may reduce the chances that they achieve their goal. A disconnect between someone's basic needs and their outward goals can lead to what is called *motive-goal incongruence* [147].

Likewise, when an individual's personal goals do not align with those of their organization, it can lead to stress and job dissatisfaction [148]. In such cases a client would look to help shift the goals of the organization or find a workplace that is a better fit. The best goals are also ones for which there is agreement and compatibility for both partners in a relationship and/or the family as a whole. Often a financial planner is in a position to help couples talk about goals and look for win-win scenarios.

FINANCIAL SELF-EFFICACY

When you are challenged, do you dig deep and find the energy and resolve to overcome that challenge, or do you raise the white flag and give up? When you made the decision to move forward or give up, was it related to your own belief in whether you could meet that challenge? Many of the goals that we take on are related to our self-efficacy. Self-efficacy is a core belief in our ability to succeed in a given situation or context and have a great impact on how we think, behave, and feel [149]. Self-efficacy comes from past performance, where someone knows they can achieve something because they have in the past. For example, if a client successfully saved for a new car as a teenager, they have a higher likelihood of thinking they can save for a new home, their children's college, or their retirement. We can also gain self-efficacy from social persuasion through modeling and encouragement from others. Think about the bench press spotter at the gym telling the lifter, "Come on. Two more reps. You can do it."

THE ADVISOR AND CLIENT FINANCIAL SELF-EFFICACY

The financial planner can be a powerful influence in helping build client's financial self-efficacy through several means. For example, the planner can share stories of clients in similar financial circumstances who achieved their goals, illustrating a concrete path toward success. The financial planner can also take large and perhaps overwhelming goals and break them into smaller, more manageable steps. Throughout that process, the planner can check in with the client and celebrate the small successes to remind the client that they are making progress and are on track to meet their larger goal. The planner could also take time to address any potential barriers to achieving client goals and discuss them. As always, avoiding jargon and being very specific regarding next steps is critical, as the planner wants to do everything in their power to make their financial self-efficacy as simple and straightforward as possible. What follows is a review of some research on goals and goal-setting that can be useful for financial planners in their work with clients.

NINE THINGS EVERY FINANCIAL PLANNER SHOULD KNOW ABOUT GOALS

1. *Cue clients around goals.* Clients will often come to financial planning with some goals in mind, but there are likely things they have not yet thought about. Rather than just asking a client to share their goals, the advisor can follow up with prompts to see what else may be important to the client, even though they may not have thought about it yet. For example, with a client who came in for help with investing, a planner could also ask: "Have you thought about educational planning?" "Do you have any mid-term financial goals, such as a new vehicle?" "How about saving for a vacation?"

2. *Encourage clients to set more goals.* The more financial goals a client has, the more money they are likely to set aside to achieve those goals. A major financial services firm told us that they have seen a direct connection between the number of financial goals a client has set and the amount of money they end up managing for the client. By encouraging clients to set more financial goals, and save toward them, financial planners are also helping clients increase their financial security and overall net worth.

3. *Encourage clients to set some nonmaterialistic goals.* We tend to have a higher success rate in achieving intrinsic than extrinsic goals. In fact, studies have found that the more focused people are on material items, the more likely they are to have debt, worse health, lower-quality relationships, and have lower work and academic motivation [150]. If we are motivated to do something because we love it, we also tend to be happier and, in a lot of cases, more successful.

4. *Encourage clients to get specific about their goals.* In a study where researchers had participants visualize their top three savings goals and create visual representations of those goals (e.g., a vision board), participants reported a 73% higher rate of saving three weeks later [151]. Rather than using a vision board with clients, financial planners can help clients gets specific about their goals conversationally, by asking them questions such as, "Could you paint me a picture of your ideal retirement? Where do you see yourself? What are you doing? Who is part of it?"

5. *Name accounts that correspond to their goals.* Naming accounts after a goal brings the account to life. It is not just an amorphous account with money in it. An application of mental accounting, it is a specifically designated account dedicated to helping the client fulfill one of their fundamental human needs. In some cases, accounts dedicated to a specific goal can lead to a higher self-regulation in meeting those goals. Seeing the specific progress they are making toward a goal with an actual number beside it can help motivate a client to continue to work toward that goal [152].

6. *Automate to achieve goals.* Once goals have been established, encourage clients to set up automated contributions to those goals. Automation helps in several ways. First, it helps capitalize on our status quo bias – our natural preference to keep things just the way they are. It also helps by instilling cognitive dissonance as a protection against sabotaging the goal.

7. *Revisit their goals mentally.* When meeting with a client, revisit their goals and the progress toward achieving those goals. An ongoing focus on the status of the goals acts as both a reminder and a cue to the client to continue to work toward meeting their goals.

8. *Anticipate obstacles and have a plan for overcoming them.* Studies have found that thinking only about positive future outcomes can decrease the likelihood of achieving our goals, often due to a lack of effort [153]. However, when visualizing our goals is combined with thinking

through, and planning for, obstacles we may face, it increases the likelihood that we will achieve our goals. Financial planners can offer value to clients in helping them plan for obstacles to goal attainment through scenario-planning approaches.

9. *Monitoring goals.* Checking in regularly on our progress toward a goal significantly increases the likelihood that we will achieve that goal [154]. In a study of individuals who were on a weight loss program, individuals who weighed themselves every day and quantified their progress lost more weight than those who did not [155]. Checking on our status can impact our behavior, whether it is facing the scale the next day or looking at our savings or investing.

KEY POINTS

- There are several universal basic needs that drive our behavior, including competence, connection, and autonomy. If some of these basic needs go unmet, clients may exhibit financial behaviors to try to meet them, regardless of whether they are consistent with their financial plan.
- The financial planner can help build a client's financial self-efficacy through regular monitoring of client progress toward their goals as well as breaking larger goals into smaller, more manageable parts.
- The financial planner can be a primary resource in helping the client both meet and formulate their financial goals. This could include mental accounting, automation, and creation of nonmaterialistic goals.

CFP BOARD LEARNING OBJECTIVES COVERED IN THIS CHAPTER

H.66. Behavioral finance

a. Identify how cognitive biases and heuristics can impact financial decision-making.
b. Describe how a client's psychology, such as their financial comfort zone, socialization, money beliefs, and past financial experiences and behaviors, impact their objectives, goals, understanding, decision making, and actions.

PART V

INTEGRATING FINANCIAL PSYCHOLOGY INTO FINANCIAL PLANNING

In the previous parts, we outlined the core elements of a client's financial psychology, values, and goals as well as the principles of counseling and communication. We now turn to some of the key issues related to financial psychology that affect financial planners on a daily basis. When we speak to practitioners and firms, one of the first things they ask about is how they can get their clients to take action. – specifically, when the client has not adopted elements of their financial plan, they need to decide to move forward with the plan, or they just plain disappear. So, we have devoted an entire chapter to that topic. As with the rest of this book, we are working to bring relevant research from psychology into practice.

We also devoted a chapter to helping clients manage crisis events. In many cases, when a serious issue arises in a client's life, the planner is the first to know – and in some cases, the client has no other professional in their life who they will talk to about it. We built a model based on research and best practices in other disciplines that can provide the advisor with guidance on how to navigate crisis situations. This part also includes a chapter on client assessment in financial planning. Financial planners use assessments with every client (e.g., risk tolerance questionnaires), and a book on the psychology of financial planning would not be complete without discussing the need for financial planners to better know and serve their clients by using sound, valid, and reliable assessments.

Finally, we talk about the role of the financial planner. We focus on two components here. First, we want to make sure there is clarity regarding the lines within which a planner can operate without attempting to be a mental health provider. Although we have mentioned this important point throughout the book, we feel that it is important to draw the lines even more clearly here. The second component of the final chapter is our thoughts on how the growing field of the psychology of financial planning will change the role of the planner going forward, to help planners better serve their clients.

CHAPTER 17

Getting the Client to Take Action: Motivational Interviewing in Financial Planning

We all have clients who seem to get stuck at some stage in the financial planning process – perhaps a prospective client who disappears and who we do not hear from again, a client who won't adopt the financial plan, or a client who just doesn't follow our advice. In other cases, market fluctuations can cause our clients to get skittish about their investments and call us with a knee-jerk reaction, wanting to make a change that goes against their best interests. There are two different scenarios here. The first is the client who starts their engagement with us. What can we do on the front end to keep them engaged, make decisions, and take action that is consistent with their plan? Second, what about the client who "ghosts" us or somehow strays from our plan for one reason or another? This chapter looks at both scenarios and how we can keep our clients on track, or get our clients back on track, to take action and move forward with their financial plan. One of the most powerful psychological techniques that has been adapted for use by financial planners to help their clients take action is motivational interviewing.

Motivational interviewing is a process used in a variety of patient- and client-centered professions to help motivate individuals to adopt behaviors that are in their best interests [89]. Healthcare professionals, therapists, and educators have used this technique for decades, particularly when the patient or the client has a high amount of control over their behaviors. For example, the dentist cannot be with their patients each morning to check to see if they flossed, but the financial planner can follow up and assess whether the behaviors are matching the goals.

Motivational interviewing has been adapted for use in the financial planning profession to avoid confronting and lecturing a client about their problem behaviors [58]. For a client who is stuck, lecturing and warning them of the dangers of overspending, for example, only pushes them further away from change [156]. When a client is experiencing ambivalence around change – part of them wants to change and part of them doesn't – the more the financial planners speak from the pro side of change, the more likely the client will be to take up the defense of the con side. When this happens, the client reinforces all their arguments to maintain the status quo. Inadvertently, the financial planner who gets caught in this dance actually decreases the likelihood that their client will take the recommended action. When someone is pushing us to make a change we aren't ready to make, digging ourselves in is a normal human response that occurs in all of us. We are hardwired to want to think and do things our own way, independently. If someone is pushing us in one direction, we naturally resist, push back, or disengage. The initial push causes stress, which activates our fight, flight, or freeze response. Before we get into specific techniques financial planners can use when they run across a client's resistance to change, it is helpful to understand the process of change itself.

THE CHANGE PROCESS

Motivation leads to change. Once a client is motivated to reach a goal, they will be open to changing their behaviors to achieve that goal. For a client to change, not only do they need to realize that change is necessary and important, but they also need to believe that it's possible. Lack of awareness and lack of confidence are the two biggest obstacles to meaningful change. Psychologists have broken down behavioral change into a six-step process [157]. Whether a person is making changes to how they behave around money, their health, or trying to overcome an addiction, the change process is the same. Understanding the change process and familiarizing oneself with the stages of change serves two purposes:

1. It helps an advisor identify which stage in the change process the client is currently occupying.
2. It helps the planner understand what conversational strategies they can use to help nudge the client forward in the change process.

Once the planner understands the client's trajectory in the change process, it will be easier to guide them toward effective, enduring change. The six stages of the change process are as follows.

1.   Precontemplation

Most people in this stage of change are in denial. In the precontemplation stage, there is usually little to no understanding of the problem. Clients will exhibit a lack of responsibility for the issue, or they think there is no issue at all, even if they have an underlying feeling that things aren't working the way they want them to be. While the client may feel that their circumstances aren't ideal, they have little interest in changing their own behavior. A client may be in the precontemplation stage if they are overspending and maxing out their credit cards, pulling funds out of their retirement, or financially enabling friends or family.

Take the case of Carmen, for example. Carmen wanted to invest in her retirement but didn't feel she made enough money to save for the future. Her colleague referred her to a financial planner who reviewed Carmen's spending and assets. The planner discovered that Carmen had been paying her sister's rent for the past few years, preventing her from saving any money of her own. But Carmen's sister was now working a steady job. The planner asked Carmen if it was possible for her sister to take over her own rent payments to allow Carmen to invest in a retirement plan. Carmen wasn't ready to consider letting her sister down, even if it threatened her ability to secure her own financial future.

At this stage, a financial planner would not want to lecture Carmen about paying her sister's rent. The planner merely asked her if it was possible for her sister to assume responsibility for her rent now that she had a job. Carmen's resistance to identifying her financial support of her sister suggests she is in the precontemplation stage of change. She is not taking any action to stop supporting her sister. She may never change her approach because she may not be aware of the consequences of paying her sister's rent on her own financial goals. While an advisor may be obliged to share their concerns with Carmen about how this might impact her own financial security, a skilled financial planner would change conversational tactics once Carmen showed signs of resistance to that advice (specific conversational tactics are discussed later in this chapter).

2. Contemplation

In the contemplation stage, the client may be able to see that there is a problem in need of a solution. The client may be able to acknowledge some of the negative consequences of continuing an unhealthy behavior and could exhibit a readiness to take responsibility for the situation. This is the point at which a client may be open to learning more information that can help them examine the problem and learn about potential solutions. The client may begin to seriously consider a financial planner's suggestions for change, even if they are still not sure if they want to change, or if change is even possible.

Carmen, at this stage, might go home and add up all the money she has given to her sister over the years. Through the help of her financial planner, she may begin to realize how much her retirement savings would have grown had she put that money in a tax-deferred retirement account instead of giving it to her sister. She may be struggling with telling her sister that she needs to pay her own rent, even if she's starting to see that it would benefit them both and allow for a healthier relationship between them.

Although Carmen might still not be ready to address the issue, she is now aware of the problems and is open to thinking through the implications of her sister's growing financial dependence on her own financial well-being. Her financial planner takes the abstract and makes it concrete, helping her see the financial implications of paying her sister's rent. At this stage, a skilled financial planner is not lecturing Carmen, but rather using good listening skills, reflections, and summaries to help reinforce and support the client.

In this stage, if change happens, it will usually take place within a year. A client may be in the contemplation stage if they know they are spending their entire paycheck without contributing to savings, but they aren't ready to take an honest look at their spending and commit to cutting back. When a client is experiencing ambivalence, the planner should take caution not to be confrontational. The more confrontational or directive a financial planner is in this stage, the more likely they are to push the client further away from change. When a financial planner confronts a client who is ambivalent, they bring out the client's internal debate, making it an external debate, which a client is hard-wired to fight against (see status quo bias). With every nudge for the client to make a change, the client will respond with an argument against it. This will reinforce the client's case opposing the change and make it harder for the change to occur.

3. Preparation

The preparation stage is all about getting ready to make a change. At this part of the process, the client may be seeking guidance or information and figuring out plans to make a change within the next few months. Resistance has faded and now the focus is on plotting out solutions and strategies. The client may be envisioning the life they want. Having a clear vision of a desired future and its benefits will add fuel to the client's intrinsic motivation for change, propelling them forward to the next level of the change process. If a client is in a financial planner's office asking about the next steps, they are likely at the preparation stage of change. Clients at the preparation stage are determined to make their financial health a priority. They are committed to doing things differently and ready to make a plan. Clients in this stage of change are looking toward the future, anticipating the ways their lives may improve once this problem is solved. This is often the stage at which a client may first engage a financial planner, and an ideal stage for the planner to make portfolio recommendations and help clients create a financial plan.

In the preparation stage, Carmen may be ready to ask her sister if she is feeling stable enough to pay her own rent in the next few months. They may even develop a tiered plan, so that Carmen is paying one-third less rent in the next month, followed by two-thirds less in the following month, and finally, giving her sister the full responsibility in the following month. Once Carmen is confident that her sister will pay her own rent, she can redirect that money to a retirement plan that she and her planner decide would fit best.

Although she is still not ready to take action, Carmen is not only aware of the issue but she is preparing herself to consider a course change. Her planner can offer support to help Carmen feel empowered. A skilled financial planner would also anticipate some of the obstacles that Carmen will likely face, including having what could be a difficult emotional experience in talking with her sister. This is where a financial planner might do some role-playing with Carmen, where they might ask Carmen to play the role of her sister, and the financial planner can model how to broach the subject.

With Carmen playing the role of her sister, she would then be free to act out all her deepest worries and fears about what her sister might say and how her sister might react. After learning how the financial planner might approach the conversation, they can switch roles and Carmen can practice having the conversation with her sister, while the financial planner plays the part of Carmen's sister.

4. Action

Preparation gives way to action in this stage of the process. The client is actively engaged in their quest for change and ready to put their plans into motion. It is important for a planner to be sure that the client is in the action stage of change before pressing for solutions. If a client is in an earlier stage of change around a given issue, the planner will likely fail to get the client to take action. People who feel pressured to change from outside influences (extrinsic motivation) don't usually follow through or stick with the changes they promise to make. Think about the elimination of any punishment or reward you have had in your life around a change you weren't motivated to make on your own. Once the "carrot" or the "stick" is eliminated, it is difficult to continue with the behavior. If you try to push a client through the stages of change too quickly, without going through the necessary preparation stage, they likely won't have the mindset and/or tools they need to change for good.

Most financial planning strategies assume that clients are already in the action stage. However, studies show that around any given issue at any given time, only 20% of people are in the action phase [157]. Planners have the most success with clients who are seeking advice, accepting, and appreciating the information, and are ready to act upon the planner's suggestions.

By this stage, Carmen has reduced her contribution to her sister's rent to zero and is setting up retirement accounts based on her financial planner's advice. She signed up to have her retirement payments automatically deducted from her paycheck before taxes and is looking forward to watching her savings grow.

In the action stage, Carmen is ready to receive and act on advice from her financial planner. This is the point where her financial planner *should* give advice, express their opinions, and offer solutions. Whereas listening without offering solutions may help at the precontemplation or contemplation stages, it would be counterproductive in the preparation and action stages.

5. Maintenance

Clients in the maintenance stage have an action plan in place and have implemented new behaviors into their everyday life. Depending on the nature of the change they made, this stage can take three or more months to achieve. The client has come to accept setbacks as a normal part of the process, and they have learned to navigate those setbacks so they don't derail progress. It may be helpful for the client to make a list of triggers that could lead to previous negative behaviors (e.g., overspending, financial enabling, making impulsive investing decisions), which can help the client proactively avoid them this time. For example, if a couple has a history of heated disagreements regarding money, part of the maintenance stage could involve preemptive periodic check-ins to keep disagreements around money from exacerbating.

Carmen confided in her financial planner that her sister was struggling to pay her rent on her own, since she had become accustomed to the previous arrangement. Even though her sister's income allowed plenty of room for her to comfortably pay rent, her lifestyle was making it difficult for her to take on this new responsibility. She blamed Carmen for cutting her off and made her feel guilty for being "selfish." Carmen's planner reminded her of the list of triggers that Carmen made at the beginning of this stage. At the top of the list was her sister's inability to support herself. The planner asked Carmen to look into the future and see what her life would be like if she stayed on the path of saving for retirement. This renewed Carmen's determination to stick with her retirement plan instead of giving into her sister, who could help herself.

The planner is a crucial asset to clients in the maintenance stage who want to sustain their new behavioral changes. Slipping back to old behaviors momentarily is a part of the maintenance phase. Clients can be reminded that small setbacks are expected and not an indicator that the changes are in jeopardy. Planners who anticipate these kinds of "relapses" can help clients understand that they are a normal part of the process, helping them avoid shame or regret.

6. Termination (or Integration)

This stage can also be described as integration. At this point, clients have integrated their healthy financial choices into their lives and have little desire to go back to their old ways.

Carmen visits her planner once a year to reassess her finances. Her retirement account is growing, and she is no longer living in fear of the future. Her sister curbed her spending and is now responsibly paying her rent without complaint, and their relationship is stronger than ever. Carmen wants to use this year's company bonus to make a new investment based on her planner's guidance.

This stage allows the client and planner to enjoy a long-term relationship. The client will have confidence in themselves, knowing that change is possible, and trust in the planner, who has demonstrated their ability to help the client reach fulfillment in their financial goals.

ENCOUNTERING RESISTANCE TO CHANGE

Think back to the last time your significant other offered you some unsolicited suggestions on how you could improve yourself. Perhaps it was some ideas on how you could be a better partner, a better parent, or perhaps advice on how to improve your cooking. What went through your mind when they were sharing their ideas? How did it feel? How did you react? Did you thank them for taking the time and effort to analyze your behaviors and offer their best advice on how you could improve? Or did you, like most people, get a little defensive, and share some counterarguments to their suggestions?

As established at the beginning of this book, we are hard-wired to resist change. Our brains seek the easiest, laziest way to do things, which will bring immediate rewards regardless of the long-term consequences. While we have a strong need to belong to a community, we also have a desire for self-determination, to be independent and free to choose our own destiny. Toddlers and adolescents develop by discovering who they are in the world while striving for independence within that world. A part of self-discovery for teenagers is to reject the traditions, values, and norms of their parents or culture in the interest of forming their own path, one that is aligned with their identity. It is a natural part of human development to resist change and pressure from others to change.

Resistance is an instinctual response to feeling challenged, pressured, or misunderstood. It's our inner adolescent who fights for autonomy, independence, and self-direction – and a protective mechanism that can help clients do the following [58].

- *Avoid emotional pain or discomfort.* Most people try to avoid painful feelings whenever possible.

- *Avoid rehashing painful memories or difficult subjects.* This may manifest as avoiding the sharing of personal details by saying, "I don't know" or changing the subject.
- *Protect themselves through opposition.* When a client feels like the planner is intruding, they may try to protect themselves by putting up an emotional wall so they don't have to deal with uncomfortable thoughts, emotions, or memories.
- *Maintain the status quo.* The idea of changing may be too scary or threatening to a client's sense of security. It may appear more attractive to the client to keep things the way they are – even when they are less than ideal.
- *Protect themselves from a painful truth.* Self-discovery can be challenging when there are difficult truths to face. Some people prefer to remain blissfully ignorant to the problems looming in the shadows.

CONVERSATIONAL PITFALLS TO AVOID WITH CLIENTS WHO ARE NOT READY TO CHANGE

When a client is ambivalent about change, it is important for the planner to avoid making confrontational statements. Confrontational statements will inadvertently push the clients in the opposite direction of the desired transformation. Many outdated strategies are confrontational and directive, which activate a client's hard-wired resistance. These strategies include lecturing, giving orders, warning clients about consequences, discussing the successes of other clients who have changed their behaviors, overloading them with information, blaming, scolding, pointing out the discrepancy between their goals and their behaviors, setting arbitrary deadlines, threatening to "fire" the client if they don't change, and making assumptions about a client's behavior. When a client is not in the action stage of change, all these strategies will backfire.

Clients who are exhibiting resistance may seem "difficult." In fact, it is the financial planner who is creating the resistance by trying to get the client to do something they are not ready to do. It is important to note that client resistance is feedback about the effectiveness of the financial planner [58]. When a client starts showing signs of resistance, the critical message to the financial planner is this: *Stop* doing what you are doing *immediately*. If you continue along the same conversational path, you will be decreasing the likelihood that the client will take your advice. In the next section we talk about what you *should* do instead. But first let's review some common signs of resistance that financial planners can look for in clients to gauge whether they are being effective [58].

Interrupting

Clients who interrupt are usually trying to signal that they are not feeling heard. If a planner notices that they are being interrupted, it could be an indication that they have been doing too much talking and not enough listening. Interruptions can also be a sign that the client is not ready to hear what the planner is trying to convey. Interruption can take many forms, such as abruptly interjecting while the planner is speaking, talking over the planner, or suddenly changing the subject.

Arguing

When a client starts arguing with the planner, it is an obvious sign that the client is resisting change. In this state, a client may call into question a planner's expertise or accuracy or become confrontational when the planner makes suggestions. In some cases, the client may even become hostile. The more skilled a planner is, the more likely it is that they will be listening for warning signs so they can steer the interaction away from confrontation well before it escalates into an argument.

Negating

This can be a flat-out "no" or a justification for refusing to do what is necessary for change. Whenever the planner hears, "Yeah, but. . .," they've wandered into negation territory. Negating shows that the client does not want to change and is digging in. It is a sign that the client is resisting the planner's advice. In this case, it is important for the planner to evaluate whether there is a discrepancy between the planner's agenda and the client's wishes. Negation can also manifest as blaming others for their situation, refusing to take responsibility, making excuses, or dismissing the planner's guidance.

Ignoring

If a client tunes out, shuts down, starts avoiding eye contact, or offers short responses that stop the conversation in its tracks, the planner is likely being ignored. If a client doesn't understand what the planner is saying, they may check out or pretend they know to avoid embarrassment. When a client checks out of the conversation, it could be an indicator that they are not ready to discuss the topic that's being presented.

Body Language

If a client is crossing their arms, leaning back in their chair, frowning, avoiding eye contact, or shifting away, it could be a sign of resistance. It's important to note that these body signals may not always be about resistance. For instance, a person who is on the spectrum may struggle to make eye contact. Someone may cross their arms when they're cold. Body language is one element in a broader picture of client cues.

NINE EVIDENCE-BASED TECHNIQUES FOR OVERCOMING CLIENT RESISTANCE TO FINANCIAL ADVICE

Perhaps the most effective technique a planner can use with a client in the early stages of change, or one who is exhibiting resistance, is effective listening. Most people intuitively know what they need to do to make meaningful changes. They just need a safe space in which they feel heard and can openly talk their way to a solution. Strategic conversational techniques can help a planner gently guide a client toward intrinsically motivated, sustainable change [58].

When a financial planner creates resistance by giving advice the client is not ready to act on, it is critical that they *stop* what they are doing. When a planner notices resistance in a client, they may try the following techniques to help create a safe climate for change [58]. All of these techniques are designed to increase the likelihood that the *client* will take the side in support of change. They are built on a foundation of trust in the client's natural propensity toward growth and well-being. These techniques are designed to help create an environment that encourages change.

1.   Simple Reflection

Like a mirror, this technique involves reflecting the client's statements and assertions with as much accuracy as possible. The planner should be selective about which parts to reflect to the client, often choosing the things the client says that are in support of the desired change, when they are offered by the client. Financial planners can reflect back a statement or an emotion that the client is sharing. Properly selected reflections will help the client feel heard and understood, gain insight about the discrepancies between their actions and their goals, and realize the consequences they will face if they don't change their behaviors.

> *Client:*   "I'm scared to invest but I know I need to get back into the market."
>
> *Planner:*   "So you know you need to get back into the market, but you're worried about the market."

2.   Complex Reflection

With complex reflection, the planner takes an educated guess about where the client is going with what they're saying. It can feel like trying to complete the client's sentence. If it is accurate, the client feels even more understood. If it is inaccurate, the client can correct you and get to the heart of the matter.

> *Client:*   "I'm scared to invest but I know I need to get back into the market."
>
> *Planner:*   "So you know you need to get back into the market but you're worried about the market *because you've had some bad experiences in the past.*"

3.   Amplified Reflection

A planner using this technique will reflect an extreme version of the client's message. It's human nature to correct an exaggeration. Through the client's tendency to correct the amplified reaction, they often find themself arguing in favor of making the desired change, rather than fighting against it. If the client agrees with the amplified reflection, it just serves as a complex reflection but shows the planner how adamant the client is about maintaining the status quo. Planners should use this technique with caution and discretion. While it can be powerful, if implemented incorrectly, it can come off as condescending or sarcastic. Empathy and genuine concern should be at the forefront when using this reflection tool.

Client: "I'm scared to invest but I know I need to get back into the market."

Planner: "You're so scared to invest that you're considering never doing it again."

4. Double-Sided Reflection

This technique can help the clients explore the pros and cons of taking action. When the planner reflects both sides of the client's ambivalence, the client is liberated from feeling pressured to argue for the status quo. In addition to meeting the client where they are, smack dab in the midst of their struggle, a double-sided reflection works as a type of experiment. The client will often pick up the side of the argument they are feeling most attached to at that moment. Often this technique can help a client look at the pros and cons of taking action more objectively. Our favorite way of using this technique is visual, with our hands:

Client: "I'm scared to invest but I know I need to get back into the market."

Planner: "So on the one hand (the financial planner presents their left hand) you're scared to invest, but on the other hand (the financial planner presents their right hand) you know you need to do it."

5. Shifting the Focus from What's Not Working to What Is Working

When a client is showing resistance to a financial planner's advice, sometimes it makes sense to shift the focus away from the impasse. When a person is hyperfocused on maintaining the status quo, it might indicate that they are in a precontemplative state of change. When a financial planner deems that little progress can be made at the moment in moving the client toward taking action, they can simply change the subject, and focus on an area where success is more likely to occur. The planner may decide to revisit the topic at a later time, perhaps after they have enjoyed some success in the relationship with the client, who has taken action in other areas of the financial plan.

Client:	"I'm scared to invest but I know I need to get back into the market."
Planner:	"That makes a lot of sense. Let's focus on reviewing your insurance needs for now and we'll revisit the topic of investing later."

6.   Reframing

When we are feeling stuck, it can help to look at an issue from a different angle. With the technique of reframing, we are attempting to offer up an alternative meaning to a situation. By looking at an issue through a different lens, clients may be able to better receive new information and can generate new solutions. This is a "thinking outside the box" technique that can offer the client an opportunity to get unstuck in their thinking. Reframing is an advanced technique that may not come naturally to a financial planner at first but is a skill that can be developed over time. In the example we have been using throughout this section, we might assume that the client has some self-awareness that they have made a mistake by getting out of the market. They may even have some regret and feel embarrassed or bad about their previous decision. In the following reframe, the financial planner attempts to cast the same situation in a different light, perhaps reducing the client's feelings of regret, and spark change by highlighting that the client is wiser and stronger after having had this experience:

Client:	"I'm scared to invest but I know I need to get back into the market."
Planner:	"I bet you've learned some very important things about investing that are going to help you move forward."

7.   Agreement With a Twist

People relax when they feel that others agree with them. They aren't as determined to prove a point and that makes them more open to receiving what others have to say. This technique involves agreeing with the client and then adding a twist that will redirect the client away from resistance. In other words, it combines agreeing with the client and normalizing their experience, followed by a reframe. When the client feels validated, they are more willing to accept new ideas.

> *Client:* "I'm scared to invest but I know I need to get back into the market."
>
> *Planner:* "That makes a lot of sense. Many people are in your same situation. And I bet you've learned some very important things about investing that are going to help you move forward."

8. Emphasizing Self-Determination

Nobody likes being told what to do. When a financial planner notices signs of resistance in a client, it might make sense to honor and support the part of the client that is seeking to gain control and assert their independence. Clients who feel like they are in control and in charge of their choices will be less resistant to change.

> *Client:* "I'm scared to invest but I know I need to get back into the market."
>
> *Planner:* "I respect your right to choose for yourself if this is something you would like to do. You have every right to decide whether this would be right for you."

9. Arguing Against Change

This powerful technique may seem counterintuitive, but it can be quite effective when used at the right time and delivered skillfully. This is not like reverse psychology, which is used to subtly encourage people into choosing the thing they are resisting. Arguing against change can take several forms, including "go slow" messages, which, paradoxically, often make people want to move faster. The planner must be willing to support the client's choice against making a change that could improve their lives, trusting that the client is making the decision they think is best for them at this time. If the planner perceives that the client is being motivated by external forces, like appeasing a demanding family member, this technique may guide the client back to their intrinsic motivation. Siding with the client's opposition to change can externalize their ambivalence in the opposite direction, with the advisor taking the side of maintaining the status quo. It may even help to remind them why they decided to seek the help of a financial planner in the first place.

Client: "I'm scared to invest but I know I need to get back into the market."

Planner: "Well, I think it is important to point out that investing is not always the best thing for everybody. If you are feeling like it's a bad idea, maybe we shouldn't rush into it."

TAKING "NO" FOR AN ANSWER

When a client says "no," it is not an invitation for a planner to try to persuade them to say "yes." A "no" is a message to the planner that they should invite the client to communicate or elaborate on their point of view. The planner should employ their exquisite listening skills to allow the client to explore and convey their own truth. This can solidify the bond between client and planner, while empowering the client to resolve their own resistance to change. Often by using a simple reflection, the financial planner can hold a mirror up to the client's resistance and the client will become more motivated to take action.

KEY POINTS

- Effective financial planners recognize resistance as a part of the change process and welcome it as a necessary element. When planners respect a client's natural inclination to resist, they help the client realize and take steps toward their financial goals.
- Effective financial planners are skilled at recognizing intrinsic versus extrinsic motivation through techniques like motivational interviewing. They are able to pinpoint which stage of change a client is in, recognize resistance, and use reflection techniques to create a safe environment that fosters a willingness to change on the client's own terms.
- Within all client behaviors, the financial planner has to continue to be vigilant in recognizing cues and most importantly, trying to uncover the root causes of these actions (or inaction). By understanding the causes, the planner can use a variety of tools to help the client get back on track toward their financial goals.

CFP BOARD LEARNING OBJECTIVES COVERED IN THIS CHAPTER

H.68. Principles of counseling

a. Explain the applications of counseling theory to financial planning practice.
b. Demonstrate how a planner can develop a relationship of honesty and trust in client interaction.
c. Select appropriate counseling and communication techniques for use with individual clients.

CHAPTER 18

Helping a Client in Crisis

Sharon is scared. She doesn't know what to do, so she called her financial planner, Ricardo, for some advice. Earlier that evening she had to call 911. Steve, her husband of 40 years, had started acting paranoid. He had been angry with his doctors for weeks, and it all came to a head that day. Years ago, he was diagnosed with dementia but that night he was refusing to take his medication because he was convinced that his doctors, and now Sharon, were trying to poison him. He became belligerent and knocked over a lamp and was acting aggressively toward her. Sharon had never seen her husband lose his temper like this and she was afraid that he might hurt her. The police took Steve to the emergency room to have him evaluated, and the attending physician asked Sharon if she had power of attorney, so that she could make medical decisions for Steve. Although she had a solid estate plan with a springing power of attorney, Steve had not yet been declared legally incompetent. Sharon was also worried that Steve might try to access their accounts and do something with their money that was not in line with their financial goals, since he was acting so erratic. Sharon was stressed, worried, and was reaching out to Ricardo for his advice and support. If you were Ricardo, what would you do?

CRISIS EVENTS WITH SEVERE CONSEQUENCES

Clearly Sharon is in the midst of a crisis. For the purposes of our discussion, we define a crisis as an event the client experiences as extremely difficult,

215

emotionally troubling, or potentially dangerous. Client crisis events where the financial planner is likely to be involved include:

- The death of a client, a client's spouse, or someone close to the client
- The deteriorating physical or mental health of a client, a client's spouse, or someone close to the client
- A client, a client's spouse, or someone close to the client who has just received a distressing diagnosis
- Significant financial loss, including job loss, housing loss, business failure, investing/speculation losses, and so on that can lead to depression and/or suicidal thoughts
- Significant family or marital conflict around money
- A tumultuous separation or divorce
- Dealing with a natural disaster, such as the loss of a home, other property, or dislocation due to fire, tornado, hurricane, or flood
- Stressful family/household transitions, such as the birth of a child, empty nest syndrome, or caretaking of a family member with special needs or illness
- Caretaking of a new dependent, such as an elderly parent
- Diminished capacity of a client, spouse, or family member
- Any other event that the client experiences as intensely difficult, emotionally troubling, or potentially dangerous

Anyone who has experienced a crisis can relate to the way it can shock us to our core. A traumatic event can cause a "psychological earthquake" [158]. It shakes up our lives and shatters our illusions of safety. Traumatic events can also shatter our assumptions about the world around us. Many of us create an illusion of safety by looking for culpability in others when a crisis happens. It's a protective mechanism that helps us feel safe in a world that can sometimes be unsafe. For instance, if someone is injured in a car accident, one might ask if they were wearing their seatbelt. If not, one could make themselves feel more in control by reassuring themselves with a thought like, "Well, I always wear my seatbelt, so that won't happen to me. I am safe." This assertion, "If I do the right thing, I can prevent bad things from happening to me," helps us function in the world without having to live in fear of not being in control of our safety. Yes, we see that bad things can happen to other people. But we don't expect those things to happen to us.

THE IMPORTANCE OF THE CLIENT–PLANNER RELATIONSHIP

Human beings thrive when we feel like we are part of a "tribe" or community, and we struggle when we are isolated from that tribe. At the very least, a supportive financial planner can help a client feel less lonely during a crisis, which is a valuable service in and of itself. Loneliness is a common human condition, whether crisis is a factor or not. Forty percent of older adults aged 65 and over have reported feelings of loneliness, and significant and prolonged loneliness is associated with a host of physical and mental health problems [159]. Additionally, those who experience significant loneliness have a 45% increased risk for mortality [160]. Loneliness is also associated with a decline in executive functioning, cognitive functioning, and dementia [161].

When it comes to recovering from the psychological impact of a crisis event, loneliness makes a difference. Those with higher loneliness levels are less likely to have a positive post-crisis result [162]. Financial planners should check in with their retirement-age clients to make sure they have a good social support system. It's important to explain how loneliness can cause a decline in mental and physical health and encourage clients to build and invest in their social networks. Perceived quality of support is also a factor in a client's ability to successfully navigate a crisis. For example, in a study of survivors of traumatic car accidents, researchers found that PTSD was more severe in people with a perceived lack of positive social support [163].

THE FINANCIAL PLANNER'S ROLE IN HELPING A CLIENT NAVIGATE CRISIS

When a client is experiencing a crisis it can feel like a crisis for the financial planner, too. While crisis events – which can include a terminal diagnosis, the death of a client or someone close to them, a tumultuous divorce, and other life-altering events – are common in our work with clients, financial planners have not been given a model to date to help them help clients in these types of situations. Financial planners need a framework for understanding how to support clients who are experiencing a crisis with potentially severe consequences. While they are not mental health providers, financial planners are front-line workers with clients who may be experiencing a crisis. As such, financial planners could benefit from learning about some of the fundamentals of the Critical Incident Stress Debriefing (CISD) process. CISD is a process that provides a "supportive, crisis-focused discussion of a traumatic event" [164], and is used to help people process and recover from a powerful traumatic event.

CISD incorporates practical information to help normalize client reactions to crisis events, but it is not a form of psychotherapy. Rather, CISD can help enhance a client's ability to cope with stress; help them experience *post-traumatic growth*; and facilitate a return to normal functioning [164]. If a client is in distress from a traumatic event, a financial planner should consider the appropriateness of referring the client to a mental health professional. However, it is possible that the planner may be the only professional to work with a client, and, as such, having a model for working with clients in crisis is important.

SIX STEPS FOR A FINANCIAL PLANNING CRISIS EVENT

The CISD process was developed as a structured way to help people recount the incident, share thoughts, emotions, and symptoms related to the event, and learn ways to recover and restore their mental health after the event [165]. The purpose of CISD is to reduce the risk of long-term negative psychological impact of stressful events [165]. CISD is usually carried out by specialists who can help people in a group process and manage their emotions throughout the debriefing phases. We have incorporated components of the CISD process and have adapted them specifically for use by financial planners in helping clients navigate a crisis.

It is important to note that emotions may be triggered from the very beginning if a client is meeting with a mental health professional. However, when meeting with a financial planner, many clients may attempt to hold back emotions, trying to "keep themselves together" to maintain appearances. Even though they are suffering inside, they may be sensitive to how they are perceived in the context of a financial planning relationship and may not lead with the emotional component of the crisis. As such, the following steps are designed to create an opportunity for clients to feel comfortable not just talking about the facts of the situation but leaving room for the expression of emotions.

Step 1: Normalize the Client's Experience

During a crisis, a client may feel overwhelmed and even possibly embarrassed or ashamed about the situation and/or their emotional reaction to it. They may be questioning how they are handling it or worried that others may see them as overreacting. Therefore, it is important to maintain trust with the client, so they feel comfortable sharing their emotions as well as the pertinent information surrounding the crisis event. It is important to approach the conversation delicately, by assuming a nonjudgmental stance and normalizing what the client is experiencing. In the case of an existing client with whom rapport has already been established, the financial planner can remind the client that their conversation, and the details shared, will be entirely confidential.

Going back to the story of Sharon and Steve, Sharon was feeling overwhelmed and vulnerable when she called Ricardo. She was embarrassed that she had to call the police and was worried that others might judge her for not being a good wife or doing the right thing. Ricardo made sure to empathize but also normalize Sharon's experience, by saying such things as: "I am so sorry to hear that. That must have been very scary and overwhelming. It makes sense that you called the police to keep him safe, you really had no other choice."

Step 2: Encourage the Client to Talk About the Facts

This step involves encouraging clients to recount the facts surrounding the incident in broad terms, without going into excessive detail [165]. This will get the conversation started with the client. This phase is designed to break the ice, reduce anxiety, and establish that the client is in control of the conversation [164].

Given the shame that Sharon was feeling regarding her husband's dementia and the incident surrounding it, Ricardo wanted to encourage Sharon to share but not push her to do so. He let her know that he was there to listen and encouraged her to share only the details she felt comfortable divulging. He used open-ended prompts, focusing on the facts and details. Ricardo was mindful of not pushing the limits of his question too far, as some questions Sharon was comfortable answering and some she was not.

Step 3:   Ask About the Client's Thought Process

In this step, clients are asked to shift from a discussion of the facts to expanding on their thoughts about what happened. This step is a gentle transition to thoughts about the event, rather than jumping into the emotionally triggering parts [164]. In this phase, a financial planner may ask the client what their first thought was during or after the incident.

Here, Ricardo asked Sharon more about her thoughts about her husband's condition, the incident, and her concerns about the future. He listened empathically and used simple reflections as Sharon began to sort out her thoughts about the situation.

Step 4:   Ask About the Client's Emotions and Reactions

This phase concentrates on the emotional impact the event has had on the client. Emotions like sadness, anger, confusion, frustration, loss, and other reactions may come out at this time [164]. The financial planner may ask a client what the worst thing about the event was for them and then just listen when they respond [164]. This is where a planner's active listening skills come in, including reflections, paraphrasing, pacing, and summarization. Their job is *not* to give advice at this step, merely to listen. The very act of talking through the emotional experience with an attentive listener can be incredibly helpful for a client.

Ricardo asks Sharon what the most difficult portion of this experience was and the impact it has had on her emotionally. He gives her the space to talk about the daily struggles of Steve's diminished capacity and how it has left her feeling scared, isolated, and confused about what to do next.

Step 5:   Watch for Signs That the Client May Need Additional Support

This step focuses on the effects of the event, specifically regarding the intensity of the client's emotional reaction and their ability to cope [164]. The financial planner should be on the lookout for signs that the situation may be causing the client significant problems in their day-to-day functioning – for example, the situation has been so stressful that they have been missing days at work or having trouble sleeping at night. The financial planner would then normalize the client's experience and turn their focus on making the case to the client that the client could possibly benefit from the help of a mental health provider, consulting with an estate planning attorney, and so on.

In addition to the planner looking for mental health support for the client, they should also ask the client to think about the support network they have to help them navigate this crisis. It may be as simple as asking who they communicate with daily or who they see or at least talk with on the phone about the issue. Financial planners can help clients come up with strategies to use financial resources for help in a crisis, but they can be equally as helpful in reminding the client of the personal and social resources they have as well.

When Sharon told Ricardo that the situation was causing her anxiety and she was having trouble sleeping at night, Ricardo listened empathically, and said that it was understandable and normal that she would be feeling that way. He recommended that Sharon talk with a mental health provider who had experience in working with people with dementia and their caregivers. He also recommended a good estate planning attorney who could help Sharon navigate the legal system so that she would be allowed to make financial and healthcare decisions on Steve's behalf.

Step 6: Modify the Financial Plan to Address the Crisis Event

In this phase, the financial planner will turn their focus to problem-solving and any changes to the financial plan that need to be made in the wake of the crisis event. This could include specific steps the planner can take to support the client, and specific recommendations for the client.

Sharon was worried that her husband might try to access their accounts and do something that went against their years of financial planning or enlist someone else's help in doing so. Ricardo placed an alert on their accounts so that they would both be informed of any unusual requests or activities. He also suggested that they have a meeting with Sharon and her children so they could talk through the situation, express their concerns, and develop a plan.

BEFORE A CRISIS

Helping a client prepare for future financial emergencies can help them weather a crisis. Planning for emergencies is a wise move for everyone. A planner may guide their clients to create emergency savings accounts or rainy-day funds to help them through rough patches and uncertain times. Mental accounting can be useful here. A client may create different categories of savings depending on their needs. For instance, one savings account may be labeled, "Mortgage: Three Months" and it would hold three months' worth of mortgage payments. Another emergency account may be labeled "Rainy Day Tuition," and hold savings for private school tuition so the client's child won't have to change schools during a financial crisis. These accounts can be as unique as the clients.

Another way planners can help clients navigate a financial crisis is to have a game plan. If the market drops suddenly, the client will benefit from having a plan in place so they aren't making panicked decisions in the moment. For example, a client may decide to sell only if their stock dips below a certain amount for a particular amount of time. Encouraging clients to have a diverse investment portfolio can help them manage if the value of one stock drops.

There may be times when a client needs additional support beyond financial planning services. If a client is feeling stuck and the planner has run out of tools to help, it may be time to refer the client to a mental health professional. It's not uncommon for financial planners to have a tax accountant or attorney to consult with as needed. Having a qualified mental health provider as part of their referral network can prove just as useful. For instance, if a client comes in asking if their life insurance will cover suicide, it can be lifesaving for the planner to be able to connect the client to a licensed mental health provider.

AFTER A CRISIS

If an individual can successfully navigate a crisis event, they can be stronger than ever before. In psychology, the concept of personal growth after a crisis is referred to as posttraumatic growth (PTG). PTG suggests that people who have experienced psychological trauma can be transformed after the event and see positive outcomes [166]. Posttraumatic healing can lead to positive psychological changes in a person who feels shaken up by an event. A person experiencing posttraumatic growth will come to terms with a new sense of reality, one that allows for and accepts unexpected events.

Studies on PTG have found that when people are given the opportunity to work through crisis events, they can function at a higher level after a traumatic event, including: (a) having more compassion, empathy, and deeper ties to loved ones; (b) experiencing a greater sense of gratitude and appreciation for life; (c) developing personal strength through suffering; (d) seeking a higher sense of meaning; (e) feeling better about their ability to manage crisis in the future; (f) reassessing their priorities and adjusting their allocation of time to the things that matter the most in life; and (g) opening themselves up to new opportunities and possibilities that we may not have seen before the event [166].

Financial planners can help their clients attain higher levels of functioning after a crisis event in many ways, including the following two examples.

Enhancing the Client's Sense of Financial Mastery

After the death of a spouse who managed the family's finances, for example, a financial planner might help the client work to gain mastery and a sense of control over their financial life. This could involve educating the client on the details of the family's finances and the financial plan. This could lead to higher levels of financial literacy, a greater sense of personal control, and an enhanced sense of self-esteem in the client.

Finding a Deeper Sense of Meaning and Purpose

After a crisis event, people go through a cognitive adaptation process. This includes searching for a sense of meaning to attach to the event in the hopes of making it make sense. People may ask, "Why am I here?" and "What really matters now?" Those in cognitive adaptation may experience a deeper connection with their spirituality or higher power. When clients are reevaluating what matters most after a crisis event, financial planners can help them develop new goals that are more in line with their values and revise their financial plan and strategies to help them achieve their newfound goals.

Although financial planners are not mental health providers, we are on the front lines when it comes to the life situations and crises of our clients. In many cases, we are the ones our clients turn to when trouble arises, as many crisis events have financial implications. As a trusted advisor involved in some of the most intimate areas of clients' lives, we must be prepared to sit with them in their emotions and help them navigate some of life's most difficult situations.

KEY POINTS

- Financial planners are in a key position to help their clients plan for and navigate crisis events with severe consequences.
- The planner can use a six-step process that provides a framework for helping a client navigate a crisis with severe consequences.
- If a client is in significant distress, the financial planner should refer the client to a mental health professional.

CFP BOARD LEARNING OBJECTIVES COVERED IN THIS CHAPTER

H.70. Crisis events with severe consequences

a. Plan/prepare/categorize and label funds to help clients navigate an unanticipated financial emergency.

b. Analyze how different types of financial or economic crises impact clients (e.g., market correction or economic decline).

c. Evaluate the potential impacts on short-term and long-term goals, including unexpected job and/or income loss and adverse health events.

d. Identify solutions to unanticipated asset allocation changes, adjustment for changes in risk tolerance, and adapting to new norms.

e. Communicate potential solutions, including government-offered solutions.

f. Describe the advisor's role in monitoring cognitive biases.

g. Demonstrate empathy, reliability, and competence in helping clients navigate the implications of a crisis.

CHAPTER 19

Assessment in Financial Planning

Individual differences in a client's personality, attitude, and experiences impact how they save, spend, invest, and otherwise manage their financial lives. Personality characteristics, such as conscientiousness, can predict a host of positive money behaviors [167], whereas money beliefs, such as money avoidance, are negatively related to net worth [168]. In addition, a lack of congruence between spousal money attitudes can create marital strife, and at the same time, investing-related attitudes, such as risk composure, can predict how a client will react during a market downturn. In summary, the very outcomes we help clients obtain are influenced by their unique characteristics. Knowing your clients' underlying money-related personalities, beliefs, and attitudes can help a financial planner:

- Align an investment strategy with the client's psychological risk tolerance
- Communicate effectively with clients by understanding their attitudes about saving, spending, investing, and other aspects of financial management
- Identify unique strengths in your client related to money management that they may not recognize
- Allow you to provide ongoing education and guidance, based on your client's experiences and background

225

It makes sense for financial planners to use a scientific approach to understanding clients' personalities, attitudes, beliefs, and motivations related to money. An assessment is the most common avenue to measure many key client characteristics. This chapter focuses on the characteristics of a good assessment and how financial planners can use them to better serve their clients.

OBSERVATIONS

We evaluate those around us, whether subconsciously or deliberately. Our evaluations are influenced by our biases, backgrounds, and experiences. In other words, our judgments are often *subjective*, and therefore, potentially inaccurate. On the other hand, if we work with a client for decades, we *might* get a better sense of them and what they will do during the next market downturn or when faced with a significant life event. That is the benefit of experience. But what about a new client? It could be immensely helpful if we can predict whether a new client will struggle to follow a spending plan or stay in the market during a crisis.

Errors in judgments, or biases, are critical to avoid in investing (e.g., avoiding herd mentality or the endowment effect). But we are equally vulnerable to them when it comes to evaluating others. Some of the most common biases in evaluating others include the following:

- **Halo effect:** An error in judgment that attributes positive characteristics to a client based on a single, positive characteristic. For example, if a client is consistently early to meetings, you may erroneously attribute other positive characteristics, like being friendly or loyal to your services, to that client.
- **Contrast effect:** We compare clients, making judgments about them relative to other clients. If on day one you meet a client who is extremely emotional about estate planning, the client you meet on day two, who is only slightly emotional, may seem calm in comparison, when in fact, they may both be prone to being fearful about the future.
- **Similar-to-me bias:** We often are more lenient with others when they are like us. For example, if a client is a fan of your favorite college football team, or if they grew up in the same city, you may have more positive feelings about that client. These positive feelings may lead

you to give this client the benefit of the doubt when it comes to not following through on tasks related to onboarding.

- **Central tendency:** This error in evaluating others is often seen when managers are rating employees in the context of performance. Central tendency effect is the tendency to rate "down the middle," or to not choose any extreme scores. In the context of financial planning, this could result in viewing all clients as similar for characteristics like the ability to follow a plan, when in fact, clients can be significantly different in this area.

An observation process may be less than ideal for getting an accurate picture of a client's personality or attitude around money. Given the potential errors in ratings in an observation, it is important to consider more formal assessment procedures, such as interviews and tests.

INTERVIEWS

Interviews can serve as a type of assessment. They have the benefit of not only helping to establish the relationship with the client and develop trust, but can also serve to gather information, establish boundaries in the relationship, and help the client make decisions [169]. There are two types of interviews in assessment: unstructured and structured.

Unstructured Interviews

An *unstructured interview* is one in which the topic and questions are chosen at random and not applied consistently across clients. These types of interviews serve in a similar fashion as information observations in that there is little structure to the evaluation:

- The characteristics measured are not often defined.
- The questions are not established beforehand.
- The way in which the results of the interview responses are going to be rated or used is not described.

Unstructured interviews are common in the onboarding process with a client, particularly when establishing rapport. You are very likely to alter the types of questions depending on the client and the situation. In an unstructured interview you might learn about the client's characteristics related to financial management or you might not. As such, unstructured interviews lack efficiency and validity as well as the ability to accurately measure client characteristics in a consistent fashion, making them less than ideal.

Structured Interviews

Structured interviews are designed to measure specific characteristics using a predetermined sets of questions. Structured interviews add consistency to the client onboarding process or to interviews with clients as they move through different stages of life. Structured interviews can be designed to measure specific client characteristics that are applied across all clients. A structured interview process can be implemented alongside the *unstructured* component to blend both the benefits of rapport-building as well as a more structured data gathering process.

Tests

A test is a "systematic and often standardized process for sampling and describing a behavior of interest" for clients [170]. Compared to observations, references, and interviews, tests are a more robust assessment tool. Tests in financial planning are often used in measuring psychological risk tolerance, allowing planners to make inferences about a client's preferred investment style. However, many financial planners are now using tests to assess other key client characteristics that have been identified by CFP Board [171].

The ability of a test to measure a specific client characteristic is dependent upon how the test was developed. Constructing psychological tests requires time, effort, and expertise. Psychometricians are trained in item writing, statistical analyses, and ongoing evaluation of tests in terms of their reliability and validity (see the following section). *Therefore, for most financial planners, creating a homegrown test is not advised.*

Any tests you are considering using with clients should have documentation associated with it (either articles from peer-reviewed, academic journals or formal technical manuals). This documentation should, at a minimum, explain the rationale for the development of the test (why it was created), the intended audience for the test, and how to implement the test and interpret the results.

Evaluating Tests for Financial Planning

Financial planners and firms should consider the following criteria for reviewing a test for potential use in financial planning:

- *Construct identification*: The first step is to understand what is being measured by the test. This should be clearly defined by the test author.
- *Test design*: Who wrote the items and how were they evaluated during the writing process? Test authors should provide an overview of the way in which the test was constructed.
- *Reliability:* Reliability means that time after time, your clients will get the same scores on whatever characteristic is being assessed. The test authors should describe the *reliability* of the test based on statistical analyses. Common analyses you might see include *test-retest reliability* or *internal consistency* (or alpha) reliability, which serves as an estimate of multiple test-retest administrations. In most cases, a reliability coefficient of .70 or higher is acceptable, depending on the type of test.
- *Validity*: Validity refers to the accuracy of the assessment in measuring a specific characteristic. At a basic level: Is the assessment "measuring" what it says it's measuring? If an assessment does not have evidence of validity, it may be a waste of both time and the cost of administering the assessment, neither of which is beneficial to your business or the client experience. Validity involves improving the precision associated with measuring characteristics, often including removing subjectivity from the process to eliminate our (or others') biases in rating others.

Financial planners typically use a combination of observation, interviews, and tests in assessing their clients. To use assessments in an effective and ethical manner, financial planners need to understand the strengths and weaknesses of the assessments they use. Through valid and reliable assessments, financial planners can better communicate and serve their clients based on their own personality and characteristics as well as predict how clients may react under different market conditions and life events.

KEY POINTS

- A client's individual differences impact how they manage their financial lives.
- The financial planner needs to assess a client's attitudes in a variety of areas, including risk tolerance, cognitive biases, and money beliefs.
- Financial planners need to understand the strengths and weaknesses of the assessments they use.

A special thank you to Dr. Sarah Stanley Fallaw, president of Data-Points, for her generous contributions to this chapter.

CFP BOARD LEARNING OBJECTIVES COVERED IN THIS CHAPTER

H.65. Client and planner attitudes, values, biases

a. Analyze a client's degree of risk tolerance and loss aversion and ensure recommendations are consistent with a client's risk propensity, attitudes, composure (e.g. past behaviors during market corrections), capacity, knowledge, and needs.
b. Explain how a client's psychology, background, preferred learning style, and values (socially conscious investor, etc.) impact the financial planning process.
c. Explain how a client's values, including cultural and religious values, and attitudes may impact their goals and the financial planning process.

H.66. Behavioral finance

a. Identify how cognitive biases and heuristics can impact financial decision-making.
b. Describe how a client's psychology, such as their financial comfort zone, socialization, money beliefs, and past financial experiences and behaviors impact their objectives, goals, understanding, decision making, and actions.

CHAPTER 20

The Role of the Financial Planner: Ethical Considerations in the Psychology of Financial Planning

Money is one of the top stressors in the lives of Americans, and chronic stress can have devastating impacts on a person's mental health, relationships, and physical health [172]. But the question is this: If someone is experiencing financial stress, who do they see to help them? Unfortunately, it is not a mental health professional. Studies have shown, for example, that mental health providers tend to be more money avoidant and have even lower levels of financial health than many other professions [59]. This is where financial planners come in. Financial planners are in a unique position to help clients deal with the biggest source of stress in their lives, and as such, often play a therapeutic role in their clients' lives. In many ways, financial planners are akin to that of other "healers" in our culture, such as mental health and medical professionals [173]. The role of the financial planner is to first understand their client, which encompasses all the instinct, biases, and behaviors that impact their financial well-being. Second, we then use the tools at our disposal to help clients improve their financial lives, meet their goals, and reduce their stress.

231

A FINANCIAL PLANNER IS *NOT* A MENTAL HEALTH PROVIDER

While meeting with financial planners can be therapeutic, they are not mental health therapists. Integrating psychology into financial planning can be confusing without a clear understanding of the boundaries between the roles of a financial planner and a mental health provider. These boundaries are important for many reasons, including the need to abide by the strict ethical codes that have been established in the mental health profession, which are described in more detail in Figure 20.1.

This illustration is designed to highlight the difference between the role of the financial planner and that of a mental health professional. *It is critical to understand that a financial planner is* not *a mental health provider.* In fact, it would be unethical for a mental health provider, acting in their role as a mental health provider, to also manage their client's money. As such, when a client is exhibiting mental health–related concerns – including a money disorder (e.g., compulsive buying disorder), anxiety, or depression – a financial planner would not attempt to "treat" the client. When a client exhibits signs of a mental disorder, the financial planner should consider making a referral to a mental health provider who can diagnose and treat the potential disorder. The financial planner would never attempt to "diagnose" a client, but rather, make a referral because the client is exhibiting behaviors that appear to be impairing their functioning in one or more areas of their life (e.g., emotional, occupational, and/or relational functioning) and are getting in the way of the financial planning process. The referral could happen at the beginning of the financial planning process or at some point later in the relationship.

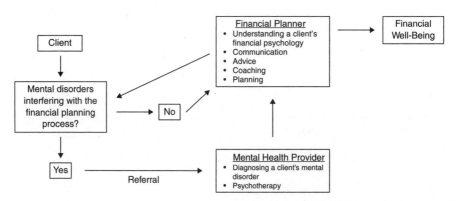

FIGURE 20.1   The roles of financial planners and mental health providers

WHEN AND HOW TO REFER

A financial planner will often make referrals to other professionals, such as a CPA, an estate planning attorney, or an insurance specialist. At some point a financial planner is also likely to encounter times when the best option would be to refer their client to a mental health provider. For instance, if a client is experiencing panic attacks related to their financial concerns, a referral to a mental health provider may be in order. The client will not be able to hear or follow through on the planner's recommendations if they are in a state of acute anxiety. It is reasonable for the planner to postpone tackling certain aspects of the financial planning process until the client is getting help for their anxiety, or they may decide to work in tandem with a mental health provider, depending on the severity of the client's needs.

The best way to know when to refer a client is if they seem stuck and the planner has run out of all the tools they are qualified to use. A planner who understands their client's financial psychology, is comfortable with a client expressing emotions, is a good listener, and can skillfully employ one or more of the communication and counseling tactics in this book may be able to help facilitate behavioral change in their client. However, despite a financial planner's best efforts, some clients may struggle to move forward and/or keep engaging in financially self-destructive behaviors despite the consequences.

Some indicators that it may be time to refer the client to a mental health provider include the following:

- Severe symptoms of depression or anxiety
- Addiction, compulsive behaviors, or money disorders
- A history of trauma surrounding money
- A chronic inability to implement financial plans or change destructive behaviors
- High conflict between couples and/or families
- A chronic inability to communicate openly and transparently about finances
- Other mental health issues that are negatively impacting a client's emotional, occupational, or social abilities and functioning

It is important to use discretion when deciding whether to refer a client to a psychotherapist. The planner should refrain from making assumptions about the client based only on the circumstances. A client with a previous money disorder, for example, may be at a place in their life where they are ready to make the necessary changes based on the financial planner's recommendations. A skilled planner may be the right professional to guide the client out of their old behaviors and into a healthier course of action. That is why it is crucial for a planner to consider the client's behaviors, emotions, and history, as well as their own reactions and emotions.

If the planner is feeling uncomfortable, fearful, or nervous around a client, it is a good indicator that they should consider bringing in another professional to help. Sometimes referring a client to someone else is the best thing a planner can do for them. It is important for the planner to understand that making a referral does not equal quitting or an admission of incompetence. Rather, it is a sign that the planner is skilled and practiced enough to recognize the signs that the client would benefit from the expertise of a professional from a different field. During every interaction, whether the planner decides to refer or not, the client's needs and well-being should be paramount.

ETHICAL CONSIDERATIONS

The psychology of financial planning requires the planner to be aware of what is happening inside the client's mind. While it can be beneficial for a planner to understand a client's psychology, it is important for financial planners to understand their own professional limitations. A planner can distinguish the appropriate guidelines and boundaries around inner psychological work with clients by examining the Ethical Principles of Psychologists and Code of Conduct from the American Psychological Association [174], and the Code of Ethics and Professional Responsibility for the Certified Financial Planner [175] Board of Standards [176]. Both codes require that a practitioner work only within the boundaries of their professional competence.

Another critical ethical consideration for mental health practitioners is to avoid *multiple relationships* with clients [174]. It would be unethical for someone acting in the role of a mental health therapist to also work in the role of financial planner with the same client – even if they are qualified to do both. To protect clients and maintain the sanctity of the mental health therapist–client relationship, the mental health provider must avoid having such multiple relationships with their clients, as it could put their clients at risk. For example, if a person and/or a firm is providing mental health therapy *and* financial planning to the same client, what if a client relies on their therapeutic support but is unhappy with the financial planning element? To maintain the therapeutic relationship, which may be essential to their mental health stability, they might feel compelled to stay with the financial planning component even though they believe that doing so is no longer in their best interest. This type of situation puts the client's best interests at risk, which is why it is strictly forbidden under mental health practitioner ethical guidelines.

THE NEW FINANCIAL PLANNER

The role of the financial planner has evolved. What started back in 1969 with a group of insurance salesmen in Chicago has grown to a thriving profession. With the advent of technology, index funds, and easily accessible information on digital platforms of all kinds, the impact and relevance of the planner hinges upon our ability as a profession to understand, relate, and serve our clients based on their individual needs, values, and goals. Financial planners need to understand their clients' financial psychology not just because it is the right thing to do, but also because the market demands it. This new set of skills, values, and competencies will make you, your firm, and our profession even more valuable and relevant in the decades to come. Here is what we think the financial planner of the future will look like:

1. ***They Will Be a Skilled Listener***
   The financial planner listens to what their client is saying and perhaps what they are not saying. They will be attentive to how they are articulating their goals and vigilant toward their behaviors relating to their financial well-being. The financial planner listens intently and responds appropriately to what their client is saying and how they are saying it.
2. ***They Will Be an Excellent Communicator***
   Good financial planners are good communicators. The financial planner of the future will be able to articulate complex information in easily accessible terms, knowing full well what the client is grasping and what they are struggling to understand.
3. ***They Will Be a Coach***
   The financial planner is no longer just the gatekeeper to financial tips or even clients' individual accounts. Now, the financial planner is

a coach, offering specific advice that relates both to the biases, behaviors, and goals of their client, but also coaching when major life events or market volatility occurs. Our clients are more informed now than ever. Many know what they should do, but given their instincts, biases, and financial flashpoints, they need a coach who can help them overcome their mental hurdles to get them to financial well-being.

4. ***They Will Always Be a Planner***

The financial planner will continue to think about the horizon ahead, including the challenges, goals, and opportunities. The planner may be the only one who asks a client what they want from their life's work or how they envision an average Tuesday during their retirement.

5. ***They Will Be a Client's Financial Wellness Mentor***

The financial planner has always been seen as a client's financial "quarterback." They may not know how to fix a tax or an estate planning matter, but they can detect a problem and refer the client to an accountant or attorney. Going forward, we envision a new level of collaboration, one where the financial planner is working with mental health professionals to refer clients and collaborate with them as needed. As mentioned earlier, financial planners are not mental health professionals by any means, but they can collaborate and refer clients as necessary.

This book will equip you and your firm to deliver the type of planning that will impact your clients in profound ways. We hope that all the content, both here and in the accompanying toolkit, provides you with a better understanding of your own biases and worldview that can only help you engage and better serve clients from diverse backgrounds. We also hope that these two resources can provide you with the specific techniques and actionable solutions to help you serve whoever walks into your office, or is on your next video call, more effectively. Our hope is that you can use your newfound understanding of money and behavior to improve your clients' lives in meaningful ways.

KEY POINTS

1. Financial planners are one of the only types of professionals who can help deal with one of the biggest stressors in clients' lives – money.

2. Financial planners can use their understanding of a client's financial psychology to help improve their client's financial well-being. *But it is critical to understand that a financial planner is not a mental health provider.*

3. The new financial planner has evolved. The new financial planner is a skilled listener, excellent communicator, a coach, a financial wellness mentor, and, as always, a planner.

References

1. Thaler, R. H. (2000). From Homo economicus to Homo sapiens. *Journal of Economic Perspectives*, 14(1), pp. 133–141. doi:10.1257/jep.14.1.133.

2. Moll, J., Krueger, F., Zahn, R., Pardini, M., de Oliveira-Souza, R., and Grafman, J. (2006). Human fronto-mesolimbic networks guide decisions about charitable donation. *Proceedings of the National Academy of Sciences*, 103(42), pp. 15623–15628. doi:10.1073/pnas.0604475103.

3. Klontz, B., and Britt, S. L. (2012). How clients' money scripts predict their financial behaviors. *Journal of Financial Planning*, 24(11), pp. 33–43.

4. Klontz, B. T., Sullivan, P., Seay, M. C., and Canale, A. (2015). The wealthy: A financial psychological profile. *Consulting Psychology Journal: Practice and Research*, 67(2), pp. 127–143. doi:10.1037/cpb0000027.

5. Kim, H. J., Hong, J. S., Hwang, H. C., Kim, S. M., and Han, D. H. (2020). Comparison of psychological status and investment style between bitcoin investors and share investors. *Frontiers in Psychology*, *11*. doi:10.3389/fpsyg.2020.502295.

6. Killingsworth, M. A. (2021). Experienced well-being rises with income, even above $75,000 per year. *Proceedings of the National Academy of Sciences*, 118(4). doi:10.1073/pnas.2016976118.

7. Jebb, A. T., Tay, L., Diener, E., and Oishi, S. (2018). Happiness, income satiation and turning points around the world. *Nature Human Behaviour*, 2(1), pp. 33–38. doi:10.1038/s41562-017-0277-0

8. Statista. (2021). *Average (median) household income 1990–2018.* Available at: https://www.statista.com/statistics/200838/median-household-income-in-the-united-states/ (accessed May 14, 2022).

9. Smith, H. J., and Pettigrew, T. F. (2015). Advances in relative deprivation theory and research. *Social Justice Research*, 28(1), pp. 1–6. doi:10.1007/s11211-014-0231-5.

10. Kahneman, D. (2011). *Thinking, Fast and Slow.* New York: Farrar, Straus and Giroux.

11. Klontz, B. T., Horwitz, E., and Klontz, T. (2021). *Money Mammoth: Harness the Power of Financial Psychology to Evolve Your Money Mindset, Avoid Extinction, and Crush Your Financial Goals*. Hoboken, NJ: Wiley.

12. James, W., and Drummond, R. (1890). *The Principles of Psychology*. New York: Henry Holt and Company.

13. Leibenstein, H. (1950). Bandwagon, snob, and Veblen effects in the theory of consumers' demand. *The Quarterly Journal of Economics*, 64(2), pp. 183–207. doi:10.2307/1882692.

14. Nickerson, R. S. (1998). Confirmation bias: A ubiquitous phenomenon in many guises. *Review of General Psychology*, 2(2), 175–220.

15. Harari, Y. N. (2015). *Sapiens: A Brief History of Mankind*. New York: Harper.

16. Klontz, B. T., Seay, M. C., Sullivan, P., and Canale, A. (2015). The psychology of wealth: Psychological factors associated with high income. *Journal of Financial Planning*, 27(12), pp. 46–53.

17. Elliot, A. J., and Devine, P.G. (1994). On the motivational nature of cognitive dissonance: Dissonance as psychological discomfort. *Journal of Personality and Social Psychology*, 67(3), pp. 382–394. doi:10.1037/0022-3514.67.3.382.

18. Goetzmann, W. N., and Peles, N. (1997). Cognitive dissonance and mutual fund investors. *Journal of Financial Research*, 20(2), pp. 145–158. doi:10.1111/j.1475-6803.1997.tb00241.x.

19. Shefrin, H., and Statman, M., (1985). The disposition to sell winners too early and ride losers too long: Theory and evidence. *Journal of Finance*, 40(3), pp. 777–790.

20. Lawson, D. R., and Klontz, B. T. (2017). Integrating behavioral finance, financial psychology, and financial therapy into the 6-step financial planning process. *Journal of Financial Planning*, 30(7), pp. 53–54.

21. Kahneman, D., Knetsch, J. L., and Thaler, R. H. (1991). Anomalies: The endowment effect, loss aversion, and status quo bias. *Journal of Economic Perspectives*, 5(1), pp. 193–206. doi:10.1257/jep.5.1.193.

22. Kienzler, M., Kowalkowski, C., and Kindström, D. (2021). Purchasing professionals and the flat-rate bias: Effects of price premiums, past usage, and relational ties on price plan choice. *Journal of Business Research*, 132, pp. 403–415. doi:10.1016/j.jbusres.2021.04.024.

23. Croson, R., and Sundali, J. (2005). The gambler's fallacy and the hot hand: Empirical data from casinos. *Journal of Risk and Uncertainty*, 30(3), pp. 195–209. doi:10.1007/s11166-005-1153-2.

24. Tversky, A., and Kahneman, D. (1971). Belief in the law of small numbers. *Psychological Bulletin*, 76(2), pp. 105–110. doi:10.1037/h0031322.

25. Kahneman, D., and Tversky, A. (1979). Prospect theory: An analysis of decision making under risk. *Econometrica*, 47(2), pp. 263–292. doi:10.21236/ada045771.

26. Behavioral Economics. (n.d.). *Regret aversion*. Available at: https://www.behavioraleconomics.com/resources/mini-encyclopedia-of-be/regret-aversion/ (accessed May 14, 2022).

27. Thaler, R. H. (1999). Mental accounting matters. *Journal of Behavioral Decision Making*, 12(3), pp. 183–206. doi:3.0.co;2-f">10.1002/(sici)1099-0771(199909)12:3<183::aid-bdm318>3.0.co;2-f.

28. Segal, T. (2019). Mental accounting. Investopedia. Available at: https://www.investopedia.com/terms/m/mentalaccounting.asp.

29. Edmonds, E., and AAA NewsRoom. (2018, January 24). *More Americans willing to ride in fully self-driving cars*. Available at: https://newsroom.aaa.com/2018/01/americans-willing-ride-fully-self-driving-cars/.

30. Langer, E. J. (1975). The illusion of control. *Journal of Personality and Social Psychology*, 32(2), pp. 311–328. doi:10.1037/0022-3514.32.2.311.

31. Delfabbro, P., King, D. L., and Williams, J. (2021). The psychology of cryptocurrency trading: Risk and protective factors. *Journal of Behavioral Addictions*, 10(2), pp. 201–207. doi:10.1556/2006.2021.00037.

32. DeMarzo, P. M., Vayanos, D., and Zwiebel, J. (2003). Persuasion bias, social influence, and unidimensional opinions. *The Quarterly Journal of Economics*, 118(3), pp. 909–968. doi:10.1162/00335530360698469.

33. Behavioral Economics. (2019). 10th Behavioral Finance Conference (Miami, FL). Available at: https://www.behavioraleconomics.com/resources/mini-encyclopedia-of-be/sunk-cost-fallacy/.

34. Gilbert, D. T., Morewedge, C. K., Risen, J. L., and Wilson, T. D. (2004). Looking forward to looking backward: The misprediction of regret. *Psychological Science*, 15(5), pp. 346–350. doi:10.1111/j.0956-7976.2004.00681.x.

35. The Decision Lab. (n.d.). *Regret aversion – Biases & heuristics*. Available at: https://thedecisionlab.com/biases/regret-aversion.

36. Kumar, A., and Dhar, R. (2001). *A Non-Random Walk Down the Main Street: Impact of Price Trends on Trading Decisions of Individual Investors*. Yale School of Management RePEc - Econpapers. Available at: https://econpapers.repec.org/paper/ysmsomwrk/ysm208.htm (accessed May 14, 2022).

37. Taylor, S. E., and Fiske, S. T. (1975). Point of view and perceptions of causality. *Journal of Personality and Social Psychology*, 32(3), pp. 439–445. doi:10.1037/h0077095.

38. Akhtar, S., Faff, R., Oliver, B., and Subrahmanyam, A. (2012). Stock salience and the asymmetric market effect of consumer sentiment news. *Journal of Banking & Finance*, 36(12), pp. 3289–3301. doi:10.1016/j.jbankfin.2012.07.019.

39. Rense, S. (2017). This is probably why you're skipping the gym. *Esquire*. Available at: http://www.esquire.com/lifestyle/health/news/a54143/missing-gym-workouts/ (accessed May 14, 2022).

40. Soll, J. B., Milkman, K. L., & Payne, J. W. (2015). Outsmart your own biases. *Harvard business review*, 93(5), 64–71.

41. Twain, Mark, 1835–1910. *The Innocents Abroad; Roughing It*. New York, N.Y.: Library of America: Distributed to the trade in the U.S. and Canada by the Viking Press, 1984.

42. J.D. Power. (n.d.). *2019 U.S. Financial Advisor Satisfaction Study*. Available at: https://www.jdpower.com/business/press-releases/2019-us-financial-advisor-satisfaction-study.

43. Roeckelein, J., (2006). *Elsevier's Dictionary of Psychological Theories*. Amsterdam, Netherlands: Elsevier.

44. Klontz, B., and Klontz, T. (2009). *Mind Over Money: Overcoming the Money Disorders That Threaten Our Financial Health*. New York: Broadway Books.

45. Seligman, M. E. P. (1972). Learned helplessness. *Annual Review of Medicine*, 23(1), pp. 407–412. doi:10.1146/annurev.me.23.020172.002203.

46. Taylor, C. D., Klontz, B., and Lawson, D. (2017). Money disorders and locus of control: Implications for assessment and treatment. *Journal of Financial Therapy*, 8(1), pp. 124–137. doi:10.4148/1944-9771.1121.

47. Horak, N. S., Eagle, G., Stein, D. J., and Lochner, C. (2020). Gambling disorder and childhood trauma: A complex association. *Journal of Gambling Studies*, 37(2), pp. 515–528. doi:10.1007/s10899-020-09983-w.

48. Cromer, K. R., Schmidt, N. B., and Murphy, D. L. (2007). Do traumatic events influence the clinical expression of compulsive hoarding? *Behaviour Research and Therapy*, 45(11), pp. 2581–2592. doi:10.1016/j.brat.2007.06.005.

49. Mendiola, M., Mull, J., Archuleta, K. L., Klontz, B., and Torabi, F. (2017). Does she think it matters who makes more? Perceived differences in types of relationship arguments among female breadwinners and non-breadwinners. *Journal of Financial Therapy*, 8(2). doi:10.4148/1944-9771.1147.

50. Newcomb, M. D., and Rabow, J. (1999). Gender, socialization, and money. *Journal of Applied Social Psychology*, *29*, pp. 852–869.

51. Germano, M. (2019, March 27). Women are working more than ever, but they still take on most household responsibilities. *Forbes*. Available at: https://www.forbes.com/sites/maggiegermano/2019/03/27/women-are-working-more-than-ever-but-they-still-take-on-most-household-responsibilities/?sh=5ea711b452e9.

52. Business Wire. (2018, April 19). Women have fundamentally different journeys to financial wellness, Merrill Lynch Study Reveals. Available at: https://www.businesswire.com/news/home/20180419005028/en/Women-Fundamentally-Journeys-Financial-Wellness-Merrill-Lynch.

53. Cagney, K. A., Browning, C. R., Iveniuk, J., and English, N. (2014). The onset of depression during the Great Recession: Foreclosure and older adult mental health. *American Journal of Public Health*, 104(3), pp. 498–505. doi:10.2105/ajph.2013.301566.

54. Riumallo-Herl, C., Basu, S., Stuckler, D., Courtin, E., and Avendano, M. (2014). Job loss, wealth and depression during the Great Recession in the USA and Europe. *International Journal of Epidemiology*, 43(5), pp.1508–1517. doi:10.1093/ije/dyu048.

55. Sochos, A. (2018). Posttraumatic stress during the Greek economic crisis: Is there evidence for mass traumatization? *Analyses of Social Issues and Public Policy*, 18(1), pp. 265–283. doi:10.1111/asap.12155.

56. Klontz, B., and Britt, S. L. (2012). Tactical asset management or financial trauma?: Why the abandonment of buy-and-hold may be a symptom of posttraumatic stress. *Journal of Financial Therapy*, 3(2). doi:10.4148/jft.v3i2.1718.

57. Klontz, B., Britt, S. L., and Archuleta, K. L. (2015). *Financial Therapy: Theory, Research, and Practice*. Cham: Springer.

58. Klontz, B., Kahler, R., and Klontz, T. (2016). *Facilitating Financial Health: Tools for Financial Planners, Coaches, and Therapists* (2nd ed.). National Underwriter Company.

59. Britt, S. L., Klontz, B., Tibbetts, R., and Leitz, L. (2015). The financial health of mental health professionals. *Journal of Financial Therapy*, 6(1), pp. 17–32. doi:10.4148/1944-9771.1076.

60. Begina, M. A., Hickingbottom, J. L., Luttrull, E. G., McCoy, M., and Klontz, B. T. (2018). Identify and understand clients' money scripts: A framework for using the KMSI-R. *Journal of Financial Planning*, 31(3), pp. 46–55.

61. Fay, B. (n.d.). *The emotional effects of debt*. Debt.org. Available at: https://www.debt.org/advice/emotional-effects/ (accessed May 14, 2022).

62. Klontz, B., Britt, S. L., Archuleta, K. L., and Klontz, T. (2012). Disordered money behaviors: Development of the Klontz Money Behavior Inventory. *Journal of Financial Therapy*, 3(1), pp. 17–42. doi:10.4148/jft.v3i1.1485.

63. Iyengar, S. S., and Lepper, M. R. (2000). When choice is demotivating: Can one desire too much of a good thing? *Journal of Personality and Social Psychology*, 79(6), pp. 995–1006. doi:10.1037//0022-3514.79.6.995.

64. Britt, S. L., and Huston, S. J. (2012). The role of money arguments in marriage. *Journal of Family and Economic Issues*, 33(4), pp. 464–476. doi:10.1007/s10834-012-9304-5.

65. Vega, N. (2021, July 15). Nearly 40% of couples who live together don't know how much their partner makes—experts say that's a problem. CNBC. Available at: https://www.cnbc.com/2021/07/15/40-percent-of-couples-who-live-together-dont-know-how-much-partner-makes.html.

66. Kemnitz, R., Klontz, B., and Archuleta, K. L. (2016). Financial enmeshment: Untangling the web. *Journal of Financial Therapy*, 6(2), pp. 32–48. doi:10.4148/1944-9771.1085.

67. BetterHelp Editorial Team. (2022, May 2). *Dependent Personality Disorder DSM 5: Signs and symptoms. BetterHelp.* Available at: https://www.betterhelp.com/advice/personality-disorders/dependent-personality-disorder-dsm-5-signs-and-symptoms/.

68. Anderson, M. A., Gillig, P. M., Sitaker, M., McCloskey, K., Malloy, K., and Grigsby, N. (2003). "Why doesn't she just leave?" A descriptive study of victim reported impediments to her safety. *Journal of Family Violence*, 18(3), pp. 151–155. https://doi.org/10.1023/A:1023564404773.

69. National Center for Responsible Gambling. (2013). *Fact Sheet: Gambling Disorders.* National Center for Responsible Gambling. Available at: https://www.icrg.org/sites/default/files/oec/pdfs/ncrg_fact_sheet_gambling_disorders.pdf (accessed May 14, 2022).

70. American Psychiatric Association. (2013). *Diagnostic and statistical manual of mental disorders.* 5th ed. Arlington, VA: American Psychiatric Association.

71. Dittmar, H. (2005). Compulsive buying – a growing concern? An examination of gender, age, and endorsement of materialistic values as predictors. *British Journal of Psychology*, 96(4), pp. 467–491. doi:10.1348/0007 12605x53533.

72. Granero, R., Fernández-Aranda, F., Mestre-Bach, G., Steward, T., Baño, M., del Pino-Gutiérrez, A., . . . Jiménez-Murcia, S. (2016). Compulsive buying behavior: Clinical comparison with other behavioral addictions. *Frontiers in Psychology*, 7. doi:10.3389/fpsyg.2016.00914.

73. Substance Abuse and Mental Health Services Administration. (2016). *Impact of the DSM-IV to DSM-5 changes on the National Survey on Drug Use and Health*. National Library of Medicine, National Center for Biotechnology Information. Available at: https://www.ncbi.nlm.nih.gov/books/NBK519704/table/ch3.t29/.

74. Canale, A., and Klontz, B. (2013). Hoarding disorder: It's more than just an obsession – Implications for financial therapists and planners. *Journal of Financial Therapy*, 4(2), pp. 43–63doi:10.4148/1944-9771.1053.

75. Spielman, R. M., Jenkins, W., Lacombe, A., Lovett, M., and Perlmutter, M. (2014). Humanistic approaches. K. Dumper. Essay. *Psychology*. OpenStax.

76. Baumeister, R. F. (2016). Toward a general theory of motivation: Problems, challenges, opportunities, and the big picture. *Motivation and Emotion*, 40(1), pp. 1–10. doi:10.1007/s11031-015-9521-y.

77. Kaittila, A. (2018). Why do conflicts over money occur between partners? Exploring the explanations of childbearing adults in Finland. *Journal of Family Studies*, pp. 1–17. doi:10.1080/13229400.2018.1428906.

78. Eslinger, K. N., Clarke, A. C., and Dynes, R. R. (1972). The principle of least interest, dating behavior, and family integration settings. *Journal of Marriage and the Family*, 34(2), pp. 269–272. doi:10.2307/350797.

79. Sprecher, S., Schmeeckle, M., and Felmlee, D. (2006). The principle of least interest. *Journal of Family Issues*, 27(9), pp. 1255–1280. doi:10.1177/01925 13x06289215.

80. Ward, A. F., and Lynch, J. G. (2018). On a need-to-know basis: How the distribution of responsibility between couples shapes financial literacy and financial outcomes. *Journal of Consumer Research*, 45(5), pp. 1013–1036. doi:10.1093/jcr/ucy037.

81. Eriksson, M., and Ulmestig, R. (2021). "It's not all about money": Toward a more comprehensive understanding of financial abuse in the context of VAW. *Journal of Interpersonal Violence*, 36(3–4). doi:10.1177/0886260517743547.

82. Adams, A. (2011). *Measuring the effects of domestic violence on women's financial well-being*. CFS Research Brief. Available at: https://centerforfinancialsecurity.files.wordpress.com/2015/04/adams2011.pdf.

83. Gordon, S. (2019). *Financial abuse: Often the first sign of domestic abuse*. Verywell Mind. Available at: https://www.verywellmind.com/financial-abuse-4155224.

84. Fields, J., Copp, M., and Kleinman, S. (2006). *Handbook of the Sociology of Emotions* (pp. 155–178). Dordrecht: Springer.

85. Peterson, J. C., Burnes, D. P. R., Caccamise, P. L., Mason, A., Henderson, C. R., Wells, M. T., . . . Lachs, M. S. (2014). Financial exploitation of older adults: A population-based prevalence study. *Journal of General Internal Medicine*, 29(12), pp. 1615–1623. doi:10.1007/s11606-014-2946-2.

86. Consumer Financial Protection Bureau. (2022). *Reporting elder financial abuse*. Available at: https://www.consumerfinance.gov/consumer-tools/educator-tools/resources-for-older-adults/reporting-elder-financial-abuse-guide/(accessed May 15, 2022).

87. Lufkin, B. (2021, September 10). *Why does lending people money feel so awkward?* BBC. Available at: https://www.bbc.com/worklife/article/20210907-why-does-lending-people-money-feel-so-awkward.

88. Miller, W. R. (2007). *Motivational Interviewing: What it is, how it works, and how to do it*. Presentation at Hawaii Psychological Association's Annual Convention. Honolulu, HI.

89. Miller, W. R., and Rollnick, R. (2012). *Motivational Interviewing: Helping People Change* (3rd ed.). New York: Guilford Press.

90. Mehrabian, A. (1972). *Nonverbal Communication*. Chicago: Aldine-Atherton.

91. Ni, P. (2019, November 16). Do you talk too fast? How to slow down. *Psychology Today*. Available at: https://www.psychologytoday.com/us/blog/communication-success/201911/do-you-talk-too-fast-how-slow-down.

92. Klontz, B., and Klontz, T. (2016, November). *7 steps to facilitate exquisite listening*. Financial Planning Association. Available at: https://www.financialplanningassociation.org/article/journal/NOV16-7-steps-facilitate-exquisite-listening.

93. Archuleta, K. L., Grable, J. E., and Burr, E. A. (2015). Solution-focused financial therapy. In B. T. Klontz, S. L. Britt, and K. L. Archuleta (Eds.), *Financial Therapy: Theory, Research, and Practice* (pp. 121–141). Cham: Springer.

94. De Shazer, S., Dolan, Y., Korman, H., McCollum, E., Trepper, T., and Berg, I. K. (2007). *More Than Miracles: The State of the Art of Solution-Focused Therapy* (pp. 1–3). New York: Taylor and Francis.

95. Archuleta, K. L., Mielitz, K. S., Jayne, D. and Le, V. (2020). Financial goal setting, financial anxiety, and solution-focused financial therapy (SFFT): A quasi-experimental outcome study. *Contemporary Family Therapy*. doi:10.1007/s10591-019-09501-0.

96. Deci, E. L., and Ryan, R. M. (2000). The "what" and "why" of goal pursuits: Human needs and the self-determination of behavior. *Psychological Inquiry*, 11(4), pp. 227–268. doi:10.1207/s15327965pli1104_01.

97. Grable, J., Heo, W., and Rabbani, A. (2015). Financial anxiety, physiological arousal, and planning intention. *Journal of Financial Therapy*, 5(2). doi:10.4148/1944-9771.1083.

98. American Psychological Association. (2017). *What is cognitive behavioral therapy?* Available at: https://www.apa.org/ptsd-guideline/patients-and-families/cognitive-behavioral.

99. Beck, J. S. (2020). *Cognitive Behavior Therapy: Basics and Beyond: Basics and Beyond* (3rd ed.). New York: Guilford Press.

100. Burns, W. E. (2001). *The Scientific Revolution: An Encyclopedia*. Santa Barbara, CA: ABC-CLIO.

101. Clark, D. A. (2013). Cognitive restructuring. *The Wiley Handbook of Cognitive Behavioral Therapy* (vol. 1, pp. 1–22). doi:10.1002/9781118528563.wbcbt02.

102. Klontz, B. T., Zabek, F., Taylor, C. D., Bivens, A., Horwitz, E., Klontz, P. T., Tharpe, D. T., and Lurtz, M. (2019). The sentimental savings study: Using financial psychology to increase personal savings. *Journal of Financial Planning*, 32(10), pp. 44–55.

103. Snyder, C. R., and Lopez, S. J. (Eds.). (2005). *Handbook of Positive Psychology*. New York: Oxford University Press.

104. Asebedo, S. D., and Seay, M. C. (n.d.). From functioning to flourishing: Applying positive psychology to financial planning. *Journal of Financial Planning*, 28(11), pp. 50–58. Available at: https://www.financialplanning-association.org/sites/default/files/2020-09/NOV15%20JFP%20Asbedo.pdf.

105. Seligman, M. (2018). PERMA and the building blocks of well-being. *The Journal of Positive Psychology*, 13(4), pp. 333–335. doi:10.1080/17439760.2018.1437466.

106. Tugade, M., and Fredrickson, B. L. (2004). Resilient individuals use positive emotions to bounce back from negative emotional experiences. *Journal of Personality and Social Psychology*, 86(2), pp. 320–333.

107. Csikszentmihalyi, M., and LeFevre, J. (1989). Optimal experience in work and leisure. *Journal of Personality and Social Psychology*, 56(5), pp. 815–822. doi:10.1037/0022-3514.56.5.815.

108. Klontz, B. T., and Canale, A. (2016, March). When Helping Hurts: 5 recommendations for planners with financial-enabling clients. *Journal of Financial Planning*, pp. 25–28. Available at: https://www.financialplann-ingassociation.org/article/journal/MAR16-when-helping-hurts-5-recommendations-planners-financial-enabling-clients.

109. Seligman, M. E. (2012). *Flourish: A Visionary New Understanding of Happiness and Well-Being*. New York: Atria Paperback.

110. Asebedo, S. D., Seay, M. C., Little, T. D., Enete, S., and Gray, B. (2020). Three good things or three good financial things? Applying a positive psychology intervention to the personal finance domain. *The Journal of Positive Psychology*, pp. 1–11. doi:10.1080/17439760.2020.1752779.

111. Klontz, B., Kahler, R., and Klontz, T. (2016). Working with couples. In *Facilitating Financial Health: Tools for Financial Planners, Coaches, and Therapists* (2nd ed., pp. 179–196). The National Underwriter Company.

112. Oggins, J. (2003). Topics of marital disagreement among African-American and Euro-American newlyweds. *Psychological Reports*, 92(2), pp. 419–425. doi:10.2466/pr0.2003.92.2.419.

113. Dew, J., Britt, S., and Huston, S. (2012). Examining the relationship between financial issues and divorce. *Family Relations*, 61(4), pp. 615–628. doi:10.1111/j.1741-3729.2012.00715.x.

114. Medintz, S. (2005, April 1). Secrets, lies and money. *CNN Money*. Available at: https://money.cnn.com/magazines/moneymag/moneymag_archive/2005/04/01/8254979/index.htm.

115. Hays, P., Klontz, B. T., and Kemnitz, R. (2015). Seven steps to culturally responsive financial therapy. In B. T. Klontz, S. L. Britt, and K. L. Archuleta (Eds.), *Financial Therapy: Theory, Research and Practice* (pp. 87–100). New York: Springer.

116. McIntosh, P. (2003). White privilege: Unpacking the invisible knapsack. In S. Plous (Ed.), *Understanding Prejudice and Discrimination* (pp. 191–196). New York: McGraw-Hill.

117. Danso, R. (2016). Cultural competence and cultural humility: A critical reflection on key cultural diversity concepts. *Journal of Social Work*, 18(4), pp. 410–430. doi:10.1177/1468017316654341.

118. Robinson, D., Masters, C., and Ansari, A. (2021). The 5 Rs of cultural humility: A conceptual model for health care leaders. *The American Journal of Medicine*, 134(2), pp. 161–163. doi:10.1016/j.amjmed.2020.09.029.

119. Hays, P. A. (2008). *Addressing Cultural Complexities in Practice: Assessment, Diagnosis, and Therapy* (2nd ed.). Washington, DC: American Psychological Association.

120. Hays, P. A. (2013). *Connecting Across Cultures: The Helper's Toolkit* (pp. 15–16). London: Sage Publications Ltd.

121. Klontz, B. T. (2014, January). Junior achievement: Clients are wary of working with young advisors. Here's how to win them over. *On Wall Street*, 24(1), pp. 29–30.

122. Furnham, A., von Stumm, S., and Milner, R. (2014). Moneygrams: Recalled childhood memories about money and adult money pathology. *Journal of Financial Therapy*, 5(1). doi:10.4148/1944-9771.1059.

123. Paradi, J., and Fillion, P. (2015). Financial advisors are failing women: What female clients really want and how to change the dialogue. Strategy-Marketing.ca. Available at: https://www.strategymarketing.ca/wp-content/uploads/Financial-advisors-are-failing-women-What-women-really-want-and-how-to-change-the-dialogue.pdf.

124. Glynn, S. (2016, December). *Breadwinning mothers are Increasingly the U.S. norm*. Center for American Progress. Available at: https://americanprogress.org/wp-content/uploads/2016/12/Breadwinners-report.pdf.

125. Larrabee, L. M. (2019, September). Using financial psychology to better serve female clients. *Journal of Financial Planning*, 32(9), 24–27. Available at: https://www.financialplanningassociation.org/article/journal/SEP19-using-financial-psychology-better-serve-female-clients.

126. Twin, A. (2020). *What is risk tolerance?* Investopedia. Available at: https://www.investopedia.com/terms/r/risktolerance.asp.

127. Klontz, B. (2013, October). Risky business: What you don't know about your client's risk tolerance can hurt you both. *On Wall Street,* 23(10), pp. 43–44.

128. Sanders, J. G., and Jenkins, R. (2016). Weekly fluctuations in risk tolerance and voting behaviour. *PLoS ONE*, 11(7), 1–12. e0159017. doi:10.1371/journal. pone.0159017.

129. Triffin, M. (2018). *This exercise can help reveal what your risk tolerance really is*. Grow from Acorns + CNBC. Available at: https://grow.acorns.com/this-exercise-can-help-reveal-what-your-risk-tolerance-really-is (accessed May 15, 2022).

130. Otto, A. R., Fleming, S. M., and Glimcher, P. W. (2016). Unexpected but incidental positive outcomes predict real-world gambling. *Psychological Science*, 27(3), pp. 299–311. doi:10.1177/0956797615618366.

131. Suknanan, J. (2021). All new investors need to understand their risk capacity—here's how to determine yours. CNBC. Available at: https://www.cnbc.com/select/how-to-figure-out-your-risk-capacity-investing/#:~:text=It (accessed May 15, 2022).

132. Tversky, A., and Kahneman, D. (1974). Judgment under uncertainty: Heuristics and biases. *Science*, 185, pp. 1124–1131.

133. Noussair, C. N., Trautmann, S. T., and van de Kuilen, G. (2013). Higher order risk attitudes, demographics, and financial decisions. *The Review of Economic Studies*, 81(1), pp. 325–355. doi:10.1093/restud/rdt032.

134. Cokely, E., Galesic, M., Schulz, E., Ghazal, S., and Garcia-Retamero, R. (2012). Measuring risk literacy: The Berlin numeracy test. *Judgment and Decision Making*, 7(1), pp. 25–47. Available at: http://journal.sjdm.org/11/11808/jdm11808.pdf.

135. Feltz, A. (n.d.). What is risk literacy? *Risk Literacy*. Available at: http://www.riskliteracy.org/#:~:text=Risk%20literacy%20refers%20to%20one.

136. Richards, C. (2013, December 9). Overcoming an aversion to loss. *New York Times*. Available at: https://www.nytimes.com/2013/12/09/your-money/overcoming-an-aversion-to-loss.html.

137. Kitces, M. (2016). The sorry state of risk tolerance questionnaires. *Nerd's Eye View*. Kitces.com. Available at: https://www.kitces.com/blog/risk-tolerance-questionnaire-and-risk-profiling-problems-for-financial-advisors-planplus-study/(accessed May 14, 2022).

138. Singh, V. K., Goyal, R., and Wu, S. (2018). Riskalyzer. *Proceedings of the ACM on Interactive, Mobile, Wearable and Ubiquitous Technologies*, 2(1), pp. 1–21. doi:10.1145/3191766.

139. Coffield, F. (2012). Learning styles: Unreliable, invalid and impractical and yet still widely used. In P. Adey and J. Dillon (Eds.), *Bad Education: Debunking Myths in Education* (pp. 215–230). Maidenhead, UK; New York: Open University Press.

140. Blinder, D., Rotenberg, L., Peleg, M., and Taicher, S. (2001). Patient compliance to instructions after oral surgical procedures. *International Journal of Oral and Maxillofacial Surgery*, 30(3), pp. 216–219. doi:10.1054/ijom.2000.0045.

141. Grable, J. E. (2019). Optimal interior design of a financial advisor's office. *Nerd's Eye View*. Kitces.com. Available at: https://www.kitces.com/blog/scientific-interior-design-financial-advisory-office-planning-performance-lab-grable/

142. McLeod, S. (2022). Maslow's hierarchy of needs. *Simply Psychology*. Available at: https://www.simplypsychology.org/maslow.html.

143. Ryan, R. M., and Deci, E. L. (2000). Self-determination theory and the facilitation of intrinsic motivation, social development, and well-being. *American Psychologist*, 55(1), pp. 68–78. doi:10.1037/0003-066x.55.1.68.

144. Cherry, K. (2021). *Self-determination theory and motivation*. Verywell Mind. Available at: https://www.verywellmind.com/what-is-self-determination-theory-2795387.

145. Fallaw, S. (2018). *Who controls your financial success?* DataPoints. Available at: https://www.datapoints.com/2018/10/31/locus-of-control-financial-success/ (accessed May 14, 2022).

146. Mallers, M. H., Claver, M., and Lares, L. A. (2013). Perceived control in the lives of older adults: The influence of Langer and Rodin's work on gerontological theory, policy, and practice. *The Gerontologist*, 54(1), pp. 67–74. doi:10.1093/geront/gnt051.

147. Hofer, J., and Busch, H. (2017). Why Citizen Kane was unhappy: Motive-goal incongruence. *Social and Personality Psychology Compass*, 11(8), p.e12330. doi:10.1111/spc3.12330.

148. Schmidt, K.-H. (2010). The relation of goal incongruence and self-control demands to indicators of job strain among elderly care nursing staff: A cross-sectional survey study combined with longitudinally assessed absence measures. *International Journal of Nursing Studies*, 47(7), pp. 855–863. doi:10.1016/j.ijnurstu.2009.12.004.

149. Bandura, A. (Ed.). (1995). *Self-Efficacy in Changing Societies*. Cambridge, UK: Cambridge University Press. doi:10.1017/cbo9780511527692.

150. Kasser, T. (2016). Materialistic values and goals. *Annual Review of Psychology*, 67(1), pp. 489–514. doi:10.1146/annurev-psych-122414-033344.

151. Horwitz, E. J., Klontz, B. T., and Zabek, F. (2019). A financial psychology intervention for increasing employee participation in and contribution to retirement plans: Results of three trials. *Journal of Financial Counseling and Planning*, 30(2), pp. 262–276. doi:10.1891/1052-3073.30.2.262.

152. Koch, A. K., and Nafziger, J. (2016). Goals and bracketing under mental accounting. *Journal of Economic Theory*, 162, pp. 305–351. doi:10.1016/j.jet.2016.01.001.

153. Wang, G., Wang, Y., and Gai, X. (2021). A meta-analysis of the effects of mental contrasting with implementation intentions on goal attainment. *Frontiers in Psychology*, 12. doi:10.3389/fpsyg.2021.565202.

154. Harkin, B., Webb, T. L., Chang, B. P. I., Prestwich, A., Conner, M., Keller, I., Benn, Y., and Sheeran, P. (2015). Does monitoring goal progress promote goal attainment? A meta-analysis of the experimental evidence. *Psychological Bulletin*, 142(2), pp. 198–229.

155. Steinberg, D. M., Bennett, G. G., Askew, S., and Tate, D. F. (2015). Weighing every day matters: Daily weighing improves weight loss and adoption of weight control behaviors. *Journal of the Academy of Nutrition and Dietetics*, 115(4), pp. 511–518. doi:10.1016/j.jand.2014.12.011.

156. Klontz, B. T., Horwitz, E. J., and Klontz, P. T. (2015). Stages of change and motivational interviewing in financial therapy. In B. T. Klontz, S. L. Britt, and K. L. Archuleta (Eds.), *Financial Therapy: Theory, Research and Practice* (pp. 570–594). New York: Springer.

157. Prochaska, J. O., Norcross, J. C., and Diclemente, C. C. (2007). *Changing for Good: The Revolutionary Program That Explains the Six Stages of Change and Teaches You How to Free Yourself from Bad Habits*. Quill.

158. Janoff-Bulman, R. (2006). Schema-change perspectives on posttraumatic growth. In L. G. Calhoun and R. G. Tedeschi (Eds.), *Handbook of Posttraumatic Growth: Research & Practice* (pp. 81–99). Lawrence Erlbaum Associates.

159. Hawkley, L. C., and Cacioppo, J. T. (2010). Loneliness matters: A theoretical and empirical review of consequences and mechanisms. *Annals of Behavioral Medicine*, 40(2), pp. 218–227. doi:10.1007/s12160-010-9210-8.

160. Holt-Lunstad, J., Smith, T. B., and Layton, J. B. (2010). Social relationships and mortality risk: A meta-analytic review. *PLoS Medicine*, 7, e1000316. doi:10.1371/journal.pmed.1000316

161. Cacioppo, J. T., Cacioppo, S., Cole, S. W., Capitanio, J. P., Goossens, L., and Boomsma, D. I. (2015). Loneliness across phylogeny and a call for comparative studies and animal models. *Perspectives on Psychological Science*, 10(2), pp. 202–212. doi:10.1177/1745691614564876.

162. Zeligman, M., Bialo, J. A., Brack, J. L., and Kearney, M. A. (2017). Loneliness as moderator between trauma and posttraumatic growth. *Journal of Counseling & Development*, 95(4), pp. 435–444. doi:10.1002/jcad.12158.

163. Clapp, J. D., and Gayle Beck, J. (2009). Understanding the relationship between PTSD and social support: The role of negative network orientation. *Behaviour Research and Therapy*, 47(3), pp. 237–244. doi:10.1016/j.brat.2008.12.006.

164. Mitchell, J. (n.d.). *Critical Incident Stress Debriefing (CISD): Introduction and Definition of CISD*. Available at: https://corpslakes.erdc.dren.mil/employees/cism/pdfs/Debriefing.pdf.

165. Peterson, T. (2021, August 13). Critical Incident Stress Debriefing: How it works & what to expect. *Choosing Therapy*. Available at: https://www.choosingtherapy.com/critical-incident-stress-debriefing/.

166. Collier, L. (2016). Growth after trauma. *Monitor on Psychology*, 47(10), 48. Available at: https://www.apa.org/monitor/2016/11/growth-trauma.

167. Asebedo, S. D. (2018). Personality and financial behavior. In C. R. Chaffin (Ed.), *Client Psychology* (pp. 137–153). CFP Board Center for Financial Planning Series. Hoboken, NJ: Wiley.

168. Taylor, C. D., Klontz, B., and Britt, S. L. (2016). Reliability and convergent validity of the Klontz Money Script Inventory–Revised (KMSI-R). *Journal of Financial Therapy*, 6(2), p. 2.

169. Grable, J. E., and Goetz, J. W. (2017). *Communication Essentials for Financial Planners: Strategies and Techniques.* Hoboken, NJ: Wiley.

170. Hays, D. G. (2017). *Assessment in Counseling: Procedures and Practices.* Germany: Wiley.

171. CFP® Certification 2021 Principal Knowledge Topics. (2021). Available at: https://www.cfp.net/-/media/files/cfp-board/cfp-certification/2021-practice-analysis/2021-principal-knowledge-topics.pdf.

172. American Psychological Association. *Stress in America.* Available at: https://www.apa.org/news/press/releases/stress (accessed May 14, 2022).

173. Klontz, B. T., Van Zutphen, N., and Fries, K. (2016). Financial planner as healer: Maximizing the role of financial health physician. *Journal of Financial Psychology*, 29(12), 52–59.

174. American Psychological Association. (2017). *APA Ethical Principles of Psychologists and Code of Conduct, Ethical Standard 2.01: Boundaries of Competence.* Washington, DC: American Psychological Association.

175. CFP Board. (n.d.). *Code of Ethics and Standards of Conduct.* Available at: https://www.cfp.net/ethics/code-of-ethics-and-standards-of-conduct.

176. Klontz, B., Kahler, R., and Klontz, T. (2016). Doing no harm. In *Facilitating Financial Health: Tools for Financial Planners, Coaches, and Therapists* (2nd ed., pp. 35–46). The National Underwriter Company.

Index